DANGEROUS WATERS

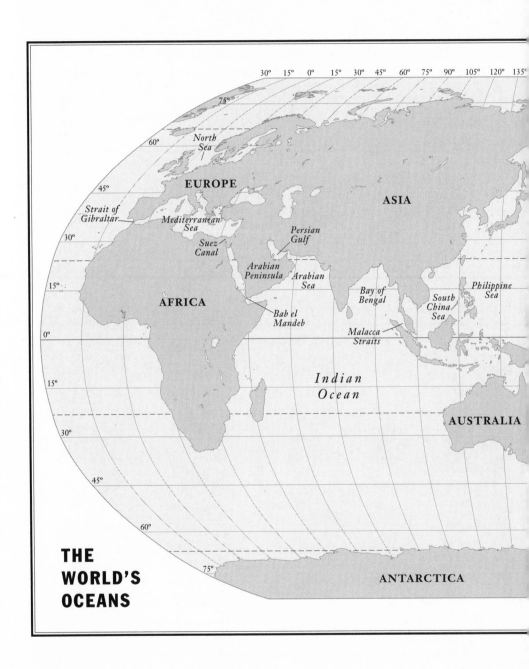

30° 15° 0° 15° 30° 45° 60° 75° 90° 105° 120° 135°

75°

60°

North
Sea

45°

EUROPE

ASIA

Strait of
Gibraltar

30°

Mediterranean
Sea

Suez
Canal

Persian
Gulf

15°

Arabian
Peninsula

Arabian
Sea

AFRICA

Bay of
Bengal

Philippine
Sea

South
China
Sea

Bab el
Mandeb

0°

Malacca
Straits

15°

*Indian
Ocean*

30°

AUSTRALIA

45°

60°

**THE
WORLD'S
OCEANS**

75°

ANTARCTICA

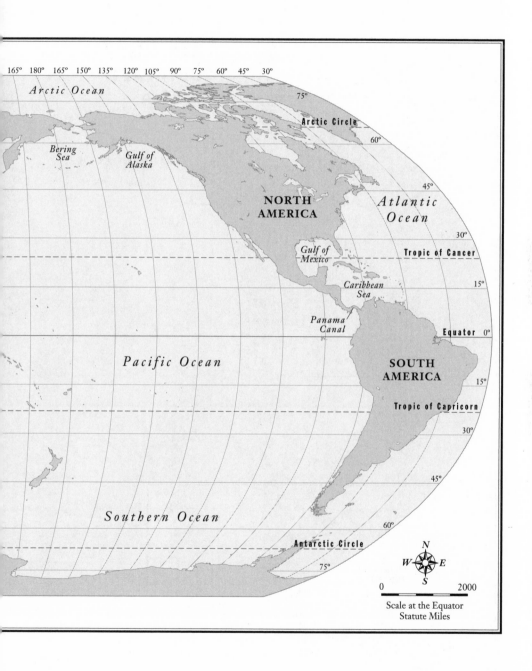

165° 180° 165° 150° 135° 120° 105° 90° 75° 60° 45° 30°

Arctic Ocean

75°

Arctic Circle

60°

Bering Sea

Gulf of Alaska

45°

NORTH AMERICA

Atlantic Ocean

30°

Gulf of Mexico

Tropic of Cancer

Caribbean Sea

15°

Panama Canal

Equator 0°

Pacific Ocean

SOUTH AMERICA

15°

Tropic of Capricorn

30°

45°

Southern Ocean

60°

Antarctic Circle

75°

N
W ✦ E
S

0 _____ 2000

Scale at the Equator
Statute Miles

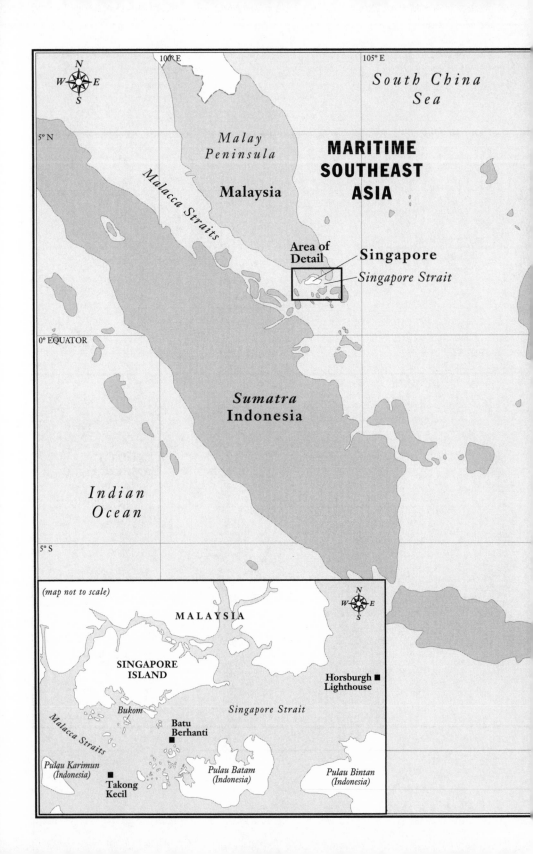

100° E

105° E

*South China
Sea*

5° N

*Malay
Peninsula*

Malaysia

**MARITIME
SOUTHEAST
ASIA**

Malacca Straits

Area of
Detail

Singapore

Singapore Strait

0° EQUATOR

Sumatra
Indonesia

*Indian
Ocean*

5° S

(map not to scale)

N
W ● E
S

MALAYSIA

**SINGAPORE
ISLAND**

Bukom

Singapore Strait

Horsburgh ■
Lighthouse

Malacca Straits

**Batu
Berhanti** ■

*Pulau Karimun
(Indonesia)*

■
**Takong
Kecil**

*Pulau Batam
(Indonesia)*

*Pulau Bintan
(Indonesia)*

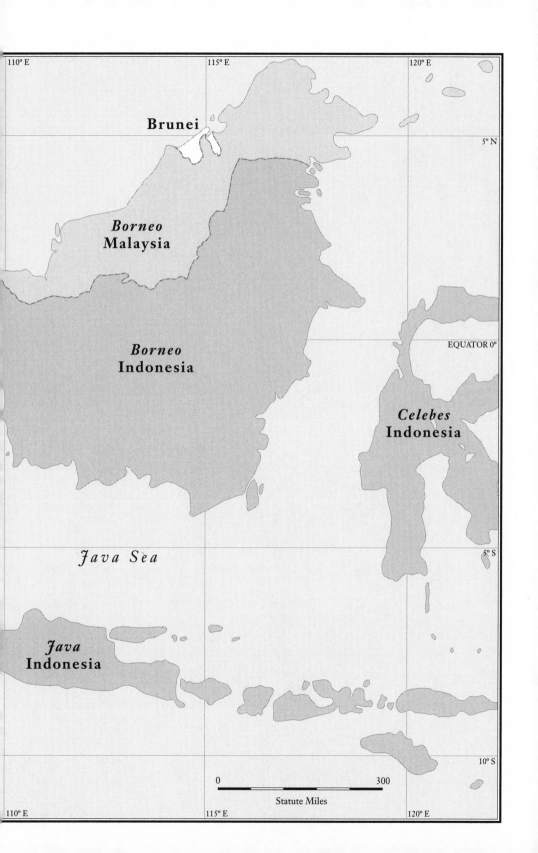

JOHN S. BURNETT

DANGEROUS WATERS

*Modern Piracy and
Terror on the High Seas*

DUTTON

DUTTON
Published by the Penguin Group
Penguin Putnam Inc., 375 Hudson Street, New York, New York 10014, U.S.A.
Penguin Books Ltd, 80 Strand, London WC2R 0RL, England
Penguin Books Australia Ltd, 250 Camberwell Road, Camberwell, Victoria 3124, Australia
Penguin Books Canada Ltd, 10 Alcorn Avenue, Toronto, Ontario, Canada M4V 3B2
Penguin Books (N.Z.) Ltd, 182–190 Wairau Road, Auckland 10, New Zealand

Penguin Books Ltd, Registered Offices: Harmondsworth, Middlesex, England

Published by Dutton, a member of Penguin Putnam Inc.

First Printing, September 2002
1   3   5   7   9   10   8   6   4   2

 REGISTERED TRADEMARK—MARCA REGISTRADA

LIBRARY OF CONGRESS CATALOGING-IN-PUBLICATION DATA
Burnett, John S.
Dangerous waters : modern piracy and terror on the high seas / John S. Burnett.
p. cm.
ISBN 0-525-94679-9 (alk. paper)
1. Pirates. 2. Hijacking of ships. 3. Burnett, John S.—Journeys. I. Title.
G535 .B87 2002
910.4'5—dc21   2002072075

Printed in the United States of America
Set in Janson

Maps by Mark Stein Studios

For Jackie.

And Koos and Mien,
in friendship.

CONTENTS

NOTE TO THE READER

Attacks on shipping by pirates and terrorists are threats to global commerce and security, but they impact no one more directly than the men and women on the front lines—those working the ships on the high seas. In the wake of September 11, their level of risk has increased considerably. Citing concerns for the security of the Very Large Crude Carrier (VLCC) featured in this book—a vessel that routinely transits hostile waters—and for the safety of its crew, the oil major that granted the author passage aboard the ship requested that it not be identified. This giant tanker carrying crude oil from the Middle East is thus referred to only with the pseudonym, the *Montrose*. The names of the crew and company personnel have been similarly changed, and the name of the oil major itself has been omitted. No other details of the investigation have been altered.

Man dies as he dreams. Alone.

Joseph Conrad

PROLOGUE

The Attack

The young Indonesian poked me in the stomach with the barrel of his assault rifle. His eyes, cold and hard, challenged me to resist. I was at the edge of doing something stupid.

I had been sailing alone across the South China Sea to Singapore in January 1992 aboard my sloop *Unicorn*. While not a large boat—only thirty-two feet long—it is stout enough for ocean passages and comfortable enough to call home. Setting off single-handed was not recommended; Indonesian harbor officials in Borneo on the other side had warned me that an oil tanker steaming through the same area had been attacked by pirates the night before.

Piracy was not a threat I took very seriously; I was more concerned with the difficult navigation through the reefs, dodging the heavy ship traffic, and getting enough catnaps during the three-day passage. Piracy was something I associated with Long John Silver, Captain Hook, and Hollywood, a childhood game to be played over the mounds of dirt, dueling with cutlasses torn from a picket fence. How could pirates climb the sheer steel wall of the hull of a big ship, I wondered?

I was approaching one of the busiest waterways in the world, shipping lanes that linked Europe to the Pacific, the Persian Gulf to Japan and China; it is a highway for six hundred commercial ships a day. It is also, I was to discover, prime hunting ground for pirates.

It was my second night out from Borneo and the atmosphere was heavy and airless. Lightning flashed off the port side from a thunderstorm over Sumatra. The reassuring loom of the Singapore City lights hovered faintly on the horizon in front of me to the west. Even without the benefit of wind, without the use of the sails, and puttering along with the small auxiliary engine, landfall, I estimated, should be early afternoon. And four or five hours after that I'd be sitting at the bar of the Changi Yacht Club, knocking back a cold medicinal ale. Then sleep. Priorities.

The merchant vessels that chugged through the shipping lanes could not see the *Unicorn* and its limp mainsail, and it was up to me to avoid them. One large container ship, its decks flooded in bright light, like Times Square on New Year's Eve, paralleled my course to starboard; fire hoses shot water out into the darkness. I watched her gradually change course, then turn sharply to port, and in disbelief I realized it was heading straight for me. A ship bearing down at eighteen knots—there was not a lot I could do. The bastard was trying to run me over! I threw the tiller hard over, increased speed to a smoky six knots; I was being chased out of the shipping lanes. I looked back and up at the towering clutter of bright lights that was about to swallow me whole. Then it dawned on me that the captain was assuming the small blip on his radar screen was a pirate boat. The ship finally returned to its original east-west course and I throttled down and slumped back, exhausted and shaking. He had run me out of the shipping lanes to where he couldn't go, apparently satisfied he had scared the daylights out of a bunch of pirates. The *Unicorn* hobby-horsed up and down on the ship's wake, corkscrewed and twisted out of control. The boom swung wildly from side to side and the engine's small propeller cavitated uselessly in the air as the stern lifted out of the water.

The sea is a lonely place at the best of times, but this was one of those moments when I realized how totally alone I could be. Even the sensation of being so isolated in the middle of an ocean with no one around for a thousand miles cannot compare to this night in the shipping lanes.

Dead tired, I was getting confused. Bright halogen lights decked the passing ships from stem to stern as part of their antipiracy defenses. With their regulation navigation lights obliterated, I had no way of knowing what they were doing, whether they were coming or going and at what angle.

I steered the *Unicorn* back to the inside edge of the traffic lanes— keeping outboard of the line of ships. The waters outside the channel were nearly as dangerous; unmarked reefs, unlit fishing boats, floats, and nets formed as much of a gauntlet as the merchant ships inside. Still, I felt safer.

Somebody was smoking nearby. Once at night off the Sri Lanka coast, I smelled cigarette smoke; a few minutes later I had to throw the tiller hard over to avoid an unlit fishing boat pulling up its nets. Only at the last moment did I spot with my binoculars the glow of a cigarette hanging from the mouth of a fishermen. There was no doubt this night. Someone close was having a smoke—a Gudang Garam, the sweet clove-scented cigarette so popular in Indonesia. Senses heightened, I tried to sort through the throaty vibrations of passing ships and strained to detect the shadows of a fishing boat that I was convinced I was about to hit.

Admitting to my own building fears, I went below to switch on the VHF radio. Just in case. The radio had seemed useless. The frequencies were either jammed with shrill whistles, a favorite Asian calling technique, or the nighttime taunts between Filipino, Malaysian, and Indonesian fishermen, anonymously calling each other: "Hey, monkey—you Indonesian monkey." "Hey, you Philippine pig—you eat your mother's shit, YOU big monkey." Tonight the radio was controlled by someone who kept the microphone keyed open next to an AM radio playing some twangy Chinese tune. A ship calling a distress or trying to get through to another would be blocked unless it had a more powerful signal. I certainly did not.

A sudden jolt threw me off balance. My first thought was that I had hit an uncharted reef or a partially submerged container that had fallen off a cargo ship.

I gripped the handrail, heart beating in my throat. Vibrations rattled the hull—another vessel, powered by a large engine, had come alongside my boat. I felt the thump as someone jumped onto the deck. Then a second. Hushed but excited voices from above sent a wave of acid horror into my gut. I froze. The sudden unexpected sound of people when you've been alone for days is terrifying. Somebody is on my boat!

I couldn't run, I couldn't hide. I felt the panic of a trapped animal. The voices were getting more agitated as the intruders stumbled around on the rolling deck. By God, I'll throw these guys off! I pulled my Indonesian machete out of its scabbard and turned to run topsides.

But this was pirate country and I had been warned. I had to calm myself and think. I replaced the knife in its sheath. I would fight only as a last resort; my life was more important than the toys on board. I would give them anything they wanted—except the *Unicorn* itself. On wobbly legs and scared to death, I pulled myself up the companionway steps.

A military-style patrol boat about the length of the *Unicorn* had tied up to me. Low slung and ghostly, the boat was only a colorless silhouette—except amidships, where the orange glow of a cigarette briefly illuminated a dark face. Two shadowy figures shrouded in terrifying silence stood opposite, pointing rifles at me. The decision not to resist was the right one. It was probably better they had guns; had they been unarmed, I might have made a mistake.

I had worked in Jakarta and had a basic knowledge of Bahasa Indonesia; I had liked those with whom I had worked and found the people generally a courteous lot. *"Salamat Datang!"* I welcomed them. My quavering voice belied my fear. I couldn't fight, I couldn't argue, I could only try to be polite, a trait that Indonesians find indispensable. It was said in Jakarta that if you are robbed in your home, the thief will apologize before killing you.

Over their shoulders I could see a third, smaller figure attempting, clumsily, to get onto my boat. Holding my breath, I walked past the guns and offered him a hand. He was just a boy, barely in his teens. He glowered and waved a long knife in my face. He didn't need any help. Then he seemed to relax.

"Terimah kasih, Pak," the boy thanked me as if he remembered his manners.

There was plenty of light from the passing ships to seaward, enough to reveal their features. One gunman was, in Indonesian terms, an old man—about forty—with sprigs of chin hair, a permanent frown, and a pinched lupine face. He wore the camouflaged uniform of the TNI, the Indonesian military. The other was a bare-chested teenager with a thin black mustache whose sullen eyes darted nervously and enviously over my boat. He was dressed only in military trousers. The patrol boat and their semimilitary attire and their modern guns gave me an instant of hope. Maybe they were police officers or customs officials, just checking my papers. However, these were international waters. And it was the middle of the night. And they wore rolled-up ski masks.

And none of them wore shoes. The toes of their dark brown feet were splayed, their leathery heels cracked. I suddenly recalled that Joshua Slocum, the first person to sail alone around the world almost exactly a hundred years ago, had spread carpet nails on the deck at night as his antipiracy weapon. It worked near Cape Horn; his pirates jumped back into the water howling and screaming after meeting the commercial end of the tacks. It was too late for me to dust the decks with nails.

I tried to refocus; why the hell would they be on my little boat, pointing guns at me? I just could not accept it—while my fear was extreme, the situation seemed at the same time ludicrous. I liked Indonesians. I thought I knew them. I had been up before a more frightening situation during an anti-American protest in Jakarta during the Gulf War and I had managed to get out of that. One-on-one with an Indonesian always seemed to work; I had found myself in the middle of rioting students in Tanjung Priok dock area who were burning the effigy of Bush senior; someone in the mob made me as a likely American and began shouting and pointing at me. I turned to an older man next to me dressed in a white robe and asked for his help. Surprised and pleased that I should ask, he led me out and away to safety.

A large tanker passed about a half mile abeam, its fully illuminated deck casting an eerie glow upon us. It was so close! There was no way to signal it, no way to call for help. I watched in frustration as the ship steamed past, its water cannon blasting into the night.

We stood facing each other. No one had ever pointed a loaded gun at me before and staring into the barrels, I became weak with fear. I knew I had to maintain some control. The older boy massaged the trigger with his forefinger. He jabbed the barrel of his rifle into my ribs, silently egging, taunting, challenging. His deep-set eyes, like black glass marbles, drilled into mine with inexplicable anger. I stood before him with my teeth clenched, unflinching, staring into those depthless sockets. He poked my gut, then jabbed harder, testing the tenderness of the meat. Emboldened, he jabbed again as if the barrel of his gun were a bayonet. The hard metal felt like a dull knife. Relaxing my stomach muscles lessened the pain. I was so close; bloody hell, one little push and he'd be overboard. I was about to do something really stupid. The older man's squeaky voice cut like a razor. "Money! You MONEY!" he said in agitated jerks of English.

"Money. Yeah, sure. Money," I think I managed. As I turned, the surly youth slammed the butt of his rifle against the back of my head. I lurched forward, falling against the wire shrouds of the mast, then slipped to my knees. He yanked me up by my hair and kicked me ahead of him toward the cabin stairs.

The three men stood awkwardly in the narrow cabin below, their assault rifles too large to point. Through tears of pain I watched the old man's eyes scan my seagoing home. The *Unicorn* had none of the toys found on most blue-water yachts. It had no radar, no sophisticated radios, no televisions, no weather fax machines, no satellite navigating system, not even any refrigeration (I had learned to enjoy bilge-warm beer), only shelves of some treasured books, a mahogany box for an old sextant, and a rack for binoculars. There wasn't much to steal.

Still dazed, I nodded for them to sit. I reached for the thermos of old coffee that I had made hours earlier and with shaky hands splashed it into some mugs and slid them across the table. There was a sickening crunch as the *Unicorn* and the pirate vessel banged against each other in the wake from a passing ship. The damage to my hull would be considerable. The sullen youth, whose eyes never left mine, watched me cringe at the sound of the two boats smashing against each other; his face brightened with a thin, cruel smile.

"*Kopi susu,*" I muttered. I nodded toward an open tin of Nestlé sweet cream. The youngest boy placed his knife in his lap, stirred in the cream with his forefinger, and slurped his cup noisily.

The old man barked something and the youngster, looking a little sheepish, hastily put down his coffee. I noticed then the similarity between the two boys. I poured myself a cup, opened a drawer, and pulled out a photo of my two sons taken years before: I was cutting a birthday cake and my face was plastered in chocolate icing; my three-year-old hung around my neck, his fingers thick with goo, and my five-year-old was doubled over laughing in the background. In passable Indonesian I told the old man they were my kids and asked him if these were his boys. The old man, who up to this point had no real face at all, broke into a crooked grin, straightened himself proudly, and said they were indeed and that he had two more sons back in Sumatra. He picked up a cup and sipped. I pushed the other two cups toward his sons; the youngest looked at his father for permission. The other pointedly ignored the coffee and kept his eyes pinned on mine; his challenging arrogance continued to test me. The old man and I spoke in stilted Indonesian about his village, somewhere on a nearby island, and my town and his admiration for America, until impatient shouts from the boat outside reminded the old man what they had come for.

There was a tense silence. The old man stared into his cup; he pulled nervously at his chin hairs. He raised his eyes and again looked over the cabin. I leaned over and pulled out my binoculars from the rack and handed them over. He slipped the strap around his neck without acknowledgment. I watched his eldest son scan the cabin, looking for his own booty. His eyes settled on an open carton of Marlboros atop a row of books. I had kept the cigarettes to exchange for fish from passing fishermen in their dugouts.

"*Rokok tidak bagus,*" I tried to joke, mimicking a current Indonesian antismoking slogan; I realized at once that I sounded like a patronizing smartass. I reached overhead and handed the carton to the humorless youth.

The old man rose. In the Islamic tradition of respect he shook my hand, then tapped his chest lightly; he turned and ascended the companionway steps in silence, followed by his sons. As the pirate boat motored off into the darkness to perhaps more lucrative prey, the angry tones of a loud and rancorous discussion drifted across the water. I imagined they were catching hell for not returning with better loot.

I went to the side, held my throbbing head between my hands to keep it from exploding, leaned over, and retched.

At the immigration office in Singapore the next day, officials told me that an oil tanker had been pirated only a few miles from where I'd had my encounter. The ship had been hijacked and had vanished.

Introduction

Once I got over the shock from my encounter in the South China Sea, I became intrigued. This was the twenty-first century. Pirates? Having been an investigative reporter, I started to nose around. I was surprised to discover that supertankers, cargo vessels, passenger ferries, and cruise ships are attacked regularly. Blackbeard is long gone but a new and violent breed of pirate is taking his place, plundering ships in most oceans of the world. Piracy, the scourge of the seventeenth and eighteenth centuries, has emerged from the history books and has returned with deadly, terrifying results. I had lived through absolute proof of its existence. I was one of the lucky ones; I escaped with my life.

It was hard to believe that today masked pirates in speedboats chase after a large cargo ship in the dead of night and, using grappling hooks and bamboo poles, scale the side, overwhelm the crew, and steal the cash from the ship's safe. Minutes later they are back in their boats counting their blessings, leaving many of the ship's crew dead or injured.

I discovered that organized crime syndicates with bases in Asia, the United States, and Europe employ pirates to hijack ships on the high seas; like the fabled ghost ships of legend an entire vessel, together with its cargo and crew, simply disappears. Years later a hijacked ship may reappear as what is known as a phantom ship with a new name and a new paint job, running drugs or carting illegal immigrants.

These modern-day pirates have little in common with the romantic rum-swilling rogues of Hollywood or of our imagination; they are not the cutlass-swinging marauders with an occasional trigger temper, an eye for a skirt, and a quest for gold. Many of today's pirates are organized gangs of poverty-stricken young men living alongside busy shipping lanes who attack slow-moving ships that lumber by, rich pickings and perfect targets of opportunity. There are others who are far more brutal, ruthless, and cold blooded, who kill. They pack grenade launchers, antitank missiles, and assault rifles and, instead of drinking rum, often are chewing khat, a leafy narcotic.[1] Many are employed by warlords, corrupt government officials, transnational crime organizations, and terrorist cells.

Victims of piracy no longer walk the plank,[2] if in fact they ever did; yet the violence is just as shocking. In a scene evoking the worst of the ancient crime, pirates in 1998 hijacked a ship, lined the crew against the railing, slipped hoods over their heads, clubbed them to death, and kicked them overboard.

Piracy is a wreakless crime that is increasing at an alarming rate in all oceans, off the coasts of nearly all continents. In 2001 seven American ships were attacked, fifteen from the United Kingdom, just some of the 335 assaults worldwide; 241 seafarers were killed, held hostage, or wounded—civilians just doing their jobs. These statistics are issued by the International Maritime Bureau of the International Chamber of Commerce, the organization that investigates maritime fraud and piracy. The statistics reflect known incidents directed at commercial shipping. They do not include attacks on all vessels nor do they include those innocent tourists, commercial fishermen, ferry passengers, or yachtsmen whose mysterious disappearances are unofficially attributed to piracy. Most acts of piracy go unreported because shipowners and captains do not want to tie up a vessel for lengthy investigations. Thus, the attacks by pirates worldwide actually number as many as several thousand each year. I reported the attack on the *Unicorn* to the Singapore Marine Police, who told me that because the incident occurred outside their territorial waters there was nothing they could do. It probably did not even rate a mention in their files.

It is not, however, just the statistics that are causing alarm. It is that one attack on the wrong ship at the wrong time, an attack that would result in the closure of one of the strategic international waterways upon which so much of the world economy depends that has industry and navies trying to find answers.

Nearly ninety-five percent of world commerce is transported by ship. The most essential of all commodities shipped in bulk is oil. Sixty percent of the world's crude oil is carried on supertankers and even larger Very Large Crude Carriers.

There are only so many ways to get from one continent to the next, from the oil fields in the Middle East, West Africa, South America, or Alaska to the rest of the world. Most of these routes pass through congested shipping lanes, narrow channels and straits, busy international canals, winding rivers, and heavily trafficked harbors. These include such vital links as the Panama and Suez Canals, the Straits of Hormuz at the exit of the Persian Gulf, the Bab el Mandab, the bottleneck at the southern end of the Red Sea leading to the Suez and Europe, the Straits of Gibraltar, and the Malacca Straits that connect Asia to much of the rest of the world. It is in many of these tightly confined stretches that modern-day pirates lie in wait and attack ships at will. Indeed, there is not a shipping lane, a navigable strait, an important canal, that is safe from those determined to take over a ship. Pirates have attacked vessels on all these waterways—not something that is well known outside the maritime community.

The Malacca Straits, on the east side of the Indian Ocean, is one of those corridors. This five-hundred-mile passage is the commercial umbilical between Europe, the Middle East, and the Indian subcontinent to Asia and the Pacific. Eighty percent of Japan's crude oil comes from the Persian Gulf, and it is shipped through these waters. A third of world commerce passes down these narrow shipping lanes. They are some of the most pirated waters in the world.

Had I not been attacked, had a tanker nearby not been hijacked the same night, I might have dismissed piracy in this new century as a product of a rich imagination. I decided to return to those pirate-infested waters and investigate the security of the high-risk, high-stakes transport of crude oil from the wellhead to the refinery to the gasoline pump.

In August 2001 I joined the British-registered *Montrose*—a Very Large Crude Carrier (VLCC) built to transport oil from the Middle East oil fields to refineries in North America, Europe, and Asia—on a passage that would take us through the Malacca Straits. At 300,000 tons the *Montrose* is a monster of a ship. Three football fields can fit on the deck of this vessel and there is still room to kick a long-distance field goal. On one voyage she carries in excess of two million barrels of crude. When refined that single payload is more than all the cars and sport utility vehicles in the United States burn in a day.

Maritime experts warn that one of these giant crude carriers like the *Montrose*—one of the largest moving man-made objects on earth—will be attacked either by pirates or terrorists in the Malacca Straits. Armed pirates at night scamper up the sides, creep aboard, take over the ship, tie up the crew; the VLCC will steam out of control down the narrow, heavily trafficked channel and collide with another ship or break up on the rocks, closing this vital commercial conduit and creating an economic and environmental catastrophe of global proportions.

Can pirates take over a ship this huge, this important? On a Very Large Crude Carrier you are above the world; the idea of being boarded and attacked by pirates seems improbable, and on the *Montrose* I shared with the captain his sense of invincibility. Yet all vessels, I was to discover, no matter how big, how fast, how modern, are vulnerable to attack. Also at risk are the highly protected ships that carry recycled radioactive waste—cargo that can be turned into nuclear weapons—as well as warships. Few could have anticipated that one of the world's most secure naval vessels, the USS *Cole*, could be attacked in the middle of a harbor in broad daylight.

I also joined the *Petro Concord*, a smaller tanker that delivers products refined from Middle East crude oil—jet fuel and diesel oil—to Ho Chi Minh City. This passage crossed the South China Sea, a lawless, disputed no-man's-land where ships are frequently hijacked by pirates in the employ of organized crime syndicates for the precious cargoes they carry. It was on this route that the *Petro Concord*'s sister ship had been hijacked. We, too, were a perfect soft target, and the voyage turned out to be a hair-raising experience.

To get an industry perspective I attended the darkly named Fourth International Meeting of Piracy and Phantom Ships. There were few expectations that this conference would have much effect on the alarming number of attacks. However, to the surprise of the delegates, the meeting concluded with a dramatic real-time high-seas chase after pirates and the rescue of a tanker hijacked in the South China Sea.

I have woven throughout this personal investigation some chilling events that cannot help but touch all of us.

The firebombing of the *Valiant Carrier*, a fully laden tanker, and the assault on its captain and his young family is so unimaginably cruel that it beggars the imagination. Yet it is representative of the horrors that occur at sea today. I have written the story of the *Valiant Carrier* as it was related to me by the captain, his wife, and children. I have taken a few liberties only in some descriptions but never with the events or with emotions themselves. Their tale of terror needs no embellishment.

There are many who are on the knife's edge in the fight against piracy; those who infiltrate organized crime to stop hijackings and live with a price on their heads, those who battle pirates in hand-to-hand combat, and those who have running gun battles while protecting lives and ships from thieves and pirates. Their stories are not hyperbolic fantasy. One of them may be in a gunfight as this is being read. If such a battle is not occurring at this moment in the Malacca Straits, it is happening in the Philippines, or off the African coast, in the Red Sea, or off Brazil, in the Caribbean or the Mediterranean.

To the men, women, and children who have been victims of pirates, to those who fight them, and those who live and work at sea today, this book is dedicated.

1

And Our Hoses Piss a Little

Montrose

We are slamming through a ball-breaking chop, looking for the big ship. Despite her size—and it is supposed to be somewhere out here—we won't see it until it rears out of the evening haze, a looming black wall. She is still north of our present position, steaming toward us down the Persian Gulf from Saudi Arabia; we should make the intercept at about dark.

The Gulf Agency supply vessel *Shamal* has been contracted to deliver me and two officers, crates of machinery, spare parts, and crew mail to the M/T *Montrose*. Too enormous to get very close to land or to belly up to a terminal, the Very Large Crude Carrier will anchor off the coast and raft up to a smaller tanker to pick up crude oil that she will deliver to the Far East. Anchoring out here in the Outer Port Limits of Dubai for a ship-to-ship transfer is not unusual; the *Montrose* is so large and so deep that there are few ports in the world that can accommodate her. We should have little trouble spotting a vessel this size with the naked eye, no matter how thick the haze, how dark the night.

The sun is beginning to set. A mistake in terms. Because of the grit blown off the desert the sun disappears far above the horizon behind a wall of bilious-colored dust. Daylight does not give up easily here on the Arabian Peninsula; it is an hour or so before the sun reaches the actual horizon and sometime later before the end of the last navigable light.

Competing weakly with the drone of the launch's big diesels, the VHF radio rattles off warnings, greetings, exchanges between ships and offices ashore; the captain tries to sing to the accompaniment of a discordant Arabic melody on the AM radio.

One of the replacement officers is a nattily dressed Pakistani; the other a large, round man with a brush mustache, a florid scrubby complexion, and a pendulous gut. They have not served together before and do not know each other. We are like three strangers finding ourselves in an empty subway car in the wee hours—we are all getting off at the end of the line, but there is nothing else in common that we know of.

The big man approaches me and belly-laughs above the din that, at this speed, we might reach our ship by tomorrow. He introduces himself as Niko, the *Montrose*'s electrician. He hands me a couple of pocket photo albums; with immense arms crossed over his stomach he stands back and watches my reaction. The first photo is of a pretty girl with big dark eyes in a wedding dress clutching a bouquet of flowers.

"Your daughter?"

"Of course. And this is her man," he says in a thick Slavic accent. He reaches over to turn a page; I feel his anticipation, the unspoken message: *If you think these are good, just wait, the show will get better.*

His daughter's new husband is an angular, sallow-faced youth in a dark suit that looks too big, perhaps borrowed. "He is a policeman; you see flags. Always flags when a policeman married. Or killed." The flag of Croatia, blue, white, and red horizontal stripes with the emblematic shield in the center, drapes over the boy's skinny shoulders like a shroud.

Faint lights on the horizon expand and brighten the darkening sky with an eerie glow. It is the *Montrose* now at anchor, still ten miles distant. The three of us—the new crew members—have begun to loosen up. What we share is that ship just up ahead; it will be my home for the delivery of crude oil from the Gulf to a refinery in Singapore, and theirs for this voyage and many others from the Persian Gulf to wherever crude needs to be hauled.

The halogen lights from *Montrose*'s deck cast an orange corona around the ship, obscuring the vessel itself. As we approach, it appears less a ship than a solid wall that rises out of the sea, a vertical sheet of steel that grows higher, darker, more threatening. The wake from the launch slaps against the ship's hull; it doesn't move—it doesn't seem like it ever could. Our boat noses up to the long diagonal gangway that extends from the deck high above. A red strobe light flashes from the mast atop the bridge. I am wonder-struck by the size of the vessel. It seems more like a flat-top mountain rooted firmly on the seabed than a machine built to plow through the seas.

The *Montrose*[3] is managed and operated by the maritime arm of what I will call, hereafter, The Group, one of the world's largest oil companies. The Group's own ship company provides this Oil Major with a fleet of tankers to transport its cargo of crude oil, refined products, and natural gas.

This is the *Montrose*'s regular run, a water-borne truck route. Our voyage will take us out of the Persian Gulf, through the Straits of Hormuz, across the Indian Ocean, down the Malacca Straits on the other side, and finally to Singapore. It will be a passage through the most pirated waters in the world. It should give me an idea of the seriousness which one ship company regards piracy, as well as the defenses that are taken to keep armed gangs off the vessel.

The *Montrose* is as long as Manhattan's Chrysler Building is tall. The 300,000 tons of crude it carries are sufficient to provide fuel oil to the entire U.S. Northeast during the winter for ten days. Could a ship this big really be taken over by pirates? I look upward from the deck of the supply vessel; figures in white boilersuits and hard hats, tiny little things, watch us from far above. I cannot imagine how pirates, no matter how determined, could climb a wall such as this.

The gangway seems endless, a walk of a thousand steps at least, something like climbing the Washington Monument. I see only the wide backside of the cheerful Croat in front of me. He is having some difficulty—not a man who is very fit.

At the top I feel like I have just successfully scaled a cliff in the Bighorns; before me, a mountain plateau, flat and extending forever. Instead of fields of wildflowers the plateau is cluttered with horizontal and vertical pipes, valve wheels, steel ladders, steel walkways, and ramps. There is a sense of overwhelming enormity; a football stadium could almost fit on this deck. The white superstructure at the far end of the deck looks like a small box planted like an afterthought to a child's building-block creation, almost fragile, a final touch before he kicks the whole thing over. The wheelhouse above the accommodation block juts out over the deck and looks like the control tower at an airport, large square windows all around. The bridge-wings extend with some architectural grace on each side of the wheelhouse, out and over the sea.

I am presented to the master of the *Montrose* in the ship's office, a brightly lighted room with a couple of desks, computers, printers, a copy machine, and a wall crammed with manuals, records, and technical books. Limp oil-blackened white boiler suits hang on a clothes rack in the corner.

Captain Gerrit Postma, bent over paperwork, is not what I expected, not the swashbuckling bearded Viking in charge of a supertanker. Instead I find a polite and intelligent fifty-three-year-old Dutchman with short gray hair, glasses, a sort of pixyish face accented by a ski-jump nose. He is not an imposing man, not tall, not distinguished; he could pass as a family doctor from Peoria. He suggests I get settled and meet him later on the bridge.

The *Montrose* is tied up to the Liberian-registered tanker *Frixos*, and we are sucking from her tanks 38,000 tons of Abadan Straight Run Fuel Oil owned by the National Iranian Oil Company. The *Montrose* is already a third full: it had loaded 141,000 tons of Arabian Light Crude at Ras Tanura, Saudi Arabia, oil owned by ARAMCO, the Saudi national oil company.

It was a fast turnaround in "Saudi"; they usually are. The crews of most ships are happy to get in and out of the country as quickly as possible, for the long arm of Saudi fundamentalism throttles all life aboard. Non-Muslims, according to the Saudi Islamic system of Wahhabism, are infidels, and Saudis interpret strictly the teaching of

Muhammad; for Westerners it is an uncomfortable place to work, live, or visit. The chief engineer aboard a sister ship to the *Montrose* tells of a Filipino crew member who signed on to the vessel in Jeddah. Before joining the ship he was searched by a Saudi customs officer, who found the seaman's cross and rosary. He flew into a rage, ripped it apart, and flung the beads over the cabin floor. Saudi Arabia can afford to treat anyone any way it pleases. A quarter of the world's known oil reserves are located within its borders, most of which goes to the United States.

The *Frixos* had loaded in the Iranian port of Bandar Mahshahr on the east coast of the Persian Gulf. This cargo, like the Saudi Arabian Light, is to be discharged on the other side of the world at the refinery on Bukom Island, Singapore. Another cargo of crude will be lifted tomorrow in Oman on the other side of the Arabian Peninsula.

About a third our size, the *Frixos* can get into ports we would never consider. Its current unglamorous career is simply to pick up oil from terminals ashore and carry it to the bigger vessels waiting in deeper waters offshore.

The two ships are tied together shoulder-to-shoulder, separated by a half-dozen giant oblong rubber fenders, each twenty-one feet long and eleven feet wide, swathed in truck tires. In spite of these the disengagement of the two vessels is the most difficult part of any ship-to-ship transfer. The two ships could bump upon disconnection, and a VLCC must not touch anything solid. This ship, in fact, never has metal-to-metal contact with anything. One tanker like the *Frixos* bumping a VLCC, no matter how slight, would tie up both ships for days, perhaps weeks, while surveyors determined how much paint was scratched. Or much worse.

It is about midnight, and I've stowed my gear in the owner's cabin—a spacious room with a double bed, couch, two large windows that face aft onto the ship's funnel and the sea beyond.

On the way to the bridge I pass the jolly Croat, who has cornered the wife of the chief engineer in the corridor: ". . . church three hundred meters above our village—in the mountains. Hey!" he calls, catching me. "I have more photos I get out of suitcase."

The bridge is the control room to this high-tech crude-oil delivery machine, and at night it possesses a near spectral quality. The two oversized radar screens on standby emit a bright blue glow that fills the wheelhouse with an eerie, watery cast. Miniature lamps of gauges, dials, readouts, alarms, switches, and buttons add tiny sparkles of bright color throughout the darkened chamber. At sea this is a cloister of voices muted and light subdued, almost cathedral-like. In daytime those on the bridge speak in day voices but, at night it is similar to the interior of a temple, hushed, respectfully quiet. The night watch is what many remember most about their days at sea.

I find the captain standing with his arms clasped behind his back, staring down at the discharge operations below. We will soon disconnect the large filler pipes and get under way. The deck lights of the *Frixos* and the lamps from our own long deck offer additional light to the normally darkened control room, and there is enough visibility to see each other.

After the initial gavotte in which the captain determines I know the difference between port and starboard, he visibly appears to resign himself that I am aboard.

Captain Postma has been in command of the *Montrose* for three months. He has been at sea and always with The Group since 1970, and, before the *Montrose*, captain of another smaller tanker for five years. He lives in the Pyrenees with his French wife, he worries about Basque terrorists, misses his two nearly grown daughters, and wonders how he will be able to handle retirement. It is a psychological conundrum, he admits. "Here I am somebody but back at home after I retire, I will look at myself and ask, *Who am I?* My wife tells me to stop talking like that, but I know I will have a problem with it. Not to my friends or family, but just—just to everyone else. To myself." It is an understandable sentiment; from commanding one of the largest, most vital machines on the planet to a life controlling weeds in the garden is not an unreasonable fear.

"So." It is a statement, nearly Germanic in character. "So, you are writing about piracy, Mr. Burnett?"

"Yes, Captain, I am."

"Oh, please call me Gerrit," he offers.

And of course, I say, please call me by my first name; but I know at the time I can never address this man as anything but Captain. "I'm particularly interested in our passage through the Malacca Straits."

"Well, I do not think pirates should be much of a problem for us," he says. "For others, for small ships, that is another matter. But for us, I think it would be very difficult for pirates to take over my ship."

He sits back on the console of lights and gauges and stares at the floor. He rubs his chin as if there was once a beard. The captain does not seem to be a man of much pretense; he appears to be down to earth and his body language, his quick eyes, seem to convey what is on his mind. It is refreshing; I'll know when to keep my mouth shut and stand back in a corner.

"And, frankly, I don't know why they would want to attack my ship. There is nothing here to steal. We are quite spare—we carry no cash aboard. We have a very good watch system, our deck lights are on in pirate areas, and our fire hoses piss a little." Considering the size of this monstrous machine called a ship, I should agree. The overwhelming sense of towering height here on the bridge, nine stories above the sea, does give the impression that no pirates could possibly board this vessel.

There are lengthy checklists for the disconnection of the big pipes through which the oil flows from the *Frixos* to ours, as well as for the separation of two vessels. Wind, current, ships' characteristics, have to be taken into account. The captain goes over it again and again.

The lines are cast free and the offshore breeze helps push the smaller tanker away; she eases slowly forward, so close I can almost jump from our bridgewing to theirs.

We begin the nighttime journey out of the Persian Gulf, south around the coast of the Arabian Peninsula to Oman for our next fill-up.

On the way down to my cabin I notice, affixed to the doors to the stairwell on every deck, the reminder that on this ultramodern behemoth, high seas piracy in the twenty-first century is a risk to the crew. Although it seems unlikely that a ship of this size is vulnerable to attack, The Group does appear to take the threat seriously:

ANTI-PIRACY PRECAUTIONS

Anti-piracy precautions will be in force whenever the vessel is sailing at night in the area from Pulau Rondo off Sumatra, in the South China Sea Area as far east as Taiwan (including all Indonesian and Philippine waters) and in any other areas such as off the island of Socotra, the coasts of Brazil, certain coasts off West Africa and anywhere pirates have been known to operate....

MUSTERPOINT IN NO.1 DECK ALLEYWAY

REMEMBER THAT THE BEST DEFENCE AGAINST A PIRATE ATTACK IS VIGILANCE. IF YOU ARE THREATENED BY ARMED MEN, IT IS NOT ADVISABLE TO RESIST THEM.

IF PIRATES SUCCEED IN ENTERING THE ACCOMMODATION DO NOT PLACE YOURSELF OR OTHERS IN FURTHER DANGER BY RESISTING OR ANTAGONIZING THE ATTACKERS.[4]

From the bridge the next morning the captain and I watch the passing shoreline. The remorseless, barren peaks of the Jabal Aswad range rise out of the blowing dust and haze. The mountains—craggy, sharp, parched, and treeless—form a five-thousand-foot barrier to the rolling hills of the Arabian Desert inside. Arabic-style homes with rounded archways, domes, flat roofs with castlelike crenellations, incongruously line the base of the mountains in the background.

According to the *CIA World Factbook* the percentage of arable land in Oman is zero, permanent crops is zero, forests and woodland zero, and pasture land five percent. However, Oman does have oil and The Group owns thirty-four percent of it.

The wellheads are located eight hundred kilometers away in the Empty Quarter, the uninhabited region at the corners of Oman, Saudi Arabia, and Yemen, territory only a Bedouin could love. Oil pipelines snake over and under the scorching, windblown sands until, like serpents, they slither up the back side of the mountains and feed Omani Export Blend, a light crude, into huge storage tanks above. The oil, gravity fed, then flows downward from the tanks in pipes that course along the seabed to a Single Buoy Mooring three miles offshore. Attached to the mooring are the two flexible floating oil-pipelines that will be connected to the ship's tank manifolds.

The pilot boat from Petroleum Development of Oman delivers the man who is going to guide us onto the mooring and some laborers to help fit the hoses to the ship's manifolds. Pilots are ship's masters who have left the high seas for a homelife. Trained with "local knowledge"—regional wind conditions, tidal flows, currents, and channel depths—these are seafarers who take over command of the ship when the vessel arrives in a port. While the pilot commands the visiting ship, the captain of the vessel maintains ultimate responsibility. I have known pilots, and they are usually soft, smarmy locals out for a little baksheesh of alcohol, cigarettes, dollars cash, or all three. This one, however, is a solid, good-looking, thirty-something Englishman, an ex–company captain with an easy manner who, after a quick handshake, gets right down to business.

He orders his crew to begin measuring the oxygen content in *Montrose*'s empty tanks. The cargo we carry never is exposed to full air; the empty tanks have been filled with inert gas, such as engine exhaust, flue gas high in nitrogen and carbon dioxide, and should be nearly totally devoid of oxygen. There is no chance for accidental ignition of flammable cargo if the oxygen content is below eight percent; anything above and the pilot will not permit the ship to be loaded.

"Let's bring it to a stop for a little while, Captain," he says while he waits for the readings.

The pilot gets word later on the handheld radio that all tanks are inert, steady at three percent.

"Come to one seventy, please. Dead slow ahead."

The Filipino helmsman repeats the command and turns the small wheel, the Pakistani officer reaches over and pushes the telegraph lever a notch, and the ship judders and begins to inch slowly forward.

The SBM, a two-story red hockey-puck-shaped mooring, is three miles away and we move at three knots, slower than walking speed. There is no hurry. While time is money for those running VLCCs at $30,000 a day, more important is the knowledge that it takes as long as a half hour to stop an object the size of a city skyscraper.

Two seagoing tugboats, large vessels by anyone's imagination but dwarfed by the *Montrose*, position themselves at the mooring and wait. We must look gargantuan to those aboard those boats; I imagine we are approaching the SBM with all the grace of a hippopotamus. One tug will keep the floating pipelines away from our ship and the other will take our ropes and attach them to the iron-and-steel pillbox mooring that supports the floating hoses. On the bow of the *Montrose* our crewmen, in white coveralls, red hard hats, and thick gloves, arrange the hawsers that will be passed down to the tugs. They are a cheerful lot. The "ratings," nonofficers, are Filipino and they banter easily in their native Tagalog, kid each other, and work steadily. White T-shirts form makeshift burnooses under their hard hats—the sleeves sweep their shoulders and effectively keep the sun off. One has raised his T-shirt up to his eyes, gangster style. He looks like he could pass as a pirate.

"*Teka, teka, teka!*—Wait!" one yells to another as he struggles with an unwieldy mooring line.

While they are pulling and straining, I stand by the *Montrose*'s anchor chain that rises to the chain pawl above my head. I have never seen a chain this big; just one side of each rusted iron link is as thick as my calf, and the width of the entire link is wider than my waist. The length of each link is half my nearly six-foot height. One link could not be lifted or moved by one man. The anchor, snug against the bow outside, weighs seventeen tons. The enormity of this monster ship is overwhelming. It is not apparent why anyone would refer to a machine this size, even if it is a ship, in the feminine.

Once we are secured to the SBM, the second tug nudges the thick orange-striped black floating pipelines toward us. From a distance they look like giant sea snakes slithering across the water's surface. One of the crew walks to the bow, turns his back, and pees against the anchor chain.

The ship's crane lifts the dripping serpents out of the water, over the side of the hull, and the crew wrestles with the hoses, lining them up with the ship's manifolds. They have put large plastic tubs under the pipes to catch any dripping oil. From what I see today and what I am to see for the rest of this investigation, no tanker that I was aboard ever left its pecker tracks.

Time was not so long ago, before protecting the environment was a matter of legislation, ships would normally empty their bilges and clean their tanks as soon as they departed a port. The telltale trail of oily scum was visible in the ship's wake and chased it for miles, remaining on the surface for days. Today, in the eyes of most masters, spilling oil is as bad as a collision. Indeed, in 2000, it was reported that a company was fined a million dollars by port authorities on the west coast of the United States when its ship spilled a single forty-two-gallon barrel of fuel oil into the harbor.

2

I Kill, of Course!

The *Montrose* is now full and fat and ready for sea. We have lifted 620,000 barrels of Omani Light and we are about to drop the floating pipelines, break off the mooring, and steam out to the normalcy and peace of the open seas. It is a nighttime departure, and an older pilot stands in the darkened bridge behind the instrument console and watches the ship's crane lower the last filler pipe into the water. He reminisces quietly about driving company tankers to Vietnam in the seventies.

There are a number of radios tuned to the hailing, emergency, ship-to-ship, and ship-to-shore frequencies, all competing for attention. A squeaky voice of some local idiot trying to sing begins to ride over one of the channels. The chief mate, supervising the parting from the mooring from the deck below, radios the progress over the babble with his walkie-talkie, and the master of the tugboat under the starboard bow radios that he is ready to push the vessel away from the mooring. It is the moment of departure.

As we drop the mooring chains to the SBM, the starboard tug pushes our bow seaward and the other pulls the floating pipeline out of our way. The *Montrose* shudders and, with movement imperceptible, creeps forward. The ship is so ponderous that you don't know that you are moving unless you fix on some stationary light onshore.

"The tug will stay on the hoses for the next ship, Captain," the pilot says. "They won't be swinging back on you." He sounds eager to be off and go home.

"Yes, good."

"Come to three zero." The helmsman repeats the order. "Dead slow, please."

It is the captain who moves the telegraph handle forward and repeats the command.

"I think you have it now, Captain," and the pilot is escorted down the stairwell to the waiting pilot boat. Postma mutters angrily to himself and twists his short gray forelocks. He walks quickly out onto the bridgewing and then returns.

"He must hurry. We can not go any faster until he is away."

"Problem, Captain?"

"We are crabbing toward that ship." He nods toward another VL tethered to an SBM on the port side a couple miles away. The captain's eyes flit from the wheelhouse docking repeater, a digital instrument mounted atop the console, to the radar screen to the brightly lit vessel on the mooring. The repeater shows our ship's forward speed as well as the speed of our bow, 917 feet in front of us, and the speed of drift of our stern, 172 feet behind us. It may seem odd that an instrument exists to measure the speed and direction of both the bow and the stern—it should all go together at the same time—but when you are steering a ship longer than three football fields, coastal currents can effect the front differently than the back. The purpose of the instrument is to monitor the precise movement of the ship as tugs fore and aft push her against a wharf. Tonight it tells the captain that our forward speed is a little more than a knot and that we are being swept sideways toward the VLCC off our port at more than a half knot. That moored VLCC is about three miles ahead and about two miles off our course line. Since it takes so long for the *Montrose* to get up speed, by the time we should be abeam the other tanker steaming safely past, we might well be on top of it. It will be that close.

The captain tries to correct the slide with five-degree course changes, but we do not have enough way on for the effort to make any difference. He cannot increase speed because the pilot and his crew are still disembarking. We are drifting inexorably closer. He walks quickly back out to the bridgewing to see if the pilot is off our ship.

"Captain, deck," the radio barks, catching him midway.

"Go ahead, Chief."

"Pilot boat clear and away."

"Thank you." He turns to me. "Now we must move."

He slams the telegraph handle to half ahead and orders a twenty-degree correction to starboard. It takes a long time for this ship to respond. The docking repeater finally tells us what we are beginning to see. The bow is beginning to move faster than the stern; we are turning. This is not a close call, not close enough to hold our breath, but it is a good lesson in supertanker seamanship. Instinctively Captain Postma saw that while the pilot was in command there was going to be a problem. He carries the savvy of any good seafarer, like sailors who make passages alone across oceans. The mark of any good sailor in command is to plan for contingencies, expect and prepare quietly for the worst, and be ready to deal with it should it ever occur. Postma anticipated the potential problem long before it became one. I wonder aloud if the pilot left too early and he simply says, "Maybe."

The caterwauling on the radio is louder and more irritating. The jerk with a VHF radio, emboldened, sings along to some Arabic song that blasts distorted out of a commercial radio station in the background, an effective way to jam the airwaves.

I am reminded of my passage across from Borneo on the *Unicorn*; all night long Indonesian seamen insulted Filipinos and Filipinos insulted Malaysians and Malaysians insulted Indonesians, calling each other monkeys, fucking monkeys, animals, and further insulting each other's mothers and sisters, while nearby vessels tried to call through.

"I have heard them sing 'God Fuck the Queen.' That made people very angry. They shout back, 'Get off the air, you bloody git!' " The captain attempts to mimic a British accent. "Sometimes they sing the Koran. And also they make fart sounds with their mouths. Anybody with a walkie-talkie can get on the radio and do what he pleases. It is very disturbing."

Behind us a VLCC approaches the mooring we just dropped. As seen through the binoculars its dark shadow looms out of the night like a wide-mouthed shark.

Here in the computerized, digitized, and rather sterilized control room of this essential vehicle of world commerce, one would think we are a little unique. However, we are not. It is that VLCC behind us that levels us. Our ship is just one of the many huge vessels that transfuse the life blood of the planet into machinery that burns it, cracks it, distills it, refines it for the needs of our temporary existence here on earth. The *Montrose* is one of many trucks of the seas, ingesting, delivering, discharging, turning back to load up and move out. Sixty percent of the world's crude oil moves by sea, and we are just one of many ships on the line. And another ship is right behind us, about to fill up at the mooring we just left.

The United States is the world's largest importer of oil; with five percent of the world's population we consume a staggering twenty-five percent of the world's total oil demand. The United States in 2001 imported about 125 million tons of oil from the Persian Gulf, forty percent more than from any other single source. Energy independence, a mantra that has been on the lips of American presidents since the oil crisis of 1973, is a pipe dream. Domestic consumption outstrips domestic production in the U.S., and barring some miraculous oil find, even if drilling does take place in the Arctic National Wildlife Refuge, the U.S. will continue to depend on oil from abroad, especially from the Middle East.[5] Japan, the world's second-largest economy, is more heavily dependent on the Persian Gulf; four fifths of its crude oil comes from this region, and all of that is shipped by VLCC. These big ships may be just watergoing trucks, but the world won't be able to survive without them any time soon.

One must wonder when it will end. The oil trade from the Persian Gulf to Asia, Japan, Europe, and the U.S. has been going on for decades, nonstop, every day of the year. The planet *is* big and the oil reservoirs are vast and there is still oil undiscovered, but I try to remind myself that this stuff is the remains of plants and creatures dating back 350 million years, give or take a million. There must have been a hell of a lot of dinosaurs.

What does crude oil, hot from the earth, look and smell like? I know crude from once scraping it off a rocky coastline. In that form it was thick, black, tarry. I have three glass vials of the cargo that we carry aboard the *Montrose:* this crude oil does not look at all what I expected—thick and black; rather it is thin, a reddish-brown liquid. The Omani Crude that we just loaded appears to be a little darker, a richer color than the Arab Light from Saudi Arabia. The Saudi oil flows easier. Neither crude is thick and tarry—each looks to be a cross between hydraulic fluid and lube oil, thinner in fact than the 40-weight motor oil we use in our cars. The Omani Light smells something like gasoline, the Saudi Light smells like lubricating oil but more powerfully gaseous. There is no doubt that the chemical properties of the two oils are different.

Our other cargo, the Abadan Straight Run Fuel Oil, is in a category of its own. It is thick, viscous, pours with the consistency of treacle, and is what I expected crude to look like. This already has been distilled by a refinery in Iran and will be refined still further. Like the crude it will probably end up in somebody's automobile.

After filling up we now weigh exactly 311,369 tons, nearly seven times bigger than the *Titanic*. That an object this solid, this heavy, this immense, actually can move is almost beyond belief. Motion is felt, but it is not movement. We equate movement with the cars we drive, the airplanes that whisk us across the skies, to objects that we observe.

When this ship leaps off its blocks from a dead start, it takes nearly two minutes simply to get moving after the propeller kicks in. Laden with cargo, it reaches hull speed of 15.5 knots—18.6 miles per hour—in about forty minutes. Not exactly a roadrunner.

Maneuvering a VLCC seems always on the edge—you coax it, you do not command it. You have no steerageway below three knots; you have to watch the computer readouts and when the propeller reaches a certain RPM, then you can push it a few knots faster. It will not turn on a dime; it will not stop on a nickel. No miscalculations are permitted on this ship.

The captain picks up the phone on the main console. "Good evening, Chief. We will go full away at 2330, if you please."

Full away on the *Montrose* is maximum cruising speed. It is also the moment the meter starts ticking; the official passage begins and the charterer, the corporation's Asian trading company, begins paying the tab for the delivery.

We are rumbling southeast into the Arabian Gulf toward the Nine Degree Channel between the coral archipelagos of the Lacadives and the Maldives, about four days away. It is during this stretch that the seas are often a little lumpy; it is cyclone season and the southwest monsoon, which brings devastating floods to India, Pakistan, and Bangladesh, lies in our path. Our course takes us around the bottom end of Sri Lanka, then nearly due west toward northern Sumatra and then southward down the Malacca Straits. The entire passage from Muscat to the Singapore area should take nine days.

The ship is remarkably quiet under way. The only sound of the 36,000-horsepower engine is from the blowers under the funnel. No roar, no deep-throated rumble. Only the nettlesome rattling of cabinets, doors, and fixtures from a surprising amount of vibration. The vibration could be from a problem with the engine itself. The *Montrose* lost a fuel pump on its huge seven-cylinder Sulzer engine during the last passage between the Philippines to Singapore and Tony Butcher, the second engineer who has been working on these same-class ships since the first one slid down the ways in 1995, says she "limped in on six legs." The timing is still just not right, he thinks.

Except for the vibration and the hint of a slow roll, you would never suppose you are aboard a ship crossing an ocean; it is conducive to a perfect, dreamless sleep.

The highlight of the ship's weekly social calendar is happy hour, held in the officers' recreation room thirty minutes before the Sunday dinner. This is the occasion when we are to wear our Sunday-go-to-meetin' clothes: the officers in uniform, others as formal as we can make it. Happy hour kicks off at 1245; unless under extreme duress I am not accustomed to drinking before the sun sinks behind the yardarm, but one does have manners.

Brian Ashdown, the chief engineer, and his wife, Angela, who always sail together, sit at one end of the bar; Chief Officer Viktor Travnik, the other Croatian on the ship, and the captain, smartly dressed in their summer whites, are camped at the far corner. Niko, father of the bride, is bartender; he offers me a beer and a big welcome and pops tabs of beer and soft drinks for the others. I don't know if he volunteered or has been ordered to the position, but by his nature I imagine his job behind the bar is self-appointed. As the ship's electrician Niko gets his hands in it. But he scrubs up pretty well—white shirt, stripes on his shoulder boards, white shorts, white socks, and polished black shoes, the normal kit for an officer of a vessel flying the British ensign. He pops a tab for the captain, then bends over to pick up a booklet of photos that has slipped out of his back pocket.

Happy hour is a time the officers feel they are no longer cogs in a wheel. Joke, jibes, simple good fun, even at the expense of "the old man," are exchanged freely—a Friday after work at the bar for those who work and live together.

The officers' rec room is always open, a place to watch local TV when in port or to watch videos or listen to CDs. The bar opens daily at 1700 hours and the honor system allows each of us to sign for his own poison. What we consume is paid for in pounds sterling and a can of beer costs 24p, about thirty-five cents U.S. The captain admits that he inspects the sheet every night to see who is imbibing more than he considers proper. Understandably he wants a limit of three, max four, beers a day per person.[6] Most of the officers are Pakistani and Muslim and they don't drink. The Filipino ratings are allowed beer only. Then there are the rest of us: Niko, who had boasted about the superiority of Croatian white wines on the launch the other day; Angela and her husband, Brian; Tony, the second engineer, myself, and the captain; it is not a difficult accounting. And the captain is keeping track.

The captain looks up at the clock and announces, "Okay, gentlemen, time to eat," and we gulp down the last of our pleasure and continue the ribald discussions at the dinner table. Angela, a spirited grandmother, turns out to be one of the guys, giving as good as she gets, for seamen often whinge about women and she is there holding up her end.

The officers' mess is a spacious bright corner room with windows facing aft and starboard out over the sea. A couple of large Korean dolls in traditional ancient dress with painted faces, gifts or talismans of the ship's builder, Daewoo Heavy Industries of Korea, stand guard in a clear plastic case against the far wall. A tall indoor tropic houseplant is strapped into a corner, neglected and unseen. A small unidentifiable shrub droops lifelessly in a flower box under the tree.

The long table in the center is covered with a white linen cloth; linen napkins tidily rolled in sterling silver napkin holders remain at each place setting. A tray of chutneys, ketchup, chili sauce, mustards, and a pepper mill are within reach for the communal grab. The captain takes his seat in a rather undistinguished position somewhere near the middle and beckons me to sit on his right. It is the place of honor, I presume. Angela and Brian and Tony sit opposite, and Niko and Chief Officer Viktor to my right. The Pakistani officers eat at the other end among themselves in companionable silence. These will be our places until signing off.

It is apparent that new blood is welcome at the Sunday meal; there is something other than the management of the vessel to talk about. And the conversation turns to piracy. Most seem to know someone who has been pirated and some, I am to discover, have their own horror stories to tell. Except Captain Postma.

"I have never met any pirates," he says. "I think they are mostly—what?—stories." Captain Postma reminds me that there have been instances in which ship masters have claimed to have been robbed by pirates but took the money themselves.

Niko puffs up and announces, "Pirates come, I know what to do."

"What's that, Niko?"

"You see watch?" he says, holding up his beefy arm. "Two hundred dollars, I pay. Pirates come, take my watch—I kill, of course!"

Angela furrows her brow. "I don't think that is a very good idea, Niko."

"No worry. You see. In morning I still have watch. You see."

Tony Butcher, second-in-command of the engine room, has a bright round head like a basketball and he is shorn bald with just a hint of a shadow around the temples. He carries that cartoonish Alfred E. Neuman what-me-worry innocence that is hard not to like.

"You are not supposed to fight back, Niko," Tony says.

"Hey, not worry, Tony. I take care."

I notice that one of the young Pakistani officers at the other end has been glancing in my direction as he eats. I sense he wants to join in the conversation, ask something. He is a wiry, erect man with a sharp hooked nose, curly black hair, fair skin, and a pleasant face.

In a quiet moment as we tuck into our food, he looks up and asks, "Are you an American?"

"Yes."

"I worked for KFC in Karachi. When I was a student."

"KFC?"

"Chicken. I have been to America. I did not like America."

"Where did you go? Maybe there are better places."

"Baltimore. And New Orleans."

"New Orleans is a great town. You didn't like it?"

"I did not like America."

"Come to think of it," I say to the young officer, "I got off my first ship in Baltimore and I don't think I liked it much either. A good city once you get to know it. But for a sailor getting off a ship—you are probably right."

"America wasn't friendly to me," the Pakistani says.

Captain Postma announces that the tradition of baksheesh is alive and well on the Arabian Peninsula. An Omani customs officer boarded us shortly after we moored up to the SBM. While the official checked the ship's stores and the bonded locker, the captain was called to the bridge, leaving a junior officer and the customs man alone in the lockup. The captain later saw the customs agent on the deck below walking quickly toward his launch, lugging three garbage bags. Taking the stairs two at a time, Postma caught up with the official just as he was about to descend the gangway.

"Normally, we give them something, but three bags was just too much! He was like Santa Claus! But what can I do? We go there all the time and we will be back, so I know that I must not make him angry. I told him to open the bags and show me what he stole, but he said he was embarrassed—'Not here, Captain, please,' " he says. "So inside I open the bags and there are cigarettes, wines, and one bagful of condiments—sauces, ketchup, mustards, napkins. He looted us.

"So. What must I do? Well, I have to give him something and I tell him to take two bags and leave the other here. We have to pay for what he steals. I am still a little angry."

The captain looks over the table, watches the last officer finish his ice cream, and with an "*Ah, bon!* Thank you," he dismisses us all.

The climb of the four outside flights to the bridge may be as much exercise as I get on this ship, although the thousand-foot deck looks enticing; I would like to jog around it, but orders from the captain are that steel-toed work boots and hard hats must be worn at all times topsides.

The sky reluctantly gives up its putrid sandy color for cleaner silvery low cloud that skits across the surface of the sea. We are away finally from the influence of land and not far from the island of Socotra off the Horn of Africa, where at this time of year the seas can turn into some of the meanest on the Indian Ocean. Today they are moderate, two- to three-meter swells and wind out of the southwest is at a steady twenty-five knots, gusting higher in squalls. In a sailboat I would have sails reefed, but from up here it means nothing. The ship rolls easily from one side to the other, and it is not at all uncomfortable.

A tanker the size of the *Montrose* returning empty to the Gulf for another bellyful has poked through the haze ahead of us; she is in ballast, high out of the water, awkward and boxlike; you could imagine that, like a melting iceberg, she is so top heavy she would roll over without warning.

The CPA on the radar flashes and Captain Postma begins to explain to the young officer on watch about the closest-point-of-approach alarm.

The captain seems to be well liked by his men; he knows their names, talks to them about their families. He has sailed with some of the older ones in the past before he became master. Like other good captains he is a bit of a teacher; he gives them an order and if there is time, he frequently explains why. This on-the-spot tutelage conveys a partnership, and no one seems to really resent his explanatory comments; one day some of them will be in command and will be instructing their protégés.

The weather is getting up. The visibility is down to about a mile in a horizontal rain. Lines of whitecaps crease the metallic-colored seas. We are beginning to roll. This is a double-hulled ship, and because of the design she rolls like a cork in any seaway. In the *Unicorn* I would be well bundled up in slop such as this, down below in the cabin with the self-steering windvane keeping the old girl on course. However, I am not in my stout little boat. I am high and dry a hundred feet above it all on the bridge, sipping my coffee, watching the radar screen.

The telex spits out a message and the captain walks to the machine, tears off the spooled paper, reads it, hands it to me. "This might be of some interest. Very useful—could happen to us as well."

I am incredulous. It is the daily situation report[7] sent to all ships from the International Maritime Bureau's Piracy Reporting Center in Kuala Lumpur. I have wondered on occasion whether I am creating this crisis about piracy, whether those who tell me there is a disaster in the wings have their own agenda. Perhaps I should be writing a book instead about the Golden Age of Piracy. We all know about that era—dashing, picaresque, and romantic; maybe piracy exists only in the lost childhood visions of my own mind. The incident that happened to me on my boat was merely a strange get-together by a bunch of sailors with guns. And so many other attacks in which entire ships, their cargo, and their crews disappear, just random robberies at sea. Yet the stark language in the situation report shakes me back to reality and I realize am I dealing with facts, not romance:

SITREP MSG:227/2001
THIS BROADCAST WARNS SHIPS IN PASSAGE IN AFRICA, THE
INDIAN SUBCONTINENT, AND SOUTH EAST ASIAN WATERS
REGARDING PIRACY AND ARMED ROBBERY AGAINST SHIPS.

WARNINGS
INCREASING NUMBER OF ATTACKS HAVE BEEN REPORTED IN THE
MALACCA STRAITS BETWEEN THE COORDINATES 01 TO 02N–101
TO 103E. THE MOST RISK-PRONE AREA IS WITHIN 25 NM RADIUS
SURROUNDING 02N–102E, WHERE THE SAME ARMED GANG OF
PIRATES SEEMS TO HAVE REPEATEDLY ATTACKED SHIPS.

SHIPS ARE ADVISED TO AVOID ANCHORING ALONG THE
INDONESIAN COAST OF THE MALACCA STRAITS UNLESS
REQUIRED FOR URGENT OPERATIONAL REASONS. THE COAST
NEAR ACEH IS PARTICULARLY RISKY. PIRATES RECENTLY
BOARDED TWO VESSELS AND KIDNAPPED THE CREW FOR
RANSOM. SHIPS ARE ADVISED TO BE EXTRA CAUTIOUS WHEN
TRANSITING THE WATERS OFF ACEH.

IN VIEW OF THE RECENT SPATE IN HIJACKINGS, SHIP OWNERS
ARE ADVISED TO INSTALL A SATELLITE TRACKING SYSTEM ON
BOARD. IMB RECOMMENDS INSTALLATION OF SHIPLOC, WHICH
HAS PROVED TO BE INVALUABLE IN THE LOCATION AND
RECOVERY OF HIJACKED VESSELS.

SUSPICIOUS CRAFT
IN POSITION: 05.38N–096.32E, INDONESIA.
*WHILE UNDERWAY, TWO SPEEDBOATS APPROACHED A CONTAINER
SHIP FROM STERN. GENERAL ALARM RAISED AND CREW ALERTED,
FIRED FLARES. AS A RESULT, SPEEDBOAT RETREATED.*

LATEST REPORTED INCIDENTS
IN POSITION 0:08.8S–044:06.2E 90 NM EAST OF KISMAYO,
SOMALIA.
*WHILE UNDERWAY, ARMED PIRATES IN THREE FISHING BOATS
OPENED FIRE AND SHOT FOUR TIMES AT A CONTAINER SHIP AND
TRIED TO BOARD HER. BOARDING WAS AVERTED.*

IN POSITION 01:56.5N–102:19.0E, MALACCA STRAITS.
*WHILE UNDERWAY, ABOUT 20 ARMED PIRATES BOARDED A BULK
CARRIER AND TOOK HOSTAGE ALL CREWMEMBERS AND ROBBED
THEIR VALUABLES AND CASH.*

IN POSITION 01:40N–104:30E, NEAR HORSBURGH LIGHTHOUSE,
SINGAPORE STRAITS.
*WHILE UNDERWAY, 12 PIRATES WITH KNIVES BOARDED A
CHEMICAL TANKER, HELD HOSTAGE THE CAPTAIN, 2/E, 4/E, A/B
AND ENGINEER CADET. THEY ROBBED THE CREW'S PERSONAL
BELONGINGS, SHIP HANDPHONE, CAMERA AND CASH. PIRATES FLED
IN THEIR SPEEDBOAT. NO ONE INJURED ONBOARD.*

IN POSITION 04:35N–95:05E, INDONESIA.
*WHILE UNDERWAY, FIVE PIRATES IN A SMALL BOAT FIRED UPON A
TANKER AND ASKED THE MASTER TO STOP THE ENGINE. THE
MASTER INCREASED SPEED. PIRATES FOLLOWED THE SHIP FOR A
FEW MINUTES THEN FLED.*

AT BALIKPAPAN ANCHORAGE, INDONESIA.
*DURING TRANSSHIPMENT OPERATIONS THE WATCHMAN ON A VLCC
SPOTTED TWO PERSONS ON THE FORECASTLE REMOVING SHIP'S
STORES FROM THE FORWARD LOCKER. WHEN PIRATES REALIZED
THEIR PRESENCE WAS DISCOVERED, THEY ESCAPED DOWN THE
ANCHOR CHAIN.*

ADVICE TO ALL SHIPS
EXTRA CAUTION IS ADVISED AT ALL PORTS IN INDONESIA, GELASA
STR, BANGKA STR, BERHALA STR, SUNDA STR, MALACCA STR,
SINGAPORE STR, PHILLIP CHANNEL, CHITTAGONG ROADS, MONGLA
ANCHORAGE, CHENNAI ANCHORAGE, COCHIN ANCHORAGE, KANDLA,
SOUTHERN RED SEA, GULF OF ADEN, THE SOMALI COAST, CONAKRY
AND NIGERIAN PORTS.

SHIPS ARE ADVISED TO MAINTAIN ANTI-PIRACY WATCHES AND
REPORT ALL PIRATICAL ATTACKS AND SUSPICIOUS MOVEMENTS
OF CRAFT TO THE IMB PIRACY REPORTING CENTRE, KUALA
LUMPUR, MALAYSIA.

Pirates boarded a VLCC at Balikpapan by climbing up the anchor chain—not hard to imagine; it is as easy to scale as a ladder. And the attack on the ship near the Horsburgh Light—the same place where the wretches boarded my boat. One attack in this sitrep occurred directly on our route—in the deep water channel in the Malacca Straits.

At least we had been warned.

One tanker pirated in these waters never had the benefit of such alerts.

3

A Dangerous Space

When the oil tanker *Valiant Carrier* was attacked in 1992, the crime of piracy was not yet much of a concern for most shipowners and their crews. Yet within weeks of the attack on the *Unicorn*, pirates struck the *Valiant Carrier* in the same area with far more tragic consequences. The story of the brutal assault on the ship's master and his family made it one of the most notable in recent history. It was in part the incident in modern piracy responsible for the creation of the Piracy Reporting Center and these daily alerts to shipping. There were no such dire warnings available at the time to help Captain Donny Monteiro, his wife, his children, and his crew.

Valiant Carrier

The taxi bounced down the dockside road toward the oil refinery pier, where Captain Monteiro's ship was loading. It had been four months since Vimala Monteiro had seen Donny, husband, father, sea captain—a short time compared to some contracts he had had. One day she would get him off the ships and back home where he would be able to help raise his son and daughter; but she knew it would be at the time of his choosing. Four months was just too long—more than half a lifetime of their baby. Vim could imagine Donny's smile when he saw his daughter.

Within minutes her life on land would be but a memory. Vimala sighed, gazing down at the infant she held in her arms. Deepak, their eight-year-old son, sat next to his mother, his nose pressed against the taxi window, and stared out at a large container ship that passed close to the dock.

The oil refinery rose above them with fat chimneys belching thick clouds of smoke, pencil-thin spires emitting bright explosive flares, oblong tubes and vertical canisters, skeletal metal fingers clawing the sky venting steam; and at ground level, a confusion of hoses, twisting pipes, cobwebs of curling silver lines, girders and buttresses, iron stairways and catwalks, huge valves, fire cannon, and storage tanks.

A line of merchant ships, imposing and stately, lined the pier, bow to stern. A Very Large Crude Carrier appeared as a long flat island out in the washed-out haze of the bay. Too large to get close to the refinery, she swung on the specially built mooring, pumping out Persian Gulf crude oil through large-diameter pipes that snaked along the seabed. The refinery turned the crude into "products"— from the heaviest bitumen for roads to liquid petroleum gas for stoves; the awaiting smaller vessels such as the *Valiant Carrier* would then deliver the finished product to virtually every nation in Asia and beyond into the Pacific.

The *Valiant Carrier* was at the end of the wharf; from a distance the tanker looked sleek, powerful—had "nice lines," Donny had written in a letter. The long shadow of his new command swallowed the taxi, and its tall black hull soon became a dark sidewall. The ship's gleaming white superstructure, the six-story accommodation quarters for officers and crew, squatted aft behind the long cargo deck that stretched nearly the length of two football fields. Emblazoned across the sheer face of the accommodation block in large red letters:

NO SMOKING
No Open Lights

The *Valiant Carrier* was big for a product carrier—from the bridge atop the superstructure a crewman up on the foredeck at the very front looked very small indeed. Strings of pipes and a long catwalk ran down the middle of the ship to its bow, an uncommon flared design that gave the vessel an air of defiance as if a challenge to any seaway.

Vimala Monteiro was no stranger to ships; she and Donny had spent their honeymoon aboard his first command ten years before. And even when their son was still an infant, their daughter's age, she had made passages with Donny and she had loved it. She loved it still—the excitement of being at sea, the new ports, the other cultures, the unusual people. Foresight of London, the ship's owner-manager, was a good company to work for. It permitted wives and even, in some cases, the children to sail with the officers; a master's contract on a ship sometimes lasted from eight to twelve months, and many marriages might not have survived without these connubial voyages. She knew some people paid thousands of dollars for a two-week cruise. She could sail to faraway and exotic places and be with her husband and he would get paid for it. Aboard his command she was someone quite special; she was the "captain's wife." And until the age of his schooling she always took Deepak. But she was now land-bound, a grade-school teacher, ineluctably connected to work and to the responsibilities of raising a family, where she was simply Mrs. Monteiro. She could never get used to the two lives she led; a single mother when he was at sea and then, with abrasive suddenness, a wife when he was on leave. At times she resented it. It had been much easier at sea.

Both practicing Catholics, they had come from different states on the Malabar Coast of southwest India; Donny from Mangalore, an ancient seaport and trading center, Vimala from Kottayam. There are sixteen hundred different languages and dialects in India, and it is common for residents of one village to be unable to properly communicate with those of a neighboring village only a few miles away.

As elsewhere in India, English was commonly used. And it was the language they spoke to each other and with their children.

With Vanisha in her arms she stood holding Deepak's hand on the cement pier, looking up at this powerful, rumbling giant of machinery that was to be their home for the next four weeks. Its freshly painted black side loomed over them. Vimala noticed immediately the long streaks of rust bleeding down the hull like an open wound—rust that had been freshly painted over but inevitably won its release. Not even the new paint job could hide the fact that the rot was never removed. Not a good sign. *Compared to his other ships,* she thought, *this ship looks like a rusty old junk, like it's falling apart.* She could not help but feel a little embarrassed for her proud captain; she knew that the condition of the ship, other than day-to-day maintenance, was not his responsibility. In fact Foresight had already determined that the *Valiant Carrier* was ready for the breakers. Built in 1976, it was well past a tanker's useful life of fifteen years of nearly nonstop port-to-port commerce: load up, sail out, arrive and discharge, turn around and do it again; a ship down is a loss of revenue. The *Valiant Carrier* hired out for $9,000 a day. A week or two idle or in port for repairs could bankrupt smaller shipping companies. Fifteen years of transporting petroleum products through tropics, midwinter Atlantic storms, South China Sea typhoons, and a punch-up or two when working onto narrow berths was a lifetime.

Deepak stood rigidly by her side looking up at the boat deck where he expected to see his father. He was an intense little boy. Dressed in spotless white shorts and yellow T-shirt, he stood with the gawky countenance of a knock-kneed heron staring expectantly across a marsh; his big curious dark eyes were surrounded by oversized horn-rimmed glasses that gave the impression he missed nothing.

Vimala found herself transfixed by this black steel wall that rose up immediately before her. As the sea reared and fell and amid the creaking of hawsers and spring lines, a moan, plangent and mournful, arose from somewhere deep within the bowels of the ship in front of her, a baleful, almost human sound.

The articulated arms of the cranes, poised over the deck like spindly arms of a praying mantis, slowly lifted the giant filler pipes away from the ship. The *Valiant Carrier* soon would be ready to depart on what had become its regular run: transporting F4 furnace oil for the factories and power plants in Indonesia. The route took them from the refinery into the crowded Singapore Straits, then out into the South China Sea. Following the coast of Sumatra, she would steam into the Sunda Straits to an anchorage where it would raft up to a larger, permanently moored mother ship and, in a ship-to-ship transfer, discharge part of its cargo. It would be an idyllic two-day passage for the captain and his family.

The captain emerged from the side doors of the wheelhouse and onto the bridgewing above them. Dressed in an open-collar white shirt, pressed white pants, gold bars on his shoulder boards, he cut a gleaming, important figure. Captain Donny Monteiro was a handsome man—not because of his uniform or his command responsibilities, she often reminded herself, but because it was simply fact—everyone agreed. Her mother joked that he looked like the actor Omar Sharif—solid jaw, carefully trimmed mustache, full black hair beginning to gray at the temples, and patient and communicative eyes. He even had a dimple in the center of his chin. He was a good father—when he had the opportunity. Vim was very proud.

Donny Monteiro was an experienced seaman; he had begun as a raw cadet when he was sixteen, working his way through the ranks until he commanded some of the largest ships afloat. The *Valiant Carrier* was not a comedown—it was simply another ship that needed a master. It was Foresight's only tanker and the run was a lucrative one, important to the economy of Indonesia. Built in Japan for the Japanese, the *Valiant Carrier* was not a dream ship for anyone but the Japanese; the corridors were narrow, the ceilings low, and the cabins for crew and officers alike were cramped.

As Donny watched his wife and children climb the gangway, he felt a sense of relief. The sea and ships and ports and men had been his life for twenty-five years. Maybe it was his age or the months at sea; seeing them, he was feeling once again that there was something incomplete about his life.

He knew that his wife, son, and baby daughter led separate lives and the role he played in their lives was peripheral. When he was at home, like many seafarers on leave, he was a man deracinated, finding himself at the edge of society, never a part of it; more like a tourist visiting the mainstream. He found it difficult to get involved in the mundane everyday acts on land and it was a strange, sometimes uncomfortable existence. Was it the life on land or was it simply people? He knew he shared the eremitic tendencies of many sailors, tendencies that bordered on misanthropy. When in a port, like so many others, he would stay aboard—why go ashore just to get on the piss when he could stay in his cabin with a good book, sip his Glenfiddich, watch a little local television? Unless it was a port he had never visited, or unless Vim was along, it was usually far more enjoyable to kick back and relax with the knowledge that his ship was moored securely to the pier, loading or discharging proceeding smoothly, catch up on a little reading, and get an undisturbed night's sleep. The days of a woman in every port—part of the seafaring myth—were long past. Today merchant shipping was highly competitive, and time was money; quick turnarounds in port and otherwise tedium; shore leave would come soon enough—four months of it.

Vim had made it easier; she eagerly made the passages with him, sharing the port-to-port adventures. And when Deepak was born, they all sailed together; it had been ideal. But now there was Vanisha. And there was Deepak's schooling and it was different. Vim seldom sailed with him anymore.

Donny greeted his family at the top of the gangway and led them along the deck. Vim noticed case-hardened steel locks on every outside door, even on small hatches; the skylight over the engine room was cinched tight by a stainless steel chain and secured by a padlock.

The door to their quarters opened to the dayroom that served as the master's office, private lounge, and conference room. Equipped with easy chairs and a sofa, bookshelves, and a desk with TV and refrigerator, it was here that Donny entertained, met with immigration, customs, and health officials in ports, where he and a few officers when off watch would gather for a whiskey or a beer and watch a video or play a few rounds of cards. It was here that his family would spend most of their days when not strolling the deck or standing with the captain on the bridge.

It was in here, too, that the ship's safe was located. The meter-high iron strongbox was hidden inside the cabinet and usually contained the crew's wages—as much as forty thousand dollars in U.S. currency—the cargo manifests, and the ship's papers. But Donny didn't care much for this ship's safe. It had a double locking system: a tumbler combination dial and a key. The combination sequence was difficult to remember and the dial difficult to turn. As was his custom, he had paid off the crew just before departure, and while the money was still aboard the ship, it was now with the individual crewmembers—in pockets, in drawers, under mattresses, wherever seafarers thought their wages were safe. Donny did keep $4,000 cash, however, in a leather pouch that hung on a hook in his bedroom.

The captain's dayroom was on the starboard corner of the accommodation block, its fixed forward windows looking out upon the long expanse of deck and to the sea beyond; its windows on the starboard side swung open to a view that would warrant top dollar on any cruise ship.

Their bedroom was attached to the dayroom, with small portholes looking out to sea. Vim was horrified. It was more like a cell, about half the size of the captain's dayroom, just large enough to have something soft to collapse on at the end of the day, a small bedside table with Donny's gold-framed photo of her and the children and space between the bed and the wall to squeeze in a small single mattress for Deepak.

With his son in tow Donny went up to the bridge to make preparations for getting under way. As Vim began to unpack, she felt familiar vibrations of the ship's propeller bite into the water; it had always been a soothing sensation, representing freedom from land, the start of the passage, the beginning of an adventure. It wasn't the first time she wished she could be back at sea. With a bundle of Deepak's clothes in her arms, she walked over to the open seaside windows and watched a tugboat pull the ship's bow away from the pier. The warm air drifted in with a faint mix of refinery sulfur, tidal mud flats, tropic flowers, and the slight fumes of the fuel oil that now filled the ship's cargo tanks.

On an impulse she opened the dayroom door leading to the outside corridor. She recalled that there was something strange written on the outside of the door that she hadn't bothered to read. Stenciled in bright red in place of the usual small brass strip announcing CAPTAIN:

DANGEROUS
SPACE
TEST AIR
BEFORE ENTRY

Good Lord! What does that mean?

Back in the cabin it was slowly becoming clear. The warning on the door, extra locks everywhere, even a dead bolt. *Why is this ship like a fortress?* Donny was a cautious man and the locks did offer extra security. But what was he expecting?

She had total faith and confidence in her husband; there was no one on earth she trusted more. She remembered a more frightening time. In 1984 she had accompanied Donny on an Iranian/Indian-owned ship delivering wheat from Bandar to Bushehr in the Persian Gulf. During the passage the Tanker War between Iran and Iraq erupted and the ship was sailing through the middle of a battle zone. She took strength in the way he was then—they had only recently been married and she was still newly in love. Donny stood at the wheel on the bridge alone—he had ordered Vimala to join the crew, who had taken shelter in the very bow of the ship, in the fore-peak with the ship's stores. The forepeak was the point farthest away from the ship's funnel; heat-seeking missiles sought out a ship's exhaust steaming out of the funnel, and the bridge was just in front of it. Vim had refused. Through the side windows on the bridge they watched a supertanker southbound overtake them. The tanker had lifted oil at the Iranian terminal at Kharg Island and was about a mile off his starboard, spitting distance in nautical terms, when two Iraqi MIGs screamed out of the desert sun, strafed the tanker, climbed back into the sky, dived again, and dropped their bombs on the hapless vessel. The tanker took a direct hit and exploded. The concussion cracked the windows on Donny's vessel. Burning oil spread quickly over the water. The MIGs peeled away from the stricken vessel and turned toward his ship. Skimming the surface like a couple of angry wasps, they aimed directly for the bridge. As Donny steered his ship away from the foundering tanker, he took her hand, drew her to him, and told her she was going to be safe. As if on cue the fighters pulled up in a roar, narrowly clipping the ship's antennae. They circled overhead for a few minutes, then flew off leaving them unharmed.

Donny could never quite forgive Vimala for refusing to leave the bridge, but he could not be displeased with her determination to stand by his side when the rest of the crew had taken cover. It was the defining moment of their marriage. She was a strong, intelligent woman and he loved that in her; he knew that while he commanded men and ships, Vim showed she had a will of her own.

"Port ten," Captain Monteiro ordered quietly. He stood before the large bridge windows and watched a tugboat towing a sand barge pass a couple miles in front of him.

The third officer, his legs planted firmly apart, repeated the instruction and turned the small wheel to the left, driving the big tanker as he might a Formula One race car; the stainless steel wheel was smaller than a car's and it turned more easily, but there the similarity ended; the ship responded with the agility of a pregnant elephant in a mudhole.

Motoring out into the busy Phillip Channel at the bottom of the Malacca Straits was one of the most demanding tasks of the entire voyage. Captain Monteiro had to maneuver 30,000 tons of explosive fuel through heavy crossing traffic; once past the first lane, he had to tuck into the eastbound lane between the vessels already in it, overtaking or squeezing in behind larger and smaller vessels—towboats, container ships, fishing boats, VLCCs, and even a sailboat or two, all going at different speeds. It was akin to running across a busy highway during rush hour; it could be done but not without first choosing your precise moment, steering for the stern of the ship coming at you, and going for it.

Except for the occasional squawk on the two radios, it was quiet on the bridge. One radio monitored the hailing frequency on Channel 16 and the other the Vessel Traffic Information Service on

Channel 10. VTIS East covered the ship movements on the straits in and out of Singapore leading into the South China Sea. Performing a similar role as air traffic controllers, the Singapore-based service advised, shifted, and often corrected the movement of hundreds of vessels a day going into and out of the narrow sea lanes that connect Asia to the rest of the world.

"VTIS East," announced a voice. "This is *Ocean Neptune*, bound for Western Petroleum Anchorage. We're abeam Horsburgh Lighthouse."

"*Ocean Neptune*, VTIS East." It was a woman's confident response. "Understood you are abeam Horsburgh Light. Be aware of container ship and VLCC Eastbound. Proceed with caution."

"Yes, ah—sir, container and VL eastbound. *Ocean Neptune*, clear."

"Vessel passing on my starboard—you are too close!" an anonymous voice blurted over Channel 16.

"Relax, Captain," came a response. "I see you—I'm bearing away."

Silence.

Captain Monteiro picked up the binoculars and scanned the traffic ahead. "Midships," he ordered quietly. "We'll keep her there."

"Right, Captain."

The bridge was a spacious and sterile chamber with large reinforced tinted windows that tilted slightly outward; the center console, extending nearly the width of the room, was imbedded with dials, gauges, readouts, radar screens, and telephones. A large thermos of hot water and Nescafé instant coffee, tea, and a box of cookies were permanent fixtures on a small ledge behind the console under the windows that faced aft.

A narrow dugout, whose two fishermen apparently thought the catch was better in the middle of the shipping lane, drifted dangerously close to the ship's path. Monteiro watched the fragile boat thrown about like a cork by the passing ship's wake; a man in front and a boy in the back fished with handlines, unconcerned about the huge ship that towered overhead within a few meters of their little boat.

"Full ahead, Homi."

"Full ahead, sir."

Homi Tarapore, the third mate, was every bit officer material, and one day he would be master of his own ship. His easygoing manner and his respect for rank held him well with those he served. He was a tall man with laughing blue eyes and a flamboyant cavalry mustache. A fitness nut, he had earned his black belt in karate, and Donny was assuming that Homi was a good man to have around. Homi walked to the "telegraph," the engine command lever mounted on a pedestal in the far corner of the wheelhouse, and shifted the handle forward to its near horizontal position to full ahead. Small bells rang within the pedestal confirming the order; down below in the engine room a similar telegraph repeated the command. In the old days, when "ships were ships" and men were however superior that they were supposed to be at the time, the order on the telegraph was greeted below with groans and oaths from the Black Gang, the stokers, sweating bare-chested men with short-handled shovels who fed more coal into the furnace to fire up the boilers. Today the engine is a big diesel manned by an engineer clad in a white boilersuit who wears steel-toed work boots, a hard hat, and foam-padded earmuffs. He sits comfortably in a glass-enclosed, air-conditioned control room before a console of dials, warning lights, gauges, pressure indicators, and push buttons, and a single lever to increase flow of fuel to the engines for more speed. However, unlike some of the more modern automated ships, the engine-room crew on the *Valiant Carrier*, from greaser to the chief engineer, still monitored the machinery by physical inspection, a periodic walk through the loud and hellishly hot engine area, feeling, touching, searching with a flashlight for any telltale leaks, breaks, and drips. Except for the belch of black soot from her funnel, there was no sudden acceleration as the *Valiant Carrier* crept up to her cruising speed of eleven knots.

"Full away."

"Yes, sir, full away."

Homi bent to the microphone on the console. "Good evening, Engineer, this is the bridge. Nineteen hundred hours. Engine full away."

"Roger, Bridge, full away at nineteen hundred."

The engineer turned valves switching the fuel type from diesel to fuel oil, a normal procedure on older ships when heading out to sea and free of the heavily trafficked shipping lanes. Diesel is a fuel for close maneuvers, speed changes, sudden stops—it is a forgiving but expensive fuel. An engine under fuel oil, while having more torque, cannot respond to emergency commands and is good only for steady, uninterrupted passage-making. To burn effectively fuel oil must be hot; the engine of a ship reducing speed to slow or dead slow cools down and the injectors clog. When the injectors are stuffed, the engine is nearly impossible to restart. The South China Sea was now just off their port bow and it was time.

"Starboard thirty," Captain Monteiro ordered.

"Starboard thirty, sir."

The dial of the electric compass before him clicked off degree by degree as the ship responded to the course change, taking a slow right turn around the Horsburgh Lighthouse.

Darkness comes on fast down here at the equator. On this night there would be no moon and soon there would be no distinction between the heavens and the horizon.

The captain set the same course he had on previous trips, a route that ran within about five miles of the reef on the east side of Pulau Bintan. The land mass offered a good radar target, and with satellite navigation he would never get any closer to harm's way than that. It was the most direct route to southern Sumatra, an undeclared and unregulated shipping lane. It was busy this evening, but the traffic was like this every hour of every day, always littered with local fishing boats. Fishermen had lived with these blundering merchantmen for the past hundred years. There was seldom a report of lost fishing boats in this area that he had ever heard about. But maybe a collision between ship and fishing boat happened regularly and was never mentioned; it was just a local boat that got in the way and perhaps the local fishermen were only missed back in the kampung, the island village to which they never returned.

In the gathering darkness Donny stood back in the shadows, his hands clasped behind his back—he might have been a ghost—out of the way and unseen, yet his presence was undeniable. Close to the horizon the sea was spotted with an assortment of boats: small longtails—open planked boats—pushed by loud mufflerless engines mounted above the stern, motored out to the little plastic floats marking their fish traps; pirogues with frayed plastic sails and two people hauling in nets; and a number of larger pair trawlers. The little boats were like a swarm of bees buzzing around a garbage can in a city park, going about their business unconcerned about the giant shadow that approached.

The guard alarm on the Furuno radar had been ringing continuously as the fishing boats darted in and out of the tanker's three-mile guard radius, and it was becoming irritating. The captain walked to the radar, flipped a switch, and the wheelhouse turned mercifully quiet. He bent to the radar and saw what he expected—the fishing fleets were not thinning out; they were increasing. The radar screen was a snowstorm of targets.

Donny went out to the bridgewing, looked up at night sky. It was a warm evening, the smells of industry and the city left far behind. The constellation Orion was at this time of year just overhead, as were Pleiades, the Seven Sisters; the Southern Cross was just above the horizon, partly obscured by the land effect of Pulau Bintan. He knew them well. Before Global Positioning System satellite navigation, and even now, he felt a personal relationship with these cold, icy motes of light thousands of light years away that most probably had long ceased to exist. It was a sailor who personified cold, inanimate objects; it was a sailor's need to attach a relationship to that which he so desperately relied on. Lovers and poets might sigh deeply about a full moon, but it was the seafarer who gave it a practical reason to exist. It was the sailor with sextant and the Polynesians a thousand years before him who used the moon and the stars to guide them to where they were going.

He turned and looked aft. The loom of the lights of Singapore City hovered in the night sky to the west. In the distance the Horsburgh Light flashed reassuringly once every ten seconds. And other than the stars above he could find no other light, no sliver of moon, no lightning. Far off to the north a ship heading up the South China Sea, perhaps to Hong Kong, Shanghai, or to some port in Japan or the Philippines, had suddenly switched on its deck lights, illuminating itself like a midtown city block. Possibly the watch standers had seen a fast-moving blip on radar; or it was merely a precaution. While contrary to international collision regulations, a fully illuminated deck was an accepted antipiracy technique. Pirates knew that a ship brightly lit was on alert for an attack; a darkened ship probably indicated that most of the crew was asleep and the ship would be easier to board undetected.

Donny had made this passage many times before, and there never had been a threat of a boarding. Still he would take some precautions; he would not let this passage be any different.

"Deck lights, fore and aft, spotlights on the poop deck," the captain ordered the third mate upon returning to the bridge.

"We won't have much visibility," the third warned. He knew the glare of the lights would interfere with the visibility ahead.

"Quite right," the captain said. "But those fishing boats won't fall asleep if they see us bearing down on them. You've got the radar. And keep an ear for the radio. If there's traffic, we can talk ourselves through it."

Donny dialed the chief officer on the phone and ordered a deck patrol—men with walkie-talkies to stand watch out on deck, port and starboard from amidships to the poop deck[8] and one on the poop deck facing aft. "There are a lot of fish boats out here tonight," the captain said, "and we don't want any unauthorized guests on board."

The chief suggested a crewman named Singh, a big deckhand with the turban. Donny thought that was a good idea; he had heard that Indonesians were afraid of Sikhs.

The captain also considered setting up the fire hoses, an effective antipiracy weapon; boarders could be blasted off the decks, the pirate boats below swamped or at least put out of commission. But the damn things were so much trouble. The ship's old air conditioning was hardly adequate in the tropics, and most of the crew kept their cabin windows open to catch the breeze. Seawater fired into the night against the wind often blew back into the crew's quarters. He decided against charging the fire hoses; with deck lights, a deck patrol, and all doors to the outside locked except to the bridgewings, there would be no boarders this night.

"Keep sharp, Homi, and call me—for any reason," the captain said, going below.

"Right, Captain."

When Donny returned to his quarters, Vim confronted him with her worst fears: "You expect something will happen, don't you? All those locks, that nonsense on the door about 'testing' the air. What is going on?"

Donny explained that the ship had been pirated once before, that the previous master, Samsher Mannas, had installed the locks as extra precautions. Mannas had thought the warning of dangerous space on the door might fool the pirates into thinking that the captain's cabin and the ship's safe were located elsewhere.

"It was a minor incident," Donny reassured Vim. It was hardly that. For Mannas it was a nightmare that chased him off the sea. The *Valiant Carrier* had been on this same route and fully laden. Despite the antipiracy patrol on deck, pirates had boarded the ship undetected. A half-dozen men armed with guns and long knives knew exactly where they were going; they knocked on the master's door, burst inside, tied his hands, beat him until he opened the ship's safe and handed over the money. The captain was found bound and gagged and unconscious some hours later by a crewman. The pirates had escaped with $40,000 within twenty minutes of boarding the ship. Not bad for a few minutes' work.

Despite Donny's assurances that the route they were taking was safe, that he had made this run so many times before, Vimala was not convinced.

"The ship is cursed. I feel it," she told him.

"There is nothing special about this ship," Donny replied. "The ship is a ship. There is nothing to be concerned about. She's old, she's tired, but she is a proper ship in good nick. She does her job and without problems. And she is not cursed."

He showed her a red alarm button on the wall that rang on the bridge and in the crew's quarters. He also told her about a similar alarm on the bridge that rang down in the cabin. "If it goes off, lock the doors and stay inside. But I tell you nothing is going to happen— it will be a good trip."

"Something is wrong, Donny. I'm scared."

Deepak sat back in one of the hard metal chairs under the open porthole. A slight breeze ruffled his hair; he was listening but his eyes were far away, reliving the movie *Hook* he had seen on television some weeks before. His thoughts were on Peter Pan and Captain Hook and Dustin Hoffman and Robin Williams and the romantic swashbuckling adventures of the sea—duels with cutlasses, good guys swinging through the rigging, saving the children, and everyone woke up and knew it was just a wondrous dream. And the good guys always won. And the children were never harmed.

On the bridge Homi was finding it nearly impossible to see the fishing boats ahead. Disobeying orders, he flipped the four switches on the console that killed the deck lights.

4

An Easy Target

The *Valiant Carrier* was just one in an endless nightly parade of slow-moving, lumbering beasts that plodded one after the other out of the Singapore Straits and into the South China Sea. As many as twenty-five vessels motor through these waters every hour, traffic from Europe, Africa, the Middle East, to Asia and beyond.

The faint single wink of Horsburgh Light marked the entrance into a sea that was unregulated and unpatrolled. Malaysia was to the north and the Indonesian island of Bintan to the south. After Horsburgh you turn left, north to China, Japan, or Taiwan, and the rest of industrialized north Asia; you turn south to go to Jakarta, Australia, New Zealand, and on into the Pacific. These waters at the bottom of the Malacca Straits were fertile hunting grounds for pirate packs. A ship enters here at its own peril.

As usual the aft decks of most of the ships were fully lit, and spotlights from the railings above beamed onto dark waters just behind the vessels; fire hoses shot streams of high-pressure water into the sea. This was a regular run for many of the ships, but there were among them some unscheduled tramps that hopped from port to port picking up odd lots, bulk cargo, an oil charter, or, if equipped, some containers.

Despite the traffic a ship and its crew are isolated and vulnerable; a ship attacked cannot expect help from another unarmed vessel. There is no law to enforce out here on the high seas, and if the absence of law and order is a state of anarchy, then there is anarchy at sea. The only semblance of law is that which the captain maintains aboard his ship and that moral authority that humans maintain within themselves. A master must rely on his own wiles to keep pirates off his ship. And God forgive him if he doesn't.

Beyond Horsburgh the *Valiant Carrier* turned southeast, skirting the northern coast of Pulau Bintan. There was no moon, little wind, no seas—perfect conditions for the ravening thugs who waited in their speedboats among the mangroves for the opportunity to strike.

Pirates no doubt saw that one vessel, brightly lighted, had inexplicably shut off its deck lights and, now darkened, steamed past with only its regulation navigation lamps. It was at this point that most vessels usually turned on their deck lights.

This is what makes piracy so easy. While a majority of the ships are on alert, there are always one or two that are not. And on this night it got better; as the dark silhouette of the *Valiant Carrier* grew larger, it was evident that she was going to be an easy score; she was a fully laden tanker, squatting low in the water with a freeboard at the stern ten feet above the surface. And her deck lights remained off.

Pirates, scenting a kill, pulled up the anchors that also served as grappling hooks, radioed a mother ship, in this case a large fishing boat, and tore out after the hapless tanker. The *Valiant Carrier* had all the chance of an injured sheep stumbling through coyote country.

⌒‿⌒

Back in his dayroom Donny and his chief officer discussed the upcoming cricket match between India and Australia, while Vim sat in the sofa sewing a button on one of her husband's white shirts. Her long black hair fell over her shoulders and she was humming softly along to an old tape of Loretta Lynn. Deepak was sitting on the edge of the other end of the sofa, his thumbs deftly working a handheld computer game; Vanisha, the seven-month-old baby, was asleep between them, a pacifier lying carelessly next to her mouth. Donny remembered that this was one of those perfect times.

Later, as Vim helped Deepak in the shower, they heard what she took to be thunder. Yet the sounds seemed to emanate from within the ship, a metallic thud against the hull, a hard sound like steel barrels rolling on the deck outside. The captain telephoned the bridge; his immediate thought was that there was a brawl among the crew. However, he knew every one of his twenty-seven sailors. This group of men was a particularly easygoing lot; fighting among them was nearly inconceivable. The din increased, became mixed with the sounds of running feet along the deck below, on the bridge deck overhead; when someone runs aboard a ship, especially on one carrying volatile cargo, something is seriously amiss. The chief officer ran out of the dayroom and down the corridor up to the bridge. Donny opened the window and looked down at the sea. Below a small boat without lights motored alongside, maintaining the same speed. Odd, he was thinking, why would that vessel be so close to my ship and without lights? Then he realized that the lights of his own ship were off.

A small ball of flame rose slowly up from the boat alongside and carved a graceful arc toward the tanker. It disappeared out of view. A sudden bright orange flash lit up the night sky as the firebomb exploded on the tanker's deck.

"They're here! Vim! Into the bedroom with the kids. Quick! Don't open the door, whatever happens outside."

Vim hurried out of the bathroom and, pulling the naked little boy behind, scooped up Vanisha from the couch. She disappeared into the bedroom and locked the door.

Another orange glow lit the darkness in the window; just as abruptly the flare was swallowed by the night.

As the chief officer reached the door to the ship's wheelhouse, it flew open. Five men burst out, swinging knives; their sneering mouths and fearsome eyes protruded through the holes in ski masks. The pirates were dragging Homi, barely conscious and tied up, by the foot, leaving behind a wide smear of blood. The chief cried out. The pirates screamed high-pitched indecipherable orders, furious machine-gun words of broken English: "No fight! No fight! You fight, you die!" One of the gang smashed him in the face with the wooden butt of a machete and he slumped to the deck.

A pirate with popping gargoyle eyes yanked the officer to his feet, pulled out a piece of plastic rope hanging from his belt, and, with the speed of a rodeo cowboy, hog-tied the chief officer's hands behind his back.

The pirates knew exactly where they were going and what they were going to do; they asked no questions but screamed that they were going to kill everyone. One of the bandits slammed the chief officer a vicious blow to the back of the head and the man fell unconscious in a heap, where they left him. Inside the dayroom one level below, the captain heard the increasing sounds of men's anger as they clambered down the stairway and approached the outside door. He had been waiting, knew they would come. But he was still not prepared. Outside the captain's office one of attackers kicked the door with the heel of his foot.

"Captain, open the door. Please!"

It was Homi. Donny froze. He knew then there was no one on the bridge, that his ship was charging down the shipping lanes unattended, out of control. And possibly on fire.

"Please, they're killing me!"

The captain had to decide. His third officer was outside, possibly dying. His wife, his children, were inside safe with him, locked in the bedroom. He had no choice. As master of the ship he could not allow any of his crew to get hurt. That was his duty.

The captain unlocked the door and the hooded pirates stormed in, hauling Homi after them. Donny saw the wall of a fist just as it smashed into his right eye. He was trying to remain on his feet when another fist slammed him in the temple, sending him to the floor. "Give money! Give money!" Donny was too dazed to respond. On his hands and knees he looked up at the wide-splayed island feet of the attackers only inches away. Their thick, callused toes and small cracks up leathery heels looked like they had never seen shoes.

Donny sensed that their high-pitched screams, their orders, their threats, contained an extra urgency, an undertone of panic, and in his confused state he wondered why. He looked over at Homi, who lay on his side clutching his bleeding stomach. Without provocation one of the pirates kicked the third officer in his open wound. The eyes of Homi's tormentor behind the black knit balaklava were swollen like those of a boxer who had taken too many left jabs. And there was blood in his teeth. Donny knew then that Homi must have put up a hell of a fight.

"Get money!" one of the masked men screamed at the captain. He reached down and grabbed Donny by the arm and propelled him toward the closet containing the ship's safe. This one was taller than the others, and he seemed to be in command. He wore a red bandanna around his neck and a frayed short-sleeved aloha shirt over a brown loincloth. A nylon-webbed belt around his waist strapped in the tools of the trade: a large screwdriver, a short-handled sledge, a rusty machete with a finely honed edge, and a coil of nylon rope. The others were similarly dressed, in lungis, loincloths, or trousers rolled up to the knees. Donny remembers that one wore a black T-shirt with the glaring face of the Hulk emblazoned across the front.

The one with the red kerchief circled, danced around the captain, shouting, "Money! Money!" He flicked a long, thin knife in Donny's face, deftly balancing it, shifting it from hand to hand. The captain remained motionless. He felt the breeze of the blade as it passed unfocused in front of his eyes. Meanwhile others ransacked the office, dumping contents of drawers onto the floor. They rummaged through the chest, through the clothes, and rifled the pockets. One flung open the cabinet door. The safe rested on the bottom of the closet, exposed, waiting.

Dazed, Donny tried to tell them there was no money in the safe, that the strongbox was broken.

They closed around him, jumped in front of him, surrounded him like a pack of rabid dogs gone mad—in a frenzy, demanding, screaming, waving their blades, baring their fangs, foaming, spittle flying, poking him, barking in Indonesian and broken English.

The tip of a blade cut cleanly across the captain's eyebrow. He felt the blood run into his eyes.

The pirate with the beat-up face reached down for Homi and spun him over onto his stomach. Kneeling in Homi's blood, he tied the officer's hands behind his back, stood, looked approvingly at his handiwork, then kicked the officer in the ribs. Homi's cry of pain was more muted. He was close to losing it. "Stop! I tell you the money is not in the safe," he pleaded. "The money is in the bedroom."

The *Valiant Carrier* plowed down the Sumatra coastline in the darkest of nights, dangerously close to the reef, on fire and out of control. The flames on the deck had not yet reached the cargo. However, coils of thick hemp rope and synthetic mooring lines, lube oil, some hose, the rope and wood slats of a Jacob's ladder, and life rings were burning. The engineers, unaware of the violence above them, kept the engines running true.

It was unlikely that the pirates intended to destroy the ship. Most probably they wanted to distract the crew, to keep them busy putting out the fires while they went for the safe; still, it was a plan going terribly wrong.

Captain Monteiro's ship was an older, double-bottomed, single-hulled vessel with a relatively thin membrane of welded steel plate. Only 17.5 millimeters—about three quarters of an inch—separated eight and a half million gallons of oil from the environment outside.

The cargo that the *Valiant Carrier* carried this night was F4 furnace oil, a refined product with low volatility and a high flashpoint—the minimum temperature at which oil gives off flammable vapors. It is said you could drown a lit cigarette in the stuff. However, the flames, fanned by the ship's speed, raged just under the strange red bullet-shaped teats capping tall pipes sticking out of the deck; these were the pressure vacuum valves that vented those ignitable vapors. When the cargo inside the tanks expands in the tropic heat, the volatile gases escape through those vents. Although it takes a greater heat to ignite fuel oil, it takes only a spark to ignite its vapors; the cargo then is no less explosive than jet fuel or gasoline. If the tanks began venting, which often occurs, the *Valiant Carrier* could blow before the pirates got a chance to finish their dirty work.

———

Inside the bedroom Vimala huddled on the edge of the bed, and little Vanisha squirmed and whimpered in her lap. Deepak, terrified, stood by her side, his hand dug into her thigh; he trembled without stop, his entire body out of control. His attention was fixed on the door that he expected would be kicked open at any minute.

With sudden desperation Vim removed her jewelry, her necklace with a gold cross, a couple of thin gold bracelets, and her wedding ring. She pulled off the two tiny gold bracelets from Vanisha's pudgy little arms; her hands were shaking and she was none too gentle, and the little girl began to scream. She put a hand over Vanisha's mouth. She prayed the baby's cries were drowned out by the commotion from the other room and the ship's engines.

"Deepu, you take these and you put them in your pocket. No one will bother you." Deepak, his eyes wide with fear, began to back away. "Just do it!" She heard Donny's voice from the other side:

"Please don't! Why don't you believe me? The money is not in the safe. I keep it in the bedroom."

With fingers she could not control, Vim unsnapped her bra and tried to feed the little girl. But the baby tossed her face from side to side, inconsolable. Vim rocked her and spoke softly. Her attempts to sooth the baby were crushed by the sounds of terror of the men, from her husband.

The door reverberated with a sudden dull thud, the sound of a body slammed against it; she expected they would burst in any second. *I will protect my children at any cost*, she vowed, and she looked around the room for a weapon, any weapon. But it was a ship, and there were not many loose moving parts—only a pillow and the gold-framed photo of her and the children.

On the other side Captain Monteiro was on his hands and knees, his head bowed as if in prayer. The tall Indonesian stood over him, the tip of his long knife pressed against the back of his neck. Donny knew the point of the blade was just about to penetrate; under pressure of the knife he crawled toward the safe.

He felt the sudden sting of the knifepoint and knew that it had drawn blood. With trembling fingers he turned the dial, praying he could remember the combination. Several times he pulled the handle, but the safe remained locked.

Finally the heavy door swung away. The few papers inside appeared to be uninteresting discarded scraps. A bloody hand reached into the box and pulled out the safe's instruction manual and warrantee papers.

The steel door to the corridor outside suddenly exploded with a shatter. It rattled on its hinges with the repeated strokes of heavy battering.

"Captain! We're all here—you all right?" It was the voice of the chief officer. "Captain, sa'ab. You in there?" The pounding on the door was deafening.

The captain tried to respond, but his voice was hoarse and weak. Muffled angry words filtered through the door.

They jerked him to his feet. The bandit with the red bandanna, furious, waved the useless papers in Donny's face. "No money. You die now." He kicked him out of the way and slid back the bolt with the butt of his machete and opened the door. A wall of a dozen enraged crew members stood opposite, hefting crowbars, fire axes, wrenches, pipe cheaters, and pieces of dunnage. Donny saw what he must have looked like in the reflection of their expressions. A shocked murmur went through the men, and they surged toward the bloodied captain and his captors. The Indonesian pressed his knife against the captain's neck.

Confronted by the wall of angry men, the pirates ripped off their balaklavas, revealing boyish native faces with corvine eyes of malice and fear. It is one thing to board a vessel under way, surprise the crew, tie up the captain, rob the safe, and get off. However, this was no longer a robbery at sea. This was a fuckup. Faced by an enraged mob they either had to take over the ship and kill the crew or escape with their lives. Somebody was going to lose. They had to see everything, and balaklavas were no longer an option.

Unmasked, they became less fearsome; they were exposed as human beings; their loss of mystery somehow equalized them. The tall bandit with the red kerchief had a small black mustache and long, stringy hair that framed an angular, boyish face. There was an older man, balding, unshaven, and slow witted, with small scared eyes and nostrils that flared like those of a peevish horse. The damage to Homi's tormentor was more severe than Donny had imagined; he was missing a tooth, one eye was swollen shut, and his nose appeared broken.

As Donny was pushed down the stairwell, some of the crew with weapons at hand backed down the stairs, looking up. Behind the pirates an equal number of crew, armed with clubs, followed. A pirate guarded the rear, taking the stairs backward, one hand holding the rail, the other slashing out with his long knife at the advancing sailors.

On the deck outside one of the gang grabbed Donny's hair and rammed him onto the railing, jerking his head back and forth, screaming, "Money! Money!" The crew charged and the pirates turned and swung their knives. The pirate pushed Donny's head over the railing and he was certain then he was about to be heaved overboard—below, the black sea moved swiftly past, white foam forming the crest of the midships wave as it rolled aft. The darkness throbbed orange from the fires on deck.

"I get the money and you get off my ship," he managed to say. A sharp, brief discussion behind him in Indonesian gave him some hope. If they threw him overboard, they themselves would get killed—their hostage, their banker, their trump, would be lost. They knew they could not possibly fight the crew. The tall bandit jerked the captain back and spun him around: "We go, you get money. No money, we kill you." The trip back to the captain's room was much like the trip from it—the small group went forward and the crew retreated, surged, and retreated. The pirates were getting increasingly agitated and Donny began to think they were on the outer edge of control.

Vim heard men's furious voices, but they were distant, outside somewhere. In the next room there was only silence.

She walked quietly to the door, eased back the dead bolt, and cautiously opened the door to the dayroom. She gasped. It looked like a slaughterhouse—blood smeared on the walls, across the floor, the room a shambles. She searched for Donny; a low moan rose from behind the overturned table.

She held her breath and looked. Homi Tarapore lay in a pool of blood, barely hanging on to life; his eyes were swollen and caked shut.

"Water," he moaned.

She looked back into the next room; Deepak was gone.

"Deepu?" There was a note of panic in her cry. A movement caught the corner of her eye. Deepak had crawled under the mattress on the floor; he peered out from under with wide, frightened eyes. She picked up the still screaming infant, hurried toward the door to the corridor, slammed it shut, and slid the deadbolt.

Vim put the baby on the floor as far away from the blood as she could and found a broken knife blade in a corner. She cut the cord from around Homi's wrist, roughly and quickly wiped the blood from his face, then cut open his shirt.

She nearly fainted. A gaping slash extended the width of his chest and exposed his ribs. *Oh, God*, she thought, *I have to help him, but what can I do?*

"Vim."

She thought she heard her name called.

"Vim!"

"Donny?" She picked up Vanisha from the floor and ran to the door. Then she remembered his orders. There was muffled activity on the other side and she was not about to open the door.

"Vim, open the door!"

"Have they gone?" she whispered.

"Why are you whispering? Yes, they're gone."

She slid back the bolt and opened the door and suddenly was thrown back by a wave of men, covered in blood and sweat. She was shocked not just by the attackers but by the sight of her husband. His fresh white uniform was splattered in blood. He wore the face of a defeated man.

The pirates just then realized there was a woman on board and they stared dumfounded at her and her baby.

—⁓

The pirate with the punched-out face lunged for the baby and grabbed her tiny fist and began to squeeze. His small dark eyes, watery and bloodshot, bore into Vim—if eyes are the windows to the soul, this man's eyes were proof of its complete absence. Vim lashed out with her bare foot, catching him in the knee, and the pirate yanked harder, trying to wrest the baby out of her arms.

"Leave my baby alone!"

He grabbed Vimala by the hair, wrenched her head back, and spat into her face. Donny, his hands tied behind his back, lowered his head and tried to charge but was knocked to the ground by a blow from behind. Another reached for Vim's dress and ripped it down the front, looking for jewelry.

"Donny, give them the money. For God's sake. Please! They're hurting Vanisha!"

"I told you—it's in the bedroom. I'll get money. Leave the baby alone!"

One of the gang slammed shut the outside door and bolted it. The crew smashed the door with crowbars and fire axes; a deafening timpani of metallic clatter added to the madness.

"You quiet! Quiet! We kill *ibu*," one of them warned, jabbing a knife at Vim, "and we kill baby."

The lights in the cabin and throughout the whole ship suddenly went out and the room turned black. No one moved. For a moment there was silence; the crew stopped smashing the door on the outside, the pirates stopped screaming in the dayroom. Only little Vanisha continued to cry, a soft, uncertain mewling that rolled in waves. In the darkness the glow of the fires on deck illuminated the faces of their captors.

"Who the hell turned off the power?" the captain shouted, turning to the outside door. He was pummeled with fists from every direction, some landing squarely in his face, others glancing off his shoulders, the side and back of his head.

The ship suddenly came back on-line and power was restored. For an instant pirates and hostages blinked and refocused in the sudden light and awkwardly stared at each other as if waking up from a nightmare. The one who had taken the baby's wrists had let it go; holding on to your victim in the dark was frightening even if it was only a baby. Control, such as it was, returned in an instant.

They spun Donny toward the bedroom and a bare foot into his back sent him crashing face-first onto the floor of the entrance. He lay for a moment without moving, turned and looked up, and in a broken voice: "I can't get the money with my hands tied."

One of the pirates cut the cord binding his hands, then retreated quickly out of the entrance to the room as if, Donny thought, they were afraid of going inside, as if they feared they would be trapped. Placing a bloody hand on the wall for support, Donny raised himself and stood unsteadily, then stumbled into the bedroom. A large black leather purse, cause of and silent witness to the terror, hung on a hook on the wall under a porthole. He grabbed the purse and made his way back into the dayroom. Several of the pirates snatched at the bag, but the gang leader barked a warning and they backed off. He sunk his hands into the bag and triumphantly pulled out a fistful of fifty- and hundred-dollar notes and stuffed them into his loincloth until his crotch bulged.

Another grabbed the purse and filled his pants.

The lead pirate ordered Donny to tell his crew to back away from the door. "We go now."

A pirate grabbed Vim by the hair, placed a knife at her throat. Another took Vanisha's tiny arm as if escorting the child; he pressed his long, thin blade against her dress. Vanisha squirmed, kicked, and bawled and Vim, her head held back by her hair, found it difficult to hold on to the baby.

"You have the money!" Vim cried. "Leave my baby alone!"

"Back off," the captain yelled out to the crew. "We're coming out. Give us some room. They've got the baby!"

Vim turned toward the bedroom, hoping to see, and hoping not to see, Deepak; she prayed he was still hidden under the mattress. Her captor, apparently thinking she was trying to escape, slammed her head against the bulkhead. She knew she was about to pass out but fought the sensation; Vanisha was in her arms.

Once outside the dayroom a furious crew stood opposite, weighing their weapons. As the pirates and their hostages moved forward, the crew retreated down the corridor, slowly, reluctantly.

The pirates screamed high-pitched, unintelligible orders at the slow-moving crew and pushed and kicked Vim and Donny forward out onto the darkened boat deck just under the lifeboats. The acrid-tasting smoke from the fires on deck, the back draft of choking soot from the ship's funnel, and the pulsing colors from the flames etched a scene out of hell onto the night. The crew taunted and slammed their pipes and their wrenches against the metal railings, challenging the pirates.

The ship steamed full speed along an uncertain coastline, unattended and on fire. Behind the pirates Captain Monteiro saw that the lights onshore were brighter, more distinct, closer; he could see that his ship, still on automatic pilot, was being set by the current and was crabbing toward the reef, where it would break up and where, he knew, they would be incinerated.

The crew charged and feinted. The pirates, penned in by the well-armed seamen, were on the verge of panic. Violence stood its ground; they had the hostages; they had a knife to the baby. But the approaching mob of outraged crew with their makeshift weapons had become an impenetrable wall. The pirates swung at the charge and the crew withdrew. It was a standoff. The pirate who held a knife to the baby began screaming in Indonesian at the mother, at the father, at anybody who would listen. He had reached his limit and his dilated eyes mirrored his own terror. One of Monteiro's men charged the panic-stricken youth and swung his iron pipe at ankle height; the pirate hopped over the bar. But his knife plunged downward toward Vim and she saw the blade as a quick flash. She braced herself for the searing pain that she knew would follow and she expected it to kill her.

Vanisha's shriek cut through the darkness. The pirate dropped his knife; his eyes darted from the bleeding child to the mother to the startled crew across from him; he was a cornered animal who knew he was about to die.

"Vanisha? Oh, God! Donny!"

The baby's shattering cries of pain, so loud, so sharp, so heart-breaking, tore through the gloom. Vanisha's blood dripped through her fingers.

In quick jerky movements Vim tried to wipe the blood off the baby's face with her hand. The blood flowed freely from somewhere above the baby's eyes. The mother's frantic attempts to locate the wound, to stop the bleeding, merely spread the blood. Vim grabbed a handful of her dress and lifted it to the baby's head and, without thought, blindly, roughly, wiped the infant's face.

Vanisha's cries stopped. The baby went limp in her mother's arms. "Oh, God, they've killed my baby!"

The crew went berserk—there were no more restraints. They charged into the pirates, blind, swinging, out to kill. The pirates slashed with their long knives and their machetes and hacked out an opening; fragile blades rang against steel pipes. Forcing an opening, they ran toward the railing, scrambled over, and jumped into the sea. A large fishing boat crept out of the shadows behind the ship and turned on its own deck lights. It stopped in the tanker's wake to pick up the men in the water, and as the ship continued, the pirate boat fell back and was swallowed by the dark.

Donny and the crew led Vim and the baby back to the cabin, but she shook her head and refused to enter. They took her to the chief engineer's cabin down the corridor and set them on the edge of the bed, where she remained stunned, in shock.

Donny raced up to the bridge out to the wings. Below, the crew was dousing the fires with hoses. From out in the night, even above the rumble of the ship's engines, he thought he heard the break of surf and saw the crest of the swells crash upon the reef with a splash of phosphorescence. It was a toss-up whether he could stop the ship or whether the reef would stop her first. He could order a "crash stop," slamming the ship into full astern, but he knew that would probably be the end of the engine; the ship's propeller would have to slow to only a few revolutions before reverse would kick in, and even that would take about six minutes. The ship would stop, but his engineers probably couldn't get her going again. Then he would have a dead ship, at the mercy of tide and current. He could try a simple stop and maintain some steerageway, steer a few degrees to seaward, and pray it was enough to avoid the reef. He took the chance. He raced back into the bridge, threw the wheel hard over, and pulled the telegraph lever back to its vertical full-stop position. It would be close.

Down below, Vim, her dress soaked in blood, sat on the bed rocking her baby back and forth, repeating her lament, "Vanisha gone, Vanisha gone." The baby let out a sudden yelp, kicked, and flailed. Vim stopped rocking, stopped breathing, and prayed that she was not imagining that her daughter was alive. The baby's crying was a joy to hear—fitful waves of distress, less of pain than of discomfort and irritation. She wiped the infant's face with a wet rag and caught her breath as she saw that the wound had exposed the child's skull.

It takes a couple miles for a ship the size of the *Valiant Carrier* to come to a full stop; it did so within about a mile of the reef. Despite the currents, strong during the spring tide of a new moon, Captain Monteiro managed to turn the ship around and head back to Singapore.

Vanisha had been seriously injured. Doctors at the Marine Medical Center in Singapore said that while the knife had penetrated the skull, it missed the brain only by a millimeter, about the width of a pencil point. The X-ray photos attest to the miracle. They also showed that there had been a significant dent where the blade had penetrated; the baby's skull appeared to push against the part of the brain responsible for memory. But the wound began to swell outward, the skull healed itself, and Vanisha is today apparently unaffected.

Many of the injured crew were treated at Marine Medical Center and released. It took forty-seven stitches to close Homi's wounds; while exposing his ribs, the slash across his stomach did not penetrate any vital organs. He is reportedly back at sea.

Captain Monteiro has often reflected on the assault on his ship, and he is quick to acknowledge that there are lessons here for all masters. He acknowledges that when Homi turned off the deck lights, his ship virtually offered the gangs lying in wait an open invitation. It's hard to imagine that today, ten years later, with so many ships under attack, there are ship masters still out there who do not take minimum defensive measures—fire hoses, deck patrol with walkie-talkies, and deck lights—when passing through known pirate country.

The IMB began issuing their daily situation reports to all ships at sea in October 1992—a few months after the attack on the *Valiant Carrier*—to warn masters of recent attacks through waters they would be sailing. The attack on the *Valiant Carrier* might not have occurred had the service been in operation at the time; two days before the attack on Captain Monteiro's ship, another vessel was attacked in the same area. Foresight, the ship's owner, said they would have diverted their ship had they known about the previous incident.

Nevertheless, and despite the daily IMB alerts to ships, the assault on the *Valiant Carrier* presaged an alarming increase in the number of pirate attacks in the years to follow. Ten years on, piracy is a crime out of control, more costly and more disruptive to commerce than ever before. Recent estimates put the cost to world trade at $16 billion a year.[9] From 1992 to the day I joined the *Montrose*, the number of attacks had increased by four hundred percent. And during those ten years it had become more violent: two thousand seafarers had been taken hostage during that period, and this accounting represents only a third of the actual attacks.

The pirates who took down the *Valiant Carrier* were never caught. Indeed, it is highly likely that they continued to attack other ships in the Malacca Straits and South China Sea and possibly are still doing so today.

Donny had described his assailants as best he could remember. I wanted to know. I wanted to know whether they were those who attacked me in the same area. But it had been ten years for Donny and it had been ten years for me. Yet, to this day, we both live with the nightmares that occasionally surface.

Just before I joined the *Montrose* I told Donny that I was to accompany a VLCC on a passage from the Gulf down the Malacca Straits. His reaction surprised me. Never again, he said, would he ever sail the Malacca and Singapore Straits. "I know many captains who refuse that route."

5

The Empty Sea

Montrose

We have steamed into what appears to be a strange hole in the wind. The seas, only yesterday so boisterous, are now flat, without dimension. There are no clouds, and the sun presses down with the force of a hot iron. The ocean is silver and reflective. Seen from an angle from the bridge above, it is smooth and formless, more like an infinite sheet of glass. Flying fish, wings outstretched, skit across the surface like skipping stones as we pass. The ship's wake follows in faithful pursuit, a long trail of disturbed wash that fans out into the glossy sheen to as far away as the eye can imagine.

There is some slight movement to the sea. Ranks of gently undulating swells roll toward us from the southwest, but they are wide apart and low, barely perceptible from up here on the bridge—except that they are felt. We move with them, pitching slowly from one side to the other. So far apart and so low, the swells go nearly unseen.

There is nothing much to look at out there. How interesting is it to stare at a flat edge? But it is so flat, so still, so empty, so available, that you are certain something is out there to be seen.

We are in the Bay of Bengal on the east side of Dondra Head, the southernmost tip of Sri Lanka; another three days and we will enter the northern entrance to the Malacca Straits.

The captain bends over the chart table and checks our latest position—there is little that demands his immediate attention up here. A captain need not spend a great deal of time in the wheelhouse; he has his well-trained officers for those chores. He certainly never spends much time out on the bridgewings unless maneuvering for cargo operations. Gone are the days when the master stands braced against the weather, his hair pasted by gale-force winds and salt spray, listening, keening for the sound of foghorn, ships' bells, keeping watch for uncharted rocks or reefs. His job today keeps him tied to the desk in the air-conditioned ship's office below, handling mostly administrative matters, managing all this. He answers faxes, telexes, e-mails, with the certainty that his chief engineer and his chief mate run the ship as they should. The master of an oceangoing commercial vessel these days is little more than an administrator who reports the day-to-day operations to the head office, whether in London, Singapore, Athens, Vilnius, Valetta, or Houston, wherever ship companies are headquartered. Captains have very little say anymore within the great corporate scheme of things; running a ship is a management job, and you might as well be managing an office building for all the respect you get from the head office. Because of instant communication, unilateral decision-making by the captain involves only the immediate operations of the ship. In the eyes of the head office a master is successful if he arrives on schedule, arrives without incident or accident, saves money on provisions, fuel, and port dues, and keeps the vessel in good enough condition that when the company decides to sell it off, it will get top dollar. Braving storms, quelling disenchanted and potentially mutinous crews, even finding landfall, are issues for C. S. Forester, Melville, Conrad, and Masefield. There is very little romance to going to sea, to being the captain of a ship. One master told me he felt he was merely a truck driver, delivering the goods. Since about ninety-five percent of world commerce is delivered by sea, the feeling is understandable. But you are, after all, the captain. You may not lead a crew of a hundred, or forty, or even twenty-seven; it may only be seventeen, yet the pressures and the responsibilities are far greater than they ever were. The ship costs $84 million to build and it carries a cargo worth $56 million. Spill your load and you could have a bill for cleanup and punitive damages of $7 billion, as did Exxon in Alaska.

A master whose ship sank beneath him was temporarily detained after the accident caused a massive oil spill.[10] It matters little that a ship is a rotten rusty hulk that its owners should never send to sea despite glowing inspection reports under a dodgy registry, or whether it sinks after a hammering by a typhoon. It is irrelevant that the captain heroically is able to save his crew, or that he is the last to leave the foundering vessel. Spill any oil and charges are not only brought against the ship company and sometimes the cargo owner but against the master and officers of the vessel.[11] The definition of a captain's responsibility has gone to the wall and many will no longer put to sea.

Yet the respect due a captain is still guaranteed on board, still sacrosanct. Captain Postma wouldn't want to be anyplace else. "You must just do your job and do it as well as you can," he says, handing a pair of binoculars to his officer on watch. "You must have passion about what you are doing. I found my passion. I don't know now how I could leave it."

Wasim, the ship's third, is the officer on watch. A short, concerned man from Karachi, he spends much of his time with his hands clasped behind his back nervously pacing the length of the bridge, even when the captain is present. Wasim speaks in stereotypical West Asian singsong that is often quite pleasant.

"At sea you are to be studying all the time," he offers. "More than at university. All your life you are studying—new regulations, new technology—and you are always moving ahead, from cadet to officer, to second mate to chief mate and to being captain. You never stop. That is what I am liking. On land you go only so far."

"Wasim has just become a father," the captain offers. "It was a boy, wasn't it?"

"Yes, sir."

Wasim says he is either signing off in Singapore or when we return to Dubai; his four-month tour is up. "I am looking very much to see my son—I have seen him on the film," a video taken by his wife's family shortly after the birth.

The captain returns to the office below. I remain with Wasim on the bridge. I am captivated by the endless expanse of quiet sea. I don't have to be in it. I am on it, plowing through it, watching our bow wave ripple out and eventually flatten in the distance. The bridge telephone rings and Wasim simply responds, yes, yes, yes. He goes to the console and pulls back the short handle of the telegraph to slow ahead. The *Montrose* shudders, the vibrating rumbling sensation of the propeller under our feet diminishes, and the ship begins to slow down.

I look to see if we are about to hit something, but there is nothing but flat, still water.

"Why are we slowing?"

"I don't know. It is not a good time for asking," he says. The bridge phone rings again and he goes to the telegraph and pulls back the handle to full stop. "But I know exactly we are stopping."

The captain arrives on the bridge. There doesn't seem to be any urgency. "No ships?"

"No, sir. No ships." All eyes go to the radar screen for confirmation. The black screen shows only the *Montrose* as a heavy yellow splotch in the center with blue bearing-lines radiating from it.

Our engine has blown a lube oil flange. This giant bloated steel container filled with vital crude oil is stopping out here in the middle of the ocean—a momentary delay in the conveyor. The captain explains that it is not serious, that the flange was spurting oil and that the chief engineer wanted it replaced before we reached the Malacca Straits. It is in the Straits that two generators, two radar, and everything else must be fully operational. A VLCC can not afford to have an engine problem in a channel that is sometimes no wider than a mile, with vessels on your tail and others charging down at you from the opposite direction.

"We should be under way in an hour or so," Postma says. "Our contract calls for fifteen knots on passage and we have been making fifteen and a half. So we can afford a little time."

Donning hard hat, boilersuit, gloves, steel-toed boots, and ear protectors, I go down into the engine room, a bright, cavernous chamber with metal walkways, grids, ladders, and pipes that surround the huge pea-green motor that drives this ship—an engine so big that its spare piston and rod, bolted and strapped to the bulkhead, is a couple meters across and three stories high. The machinery is colossal, the heat is oppressive, and the noise is violent.

Tony and another engineer, their white boilersuits blackened with lube oil, wrestle with the 24mm nuts that circle the flange like lugs on a car wheel. Tony grabs a cheater, a long pipe that he slips around the handle of the socket wrench for extra leverage. He gives a tug and slowly a stubborn nut yields. Brian, the chief, stands off to the side; there is little he can do but to hand Tony a wrench when it is needed.

"It's a known problem," Brian says. "It has happened before on this class ship. We've got plenty of spares." He picks up the new replacement—a heavy steel pipe with two flanges on each end—and hands it to me. "You can see where it would give." He points to the bead weld that rings the pipe. "That's the leak." I am a little overwhelmed; this giant engine generates 36,000 kilowatt hours, puts out enough power to light 250,000 residential homes. The machine has been turned off. This huge ship, carrying cargo upon which so many depend, wallows lifelessly, adrift in the ocean, going nowhere.

Brian wipes his hands on a nearby rag and tosses it to me. "You don't want to put the oily rags in your pocket. An engineer on a Channel ferry did that for years and the man got cancer in the testicles. There's something in the mineral oil apparently."

The flange works loose and a spray of lube oil blasts Tony in the face. No profanity, just a grunt and he continues to loosen the nuts. As automated as this ship has become, it can still be a battleground between man and machine, and I am reassured that no robotics will take the place of a man and his tools. Replacing the flange is a fairly easy job—they should all be so simple. We are under way within the hour. The chief engineer is pleased, the captain relieved.

Time for a walkabout.

Hallelujah, I have found the gym. It is a cramped little room with a ping pong table and a limp net, a broken ski machine, a rowing machine that appears to function, and a black cushioned bench with sliding weights. I have found the small outside swimming pool on the deck above and if I do jog around the deck, I will probably dive in with full gear, hard hat, works boots, and all.

It is six stories from the main deck to the bridge above, and each floor is served by an elevator. Apparently only Angie and Brian, who is overweight, use it regularly but it is not without its merit; it is another three flights down to the lower floors of the engine room and a couple more metal stairways to the levels below that. Temperatures down there reach near 40°C. No one chides the engineers; who wants the stairs when you can take the lift? The elevator is just a yellow box big enough for four people—no hotel-type full-color glossies framed on the walls billboarding its restaurant, its panoramic bar, or its Olympic-sized swimming pool. Just an admonition that during a fire, use the stairs. The ship rolls and it is a strange sensation to be inside an elevator moving upward—diagonally. What if really bad weather hits and the ship is heeling at an angle? The advice: Get out.

I walk out onto the lower sunken deck, the short deck behind the accommodation block. Most of this giant ship's innards are beneath this level, including the engine room. The design of this class of ship is distinctive. The *Montrose* has a modern swept-back look. There is no raised foredeck like on the *Valiant Carrier*, and our long flush deck runs straight from the bow to the superstructure. When she is fully laden, as she is now, the freeboard amidships, the distance between the deck and the surface of the sea, is about eight meters. It would be a real feat for pirates to clamber onto a deck this high above the water while the ship is running at sea speed. However, pirates don't board the middle of the cargo deck. They sneak up from behind within the shadow of radar coverage, and attacking from the stern, they throw their grappling hooks over the railings and scamper up the transom. The sunken deck, or the poop deck, that shorter deck behind the accommodation block, is cut away and drops four meters below the main cargo deck, and to my surprise is much closer to the water than I expected. The distance from the water to this deck is only about three and a half meters. This height poses no more of a challenge to pirates than did the *Valiant Carrier*. Anyone standing on the bow of a fishing boat or a large speedboat could be up and over the railing of the *Montrose* in seconds. Perhaps we are not so invincible after all.

It takes about five minutes to walk the length of the deck outside—around, under, alongside the myriad pipes and valves, little steel houses, cranes, and railings. There are two helicopter landing pads. The bright yellow circle on the starboard side is stenciled WINCH

ONLY in large letters, probably easily read in deep space. The actual landing zone, a large bull's-eye circle painted gray, is located on the port side, well clear of valves and pipes and railings.

I swear that from where I stand on the main deck aft, I see the bow of the ship twist one way and the rest of the ship twist another. This is a big steel container bulging with an incomprehensible amount of cargo—could it really flex? According to Tony Butcher it does and it should. The Chrysler Building, once the tallest building in the world, surprised architects seventy years ago when they discovered it swayed slightly in high winds. That building won't fall over and we won't break in two.

I wonder how many people are needed to maintain the Chrysler Building? And I am not talking about driving it. Donny Monteiro needed twenty-seven crewmen to man his ship, which was ten times smaller than the *Montrose*. And he says he could not have done with less. I haven't seen many of our crew; I rarely pass a crewman in the stairwell; occasionally someone in white boilersuit and red hard hat works somewhere on the long cargo deck. But the ship appears nearly deserted; perhaps it is just the size of the ship that makes it seem so.

The *Montrose* is registered in the Isle of Man in the Irish Sea and her Safe Manning Certificate, issued under the Convention for the Safety of Life at Sea, the international treaty to which most merchant vessels adhere, sets our crew requirement specifically at only seventeen. In addition to the master, chief mate, chief engineer, and second engineer, all with oil endorsement, the vessel must have an officer in charge of the engineering watch and ten seamen, including a cook.

This minimal crew faces sobering statistics. Eighty percent of recorded maritime accidents are attributable to human error. Human error is caused by fatigue. Manpower shortages cause overwork and fatigue. Combine that with the need to station personnel on an all-night antipiracy watch, which is the recommendation of every maritime organization when transiting hostile waters, and you can get a pretty strung-out group of sailors.

The *Montrose* could be manned with even fewer than seventeen. This ship is one of the latest, most modern of The Group's fleet and is so automated that she probably could get by with half of that number. Small computer screens are mounted on the walls of the dining

room, the ship's office, and the control rooms, all part of the Unmanned Machinery Space system. The black boxes are plugged into
an intricate computerized remote alarm system that monitors the
main engine, the generators, the pumps, the steering, the electrical
system, the bearings, and the cargo tanks. Engineers, wherever they
are on the ship, can keep an eye on the engine without laying down
their knives or forks. Indeed, no one is required in the engine room
most of the time, and unless there is a problem and the remote alarms
start ringing, no one goes below at all during the night; the engineers
all get a good night's sleep. Same on the bridge while at sea—unless
there is known heavy traffic in a shipping channel, there is only one
man on watch at any one time. That means during most of the night
there is only one person awake on the entire ship. On many vessels
sometimes even that last watch-stander nods off, and the ship just
keeps trucking onward through the night unattended, a frightening
revelation for those on small boats who cross the paths of these ships—
at sea, at night. During the day many of the officers work twelve hours
from 0800 to 2000 but the ratings, during a passage, keep banker's
hours.

The Alaska Oil Spill Commission, in its final report on the 1989
Exxon Valdez disaster, was critical of Exxon for claiming that modern
automated vessel technology permitted reduced manning without
compromise of safety or function. "Manning policies also may have
affected crew fatigue," the report stated. "Whereas tankers in the
1950s carried a crew of 40 to 42 to manage about 6.3 million gallons
of oil . . . the *Exxon Valdez* carried a crew of 19 to transport 53 million
gallons of oil."[12] The *Montrose* carries a crew of 17 to transport
84 million gallons of oil.

Because piracy has become such a concern, the British National
Union of Marine, Aviation, and Shipping Transport Officers (NU-
MAST) has some strong ideas about crew levels:

> It is no secret that the vast majority of ships at sea are being
> run at their minimum safe manning level. Telling crews to carry out
> extra watches, additional patrols, special lockouts, and to practice
> and prepare countermeasures [against piracy] is all very well—but

it may be meaningless if there are not sufficient people to put the measures into place."[13]

I recall Captain Monteiro saying that with a crew of twenty-seven, he still didn't have enough men for a piracy watch. "Running a ship is a tensed-up job, especially now that there is less staff. You can't cut back on manpower where there are pirates. If I could have spared six or seven crew to patrol the decks, then it might have had some effect."

Captain Postma says he could use more crew. He usually sails with eighteen, sometimes twenty-one with cadets. He doesn't think that is enough, but it is the figure determined by the ship's managers. The critical times aboard any tanker, when chance of fire or explosion, injury to personnel, or damage to the ship is greatest, are during loading and discharging.

"When we put to sea and everything went well [in port], well, that is a *soulagement*—the burden is gone," Postma says.

Back on the bridge I daydream again and stare out at our world. There is for me an undeniable fascination about the edge, the horizon, at sea. It is particularly compelling when the sea is so still and so empty. It is the adventurer in us that triggers a natural curiosity; we must know what is on the other side, off the edge. Perhaps that is what drove men to sail across oceans when it was perceived that the world was flat. Not to prove otherwise but simply to get to the edge and stop and look down into the abyss.

Crossing an ocean on a ship big or small is a lonely business. Like some other seamen, I am aware of the thoughts of Dr. Samuel Johnson, as quoted by Boswell:

"No man will be a sailor who has contrivance enough to get himself into a jail; for being in a ship is being in jail, with the chance of being drowned. . . .

"A man in jail has more room, better food, and commonly better company. . . .

"When men come to like sea life, they are no longer fit to live on land."

Something white catches my eye on the far edge, the very edge—where whatever it is will surely fall off. I look for it on the radar and see a faint smudge on the screen about six miles away.

With the binoculars I can identify it as a sail. The boat, clearer now, has its mainsail up and it flaps back and forth with the motion of the swells. The small yacht, about the size of the *Unicorn*, is pointed in no direction, for there is no wind to push it. It lies parallel to the swells and I know how uncomfortable it is for those aboard. Lying becalmed in a sailboat in the middle of the ocean is far worse than battling a storm; I have done both and it is a matter of control. During a storm you are alive and scared and fighting. When becalmed you don't fight, you only think, and you are at the mercy of you know not what. When there is no wind, there is no progress and with an empty surrounding horizon, a feeling of claustrophobia borne of isolation weighs on your sanity.

My wife, Jackie, and I, alone on the *Unicorn*, were once imprisoned by the doldrums, a region near the equator of calms, sudden storms, and frequently no wind at all.

We were twenty-five days into our passage across the Indian Ocean not far from here, somewhere between continents. The nearest human beings were probably about a thousand miles away; perhaps they were just over the horizon on a passing ship that we would never see. We were becalmed, dead in the water, wallowing from side to side. There was not a breeze, not even a cat's paw. One of those dread times at sea, going nowhere, drifting with the currents and waiting for wind.

The *Unicorn* hung suspended, insignificant, a solitary mote, nothing more than an infinitesimal speck afloat upon the mirror polish of a mercury sea. The intensity of the sun had reached a personal vindictiveness. Without a breeze the temperature had reached well over a hundred Fahrenheit. The air had become so thick that breathing seemed an effort. We leaned against the bulkhead on the deck outside, facing an empty future that dazzled before us. Sweat rolled past my whiskers and fell onto a sodden dime novel that I was too exhausted to read. Through the haze undefined, silver turned to gray and disappeared into a lost horizon.

We had gone without wind for six days and we were floating like discarded jetsam without purpose or direction. Jackie sat next to me, her head back, her eyes closed. Her body glistened with sweat. Her pretty face—at that moment lifeless and plain—was framed by her damp hair like a wet shroud. We were careful not to touch.

We could start the engine and motor away, but were we motoring farther into the doldrums or out of them? Our fuel was limited—we were a sailboat and we needed wind. And I was getting concerned about our water supply. With our jerricans we could hold out for another two weeks.

A cloud sat on the edge of the horizon, a small puff of cumulus. Wind? I stared it into oblivion and it disappeared before my eyes—before I got the chance to feel any hope.

I stared at some distant point off the edge of our world and thought about landfall, our next stop, Aden on the Arabian peninsula, a thousand miles in front of us. It was to be the last stop before heading up the Red Sea and into the Mediterranean, where we would find all the wonders of Europe.

Out of boredom I stood up and looked out onto the sea. Stinging sweat rolled into my eyes, but through it I thought I noticed something in the distance off the starboard, a barely discernible out-of-sync movement. The sea rolled as it had, yet out there something looked—felt—different.

The sun on our backs allowed us to see well under the surface. The surface of the sea remained still, but down below it turned dark. A great shadow hovered ominously underneath us. Land? An undersea atoll? Yet it was moving, we weren't.

The dark mass, about the size of a boxcar, began to slide through the depths and away. Moments later, the still water in the distance appeared to heave. A low rolling wave was approaching us—the whale, still just below the surface, was coming back, displacing water before it, over it.

"My God," Jackie whispered standing next to me. "Is it going to hit us?"

I grunted something unintelligible. Initially I had regarded the intrusion with relief, fascination. Finally a break, a change. Something. But I began to feel the first taste of fear as the whale continued to bull its way toward us. I saw in my mind's eye scenes of giant whales broaching under ancient longboats and hurling them and their hunters skyward.

We held on, our nerves wide open, raw, waiting for the jarring collision that would send us to the bottom. The black headwall of the monster, water splaying out away from it, bore down on us. She took my hand and closed her eyes tightly, squinching like a little girl about to be struck by an open palm.

With inches to spare the whale glided gracefully under the boat and disappeared. Minutes later the whale burst buoyantly through the surface with a force suggestive of popping from some great depth. The boat rocked violently in its wake. An explosive geyser of air and sea water belched from the whale's blowhole; we were sprayed with a fine mist and a gagging stench of digested fish. It floated about a yard from the hull, motionless, permitting us an inspection. It was a sperm whale, its hide corrugated and dark gray. A long scar sliced diagonally from the top of its back to just below its hump, the result of a more violent encounter.

Without any evident movement the whale drifted downward, a dark shadow that vanished below. We were once again alone amid a profound wilderness, a small boat left to wallow under the broiling sun and cloudless sky. Upon the sea a canoe, a sailboat, a supertanker—no matter the size—is alone and vulnerable to beast and man.

From the bridge the sailboat has been lost to the swells; I am sure those on board saw us and I sense their envy as this giant ship steamed by in the distance. Ahead the horizon is getting dusky, lowering; it means clouds, it may mean a squall and for that little boat out there, some wind. There is some activity on the radar, some solid returns from clouds about eight miles in front of us, so there is rain and they'll get wind.

I leaf through the IMB Piracy Center situation reports clipped to the wall by the chart table. There are more incidents in the Malacca Straits, the South China Sea, and off the coast of West Africa. But there is one, a few days old, that stops me cold:

AT 0440 UTC IN POSITION 12:55N–048:20E, GULF OF ADEN. THREE ARMED PIRATES IN A WOODEN BOAT APPROACHED A YACHT UNDERWAY AND ORDERED HER TO STOP. WHEN THE YACHT INCREASED SPEED, ONE OF THE PIRATES SHOT AT THE YACHT FROM HIS MACHINE GUN. SKIPPER'S WIFE BROADCAST A DISTRESS MESSAGE ON VHF 16 SAYING "MAYDAY, PIRATE ATTACK, PLEASE HELP, WE HAVE TWO CHILDREN ON BOARD." DESPITE THIS PLEA FOR HELP, A CONTAINER SHIP HALF-MILE AWAY DID NOT RESPOND. THE SAME CONTAINER SHIP HAD FIVE MINUTES EARLIER COMMUNICATED WITH THE YACHT. FINALLY THE SKIPPER OF THE YACHT FIRED BACK WITH HIS GUN AND THE PIRATE BOAT RETREATED.

Yachts are attractive targets. Pirates know that while there is probably little cash aboard, there will be valuable sophisticated electronic equipment that can be removed easily. Sailboats are the vessels most vulnerable, for they usually cannot outrun anything other than another sailboat, and a yacht swinging on its anchor in some idyllic cove is a sitting duck. Many boats disappear without a trace; struck in midocean by a whale? Hit a partially submerged container? Attacked by pirates? The twelve-year-old son of a couple sailing off the Honduran Mosquito Coast was shot and crippled for life in 2000. A Finnish couple was taken off their boat and held hostage by Somali pirates. A single-handed Canadian sailor attacked off the coast of Mexico while under way badly injured; his yacht drifted for two days until running aground. My own experience in the South China Sea. These are just some of the attacks that occur each year.

I think of that young family on the yacht going up the Red Sea to Europe. An increasing number of Americans these days buy a boat and sail away for a year or two for a trip around the world. Although this boat is not identified as such, it may have been American, for we are the ones who most frequently carry firearms.[14] I was no exception. I sailed away from San Francisco with a box of carpet tacks and a couple of guns—a little, 30-30 Winchester saddle rifle I had bought in Wyoming and my mother's Model 12 Winchester shotgun, which I sawed off as a bear gun when I lived in Alaska. It took six shots: two slugs to penetrate the bear's breast plate, two rounds of double-ought buck if the slugs hadn't stopped the animal, and the last two of birdshot to use on yourself if the bear kept coming. A bit apocryphal but it was considered a necessary defense if you lived in the bush. I traded the saddle gun in Australia for some diesel fuel and reluctantly tossed the 12-gauge pump overboard after the *Unicorn* took a knockdown in the Pacific and seawater ruined it.

Carrying firearms aboard a yacht has its drawbacks, not the least of which is that you are obligated to declare your firearms to port officials. A friend from Los Angeles on a large Baltic schooner neglected to do so in Suva, Fiji (he also had a poorly concealed mount for a .50-caliber machine gun on the foredeck of his family yacht) and was thrown in jail. Guns are a debatable option for "yachties," but from firsthand experience I'm convinced that cruising folks have a better chance of survival against pirates if they follow the golden rule of commercial ships: Don't resist, give them anything they want, and get 'em the hell off the ship.

It is certainly foolish even to consider carrying a gun if you are not prepared to use it. I knew I would have to actually pull the trigger; while I grew up as a hunter, I could never imagine shooting at another person. In fact I can't imagine hunting anymore either. Had I still been armed when I was boarded off Horsburgh, there would have been a gun battle and I would have lost.

A recent well-publicized attack on a yacht in which a gun was fired occurred in early December 2001, when four armed pirates in a dugout attacked and killed New Zealand yachtsmen Sir Peter Blake aboard the *Seamaster*, anchored in the Amazon. According to police Blake, an America's Cup winner, fired a rifle at the bandits and then was shot twice in the back. We will never know if, had Blake not been armed, he would still be alive today.

Most cruising sailors are not so well equipped or so famous. Those folks take a leave from work, rent out their homes, cash in some of their assets, and head out to sea, drawn by fantasies of a life free and unencumbered, of time to read a book, of getting away from the narcoleptic addiction of television, of getting to know your children, of exotic places and new cultures; these are the dreams that drive the adventurous to sea. The circumnavigation of the attacked family had taken them to the places most could only read about in Sunday travel sections: Tahiti, Fiji, New Zealand, Australia, Singapore, Thailand, and finally Europe. They had convinced themselves it would be a good education for the children. But they were shot at in the Red Sea.

6

Better Than Dancing Lessons

Montrose

There are no guns aboard this ship, at least not that anyone admits to. It is certainly not company policy to permit firearms on board. Incredibly there are no effective weapons on civilian ships today to ward off an attack from pirates or maritime terrorists. A ship is equipped with fire hoses and some flare guns and some fire axes. And a few kitchen knives in the galley. That's it. Firing a flare gun at someone on a ship is out of the question, although "yachties" have been known to use them effectively when firing overboard at pirates trying to board from small boats. It is unlikely that any of those pirated ships cited in the latest IMB Situation Report were armed.

Most captains know that no matter how thorough, how complete, their antipiracy defenses, or how big their ship, if pirates are determined to board, they will, especially if armed with automatic weapons. There is little they or their crew can do to stop them. While many on board would like to be armed, most agree that a shootout on a ship, especially one carrying explosive cargo, is too risky. In addition, their use also runs the risk of escalating the violence.

Guns are forbidden in most parts of the world. Outside of the United States few civilians have any experience with firearms and would not know how to use one without training. If a crewman met a pirate face-to-face and each had a gun, who would be most likely to pull the trigger?

A ship arriving in every port must declare the weapons it carries; the guns are impounded ashore by customs officers until the ship sails out of territorial waters. Yet it is when at anchor, in port, or trans-shipping cargo that many of the most violent armed attacks occur.

It is common knowledge that Israeli and Russian ships do carry firearms and they are seldom declared to port officials. After the Russians went through a spate of attacks off the Philippines, they followed the Israeli lead and equipped their vessels with small arms. In the mid-eighties an armed gang off the coast of Nigeria attacked the Soviet-flagged *Slutsk*. The Russians won the battle and took the pirates out to sea; their bullet-riddled bodies washed ashore a few days later. Word gets around. In 2001 not one Russian or Israeli ship was attacked, compared to twenty-seven ships from the U.S. and the UK.

Shipowners are looking desperately for nonviolent ways to keep pirates off their ships.

I once spread thumbtacks on the deck of the *Unicorn* in southern Mexico, after sailors on a nearby yacht reported armed fishermen had boarded them the evening before. It was a mistake. I went on deck to pee over the side in the middle of the night. I hobbled around on my punctured feet for days. Carpet tacks might have worked for Captain Monteiro. On the *Valiant Carrier* only the pirates went barefoot.

There are other more or less effective antipiracy measures. In addition to fire hoses, deck patrols, deck lights, and carpet tacks, Mammoet, the Dutch salvage company that successfully raised the Russian nuclear submarine *Kursk* in October 2001, installed a non-lethal 10,000-volt electric screen around one of its ships, with a loud-speaker system that is reportedly as loud as a jet aircraft whizzing by at 150 feet. As of this writing there have not been any reports of attempted boarding on these noisy hot-wired vessels.

Antipiracy has gone high tech. Captain Noel Choong of the Piracy Reporting Center advocates the use of a satellite tracking device equivalent to LoJack (a stolen-vehicle recovery unit) that transmits a vessel's exact location in case of a hijacking to anxious shipping company officials back on land. The unit is attached and wired secretly to the ship without captain or crew knowing its whereabouts or, in some cases, that it is even aboard the ship.[15]

Based on the same principal used to track wolves in Montana or whales in the Pacific, the transponder automatically sends a location signal to low earth orbiting satellites that is interpreted and relayed as a position report to the shipping company's computers. Although the ship's master routinely sends the vessel's location, the device provides a backup in case the captain is unable to transmit his daily report—or in case a ship is attacked. (While initially designed in response to the growing number of hijackings, the U.S. Coast Guard, in a security review following 9-11, now recommends that every ship carry such a device, "which could not be switched off, to track a ship if it is hijacked.") If a vessel disappears, the shipowner as well as the International Maritime Bureau know the location of the missing vessel and can alert law-enforcement authorities, local navies, and regional port officials that the stolen ship might be heading into their waters. The system recommended by the IMB, a little bigger than a shoe box, is mounted topsides and costs $280 per month per ship, inexpensive if you want to keep track of your fleet transiting through areas of piracy.

In September 2000, twenty-one pirates in the pay of an organized crime syndicate hijacked the tanker *Petchem*, carrying Shell product, about a hundred miles northeast of Horsburgh Light in the South China Sea. The pirates destroyed all the communication equipment, rounded up the crew, took command of the ship, repainted the funnel, and erased the name of the ship from the lifeboats and life rafts. While still within Malaysian waters a larger tanker joined it and siphoned off 2,200 tons of diesel cargo. The *Petchem* was found adrift in Singapore waters the next day, the crew imprisoned in their cabins.

Captain Choong maintains that had there been a satellite transmitting unit aboard, he and his team could have located the ship before the pirates had stolen the cargo and while it was still in Malaysian waters, where it would have been arrested. His advocacy was proven well founded when, months later, the system was instrumental in the dramatic retrieval of *Petchem*'s sister ship hijacked in the Malacca Straits.

Equipping the vessel with the tracking device is a two-edged sword, and management is not sure how to respond. On the one hand they see the device as a deterrent; on the other hand, if the company doesn't announce its vessels are equipped with the device, then the deterrent factor is eliminated but the crew might be a hair safer.

A satellite tracking device is not the only high-tech defense against pirates. NUMAST, the UK's national maritime union, has called on companies owning the big oil tankers to outfit their vessels with closed-circuit television cameras to monitor the unmanned outside decks on larger ships. Chiding the oil majors for spending more money to protect their service stations than to protect their ships, NUMAST says the CCTV unit, costing about $25,000, is "pretty small beer compared to the loss of a ship from an attack."

A more controversial deterrent, one employed with increasing frequency, is the use of "heavies"—armed mercenaries riding shotgun aboard ships through pirate waters. These sea marshals, like their counterparts on commercial airlines, provide some protection, especially to slow-moving workboats, cable layers, dredges, and towboats, ships most vulnerable to pirates. Some cruise ship companies currently employ Nepalese Gurkhas as an onboard protection force.

But aboard the *Montrose* there are no guns, no Gurkhas, no heavies. Just a small crew with a couple fire axes and pipe cheaters. Yet one can't help but get the impression that piracy is something that happens only to yachts and to smaller ships the size of the *Valiant Carrier* and the *Petchem*, to those that are easy to board and have a lot more to loose. The *Valiant Carrier* had been a target of opportunity. The *Petchem*, carrying marketable diesel fuel, was a lot more attractive to organized crime than our ship that carries $75 million of unrefined oil; the syndicates can't fence crude. The sheer size of the *Montrose*, however, does seem to indicate that there is a lot more aboard worth stealing than the cargo she carries; pirates could imagine a vessel this big, this important, has got to be carrying a shipload of goodies.

From the *Montrose*'s bridge one can be forgiven for feeling a little smug, invulnerable to the pettiness of the world below. When one spends much of his day nine stories above everything else, where tugboats, fishing boats, small pirogues, and those upon them appear Lilliputian and harmless, one develops more than just a sense of security, it is a sense of invincibility.

Captain Postma believes only trained commandos equipped with climbing lines and hooks could board his ship, because the deck is too high. "In Normandy during the war they climbed the cliffs. They were special people, of course, well trained. I don't think pirates can get aboard my ship."

Many of the *Montrose*'s crew, however, have either been pirated or know those who have. Brian Ashdown, the chief engineer, quickly dispels the notion that a VLCC can't be boarded by pirates. Pirates once attacked his tanker at a Singapore refinery. It was an event in which guns were fired while discharging cargo and one that could have sparked a catastrophe. "And you don't want to have a gunfight on a ship like this," he says.

Brian was second engineer on the VLCC *Litopia*, when it was attacked by pirates while moored at Singapore's Bukom Terminal, where we also will discharge part of our cargo. The VLCC had a flush deck that ran in a straight line from the bow to the stern, a thousand feet of high, imposing wall—no dropping sunken deck like that on the *Montrose*. The transom on the *Litopia* rose as high as the rest of its deck and was considerably higher than ours.

Over coffee in the ship's office Brian, a colorful character with fleshy jowls, dimple in his chin, and a full head of wavy unkempt white hair, recalls he was awakened in the middle of the night by a phone call from the chief officer that pirates were aboard.

"I said, 'How many gins you have last night?' 'No,' he says, 'honest to God, they're here! Aboard!' "

Five pirates armed with machetes had climbed up the stern and, holding two of the officers as hostage, went searching for the captain's cabin and the ship's safe. Two Singapore rent-a-cops armed with rifles were asleep down in the officers' rec room. When they discovered the pirates aboard, they opened fire.

"They were only thirty feet away and they bloody well missed! And they were just telling us the night before what good shots they were. They claimed they hit one or two of them, but the next morning there was no blood on the floor, nothing like that. The chief mate was pretty shook up—they had tied him up—they told him they were going to chop his ears off."

The greatest fear of any tankerman is fire aboard his ship. Brian was worried.

"We thought that the shooting was going to start something. We tripped the cargo pumps as soon as the bullets started flying. You know that you can't even use normal flashlights out on deck." In fact, on the deck of a tanker everything must be "intrinsically safe." No mobile telephones, no radios, nothing that uses batteries, not even a cigarette lighter in your pocket, is permitted. In the early days, Brian recalls, they were going to ban watches with batteries. "That was a bit over the top and they stopped that silly idea. But when the shooting started . . ."

The next day the Singapore police told the crew that if the pirates had had guns, then they would have been a rogue outfit from the Indonesian navy. "But they had knives—Indonesians from the islands across the Straits," Brian says.

I tell the chief engineer the story about the firebombing of the *Valiant Carrier* and he shakes his head in dismay and says that he doesn't understand why it didn't blow.

~

The ship's safe is in the master's quarters and I want to see it. Above Postma's door at the end of the corridor the small three-inch plastic strip simply states: CAPTAIN. There is no ruse, no warnings of "Dangerous Air."

The *Montrose*'s safe is in a corner of the captain's bedroom at the foot of the double bed. He says he never locks it. He swings open the heavy door and a few papers spill out onto the carpeted floor. A wad of Australian-made Blu-Tac, sticky putty used to affix posters to a wall, is pressed against the dial to keep it from turning. "The safe is much too difficult to use," he says, echoing most other masters I've talked to. It serves as a filing cabinet for immediate documents such as ship's papers, registration documents, load line changes, items of no interest to a looter. There is no "ship's cash" aboard the vessel. The captain says he has $700 of his own personal money and the crew members have their own cash on hand; pirates would not find the mother lode on this ship.

Whether to keep any money in a ship's safe is a matter of debate; the ship company of The Group does not. Other companies are forced to and it is often a great deal.

Pirates attacked the *Stolt Venture*, a chemical carrier, as it was westbound in the Singapore Straits abeam of Pulau Karimun. Brian Hoare, a captain for twenty-six years, said that his ship had been carrying cash in the safe to pay off the crew, a common practice for those calling in at exotic ports where U.S. dollars are hard to come by.

"I had just returned to my cabin, dead tired, ready for bed. I was in the loo peeing when suddenly a dark face appeared around the corner. He scared the wits out of me. Then there were three more in the bathroom. One of them put a knife to my throat, and another put a gun in my ear. Then more came in. They had machetes and one of them had gotten hold of our ship's fire ax. I didn't move.

"They were screaming, 'Safe! Safe!' I had about twenty-two thousand dollars on board, but I must have been worried about pirates—Karimun is a known pirate area, and I think I must have had a premonition; I had stuffed about twelve thousand dollars under the sofa and left the rest in the safe—in fives and tens so that it looked like a lot."

Most ship's masters learn to avoid the ship's safe. Like Donny Monteiro and Gerrit Postma. Brian Hoare was learning his lesson this night. "I was having trouble getting the safe open—a combination dial and key. One of them kept jabbing me with his knife to speed me up, but I was so nervous I kept getting it wrong. I was worried about the one with the ax. He kept threatening me, waving the ax over my head. He was screaming. He was very agitated—this was the one who was going to hurt me."

It was 2330 hours and the watch on the bridge was about to change. Captain Hoare was afraid the crew would discover the pirates and all hell would break. "I felt that if any of the crew came in while they held me, I was going to get my head split open. I was desperate."

After he opened the safe, they bound and gagged him and threw him back on the sofa and fled.

I wondered, what if he had had no money to give the pirates?

"I cannot imagine," he said.

Pirates, finding no money in a ship's safe but certain there was ship's money aboard, have become enraged and have tortured crews to find out where it was hidden. Donny Monteiro kept $4,000 out just for pirates. "You have to keep some money aside," Donny says. "If I said there was no money, they would have killed me. If I said I had only a hundred dollars, they wouldn't have believed me. And they would have killed me."

One idea supported by many masters to keep money set aside specifically for pirates—a pirate pot. Captain Postma thinks it is an idea of some merit.

"Maybe it would please the pirates and then—mission completed—they can piss off."

The Reverend Peter Ellis runs the Seaman's Mission in Hong Kong. He has dealt with seafarers who have been attacked by pirates, has helped them work through their traumas. The big, cheerful Anglican minister, with the girth and the disposition of a Friar Tuck, acknowledges that once pirates have boarded the vessel, the crew must cooperate, and this includes giving them what they came for.

"No cash in the safe is certainly one way in which seafarers end up being physically harmed. The frustration of going away empty handed leads to physical aggression. Many masters do not have cash in the safe because all payments for services are handled by the company through their agents. What is the difference between carrying cash for pirates and carrying spirits [as baksheesh] for port officials?"

The *Montrose*'s managers and operators are not without their own experience. One of their tankers was pirated while discharging at the Brazilian port of Santos. When the intruders found no cash in the safe, according to one officer, they became "very agitated . . . very angry" and were somewhat placated only after the officer gave them her camera and cash.

The ship company today pays off their crews by depositing salaries into home bank accounts, eliminating the need to carry large sums of cash on board, which it hopes removes a prime motive for attack. However, this assumes gangs of pirates are able to identify the ships they chase after, and can identify and not waste time attacking a ship that carries no cash—unlikely when a target of opportunity steams by them in the dark of night. And while carrying no cash might be a good idea, it is today impossible to identify a cashless ship.

Until recently, The Group's ships were painted handsomely, its familiar corporate logo emblazoned proudly on the funnel and abaft the bows. A corporation's emblem for all to see. But, as an oil major, The Group is increasingly concerned about its public image, and has removed its logo from its ships to avoid unwanted media coverage in the event of an oil spill. Crews on company ships now call their stack the CNN funnel, ships without distinction. "If anything happens, it will be a while before the CNN-TV helicopters can see that we belong to The Group," said one officer. There is nothing outwardly to identify the *Montrose* as belonging to this oil major.

This is increasingly true among many of the oil companies. At a glance, you can't tell one company's VLCC from another. In fact, Exxon-Mobil announced it would sell nine of its tankers by the summer of 2003 and then lease the ships, no longer identified as Exxon ships, back from the new Greek owners. Shell perhaps started the trend, in response to the controversial disposal of the North Sea oil rig *Brent Spar*, in 1995. Shell had proposed dumping the installation, claimed by environmentalists to contain radioactive and toxic sludge, in the North Atlantic. Environmental activists occupied the rig for months to prevent its disposal, and all of it played out in full view of the media. Today, Shell's famous yellow scallop has been wiped clean from its ships, and its company symbol has vanished from its fleet of VLCCs.

If pirates could identify us, then the word might get around that we carry no cash. Jonas Krokos, the ship company's vice president of shipping in London, put an end to the discussion of a pirate pot: "Someone once suggested that along with the sign on the accommodation block NO SMOKING, we put NO CASH like some city buses. There will always be something to steal, medical chests, crew's personal belongings, some equipment. But our policy is to never carry cash."

⌢

Captain Postma hands me a fax he has just received from the ship's agent in Singapore. It advises him that he is to anchor the *Montrose* in the lee of Pulau Karimun, where we will discharge the Omani Light Crude into another tanker for delivery to a refinery in Malaysia. It was just off Karimun that Captain Hoare's ship was attacked.

The captain, who has never been to Karimun, acknowledges that he has heard that the island is dangerous. "It was in my head somewhere, maybe the IMB piracy report, I'm not sure."

It probably was the daily sitrep from the Piracy Reporting Center that came over the wire a few days ago:

07.07.2001: TANJUNG BALAI, KARIMUN WATERS, INDONESIA. WHILST UNDERWAY, PIRATES HIJACKED A TANKER AND TOOK HOSTAGE HER ELEVEN CREWMEMBERS. ON 12.07.2001 THE INDONESIAN AUTHORITIES LOCATED THE TANKER AT THE CIREBON PORT IN CENTRAL JAVA. ALL ELEVEN CREWMEMBERS ARE SAFE ON BOARD. AUTHORITIES ARE INVESTIGATING THE INCIDENT.

More piracy attacks are recorded within a few miles of Karimun than any other place except around the Horsburgh Light. When I pass on this information, the captain wonders why he has not been warned. "It is a lightening area and the charterer says it is okay, that where we are going is safe. But they mean safe for discharge, safe for anchoring, safe draft—but they do not tell us whether it is safe for pirates. Piracy is not mentioned; I have received no warnings."

A few hours later he announces he will conduct a "pirate drill" on Monday morning as we enter pirate waters. According to the crew members I have spoken to, many of whom have worked for the company for years, this will be the first antipiracy drill they have ever seen. Only the senior officers know that the drill will be held, but I suspect that by the time the bells ring and the horns blow for the general alarm, it will have been an open secret. "I want to see the crew's reaction, to see what they can do against pirates," the captain says. "They will go to their muster station—I will call on the PA system that we are being boarded by pirates. Then I will build from that exercise." With full instructions for antipiracy precautions posted on the doors, the crew should have a good idea of their responsibilities.

The crew works only half day on Sunday, except for the watch stander on the bridge, and he gets overtime. It would seem more appropriate to hold the antipiracy drill the day before we arrive in pirate territory, but the captain has to choose his priorities: balancing a happy crew against the slim possibility of attack.

"I take the precautions," Postma says, "so that if anything did happen the company can say it did everything it could."

The ship company has some very specific procedures that it expects its masters to follow when entering pirate country:

ACTIONS TO BE TAKEN WHEN PASSING THROUGH KNOWN PIRACY AREAS:

1. Before darkness lock all doors.

2. Before darkness lock all doors of both superstructures (by the use of padlocks externally or locking bars internally) including funnel, emergency escapes should be padlocked through the releasing bolt.

3. From sunset onwards switch on deck lights around the Sunken Deck. Prepare bridgewing searchlights/Aldis lamp in order to 'blind' any craft approaching vessel.

4. Have fire hoses fixed to the railing, hydrants and nozzles left open. In certain areas such as the *Malacca/Singapore Straits* the fire pump will be running and the hoses continuously spraying.

5. Keep your cabin door locked during passage of these areas.

6. Keep a sharp lookout for any craft approaching, use bridgewing searchlights/Aldis lamp to show that you have seen it.

7. Watchkeepers to keep a sharp lookout and report anything behaving suspiciously around the vessel.

These are steps that the company assumes are adequate, that if a VLCC is attacked in the Malacca Straits it won't belong to The Group.

"We don't need that wakeup call," says Bill McKnight in the London office. Bill is the manager of Emergency Response and Industry

Standards, who makes sure that the corporate fleet adheres to the rules and regulations set out by international regulatory agencies. Just as importantly he is the designated person ashore, the liaison between the head office and the ships' masters.

The ship company had told me that its captains and crews have had some antipiracy briefings, that many had watched an educational video on piracy. The video, underwritten by the International Chamber of Shipping and the International Shipping Federation, is a dramatic, often violent recreation of pirates attacking a ship and crew members cowering in fear of getting killed as well as interviews with victims of piracy and suggestions on how to mount an antipiracy defense. It is designed specifically as a training tool to be shown to crews whose ships pass through pirate territory. Based on recommendations of the International Maritime Organization (IMO), the United Nation's marine regulatory body, the video recommends turning the ship into a fortress known as "the citadel" and keeping the crew inside, stringing barbed wire around the decks, photographing everyone coming aboard, keeping the gangway up while in port, being alert for decoy craft. It further warns that "prostitutes are a major security risk; they can provide information to pirates as well as being involved in drug smuggling." It stresses the necessity of regular antipiracy training and drills, and adhering to the policy of nonresistance.[16]

Captain Postma does not know about the video. And he says there never has been any training about piracy that he knows of. "Not for me, not for my crew."

But he welcomes it—"if done by people who knew what they were talking about—not by people in an office who have never worked on a ship. Most of my crew have never seen a pirate and it is science fiction for them. For me as well. I would like to know more about piracy. But I have never been pirated, so I don't know what to expect.

"We are told not to resist if pirates come aboard, so maybe we are talking about psychological training. We are saturated with training courses. But it would be better than dancing lessons, I think. Training for piracy, yes, maybe it is a good idea. Other masters could use it as well."

There already exists a demanding training regimen for the captains and senior officers: tanker safety, executive development, fire fighting, bridge management techniques, vibration analysis, first aid, and welding. The Filipino ratings, the nonofficers, are offered courses in tankerman, fire fighting, and first aid. Antipiracy training, according to the Vessel Particulars Questionnaire filed with the IMO a few months before this voyage, is not part of the ship company's routine curriculum.

A large poster that accompanies the training video and the *Master Guide: Pirates and Armed Robbers*, written by the International Chamber of Shipping, has been taped to the corridor wall by the mess room. It shows a group of savage-looking thugs armed with long knives and automatic rifles crawling over the stern railing of a ship. BE VIGILANT IN PIRATE AREAS! it warns.

For our run down the Malacca Straits the captain will have fire hoses spraying water outboard. He has not got much faith in them. "My hoses are not capable of producing the amount of water to splash away the pirates. The hoses now are only effective because it tells the people who want to come aboard, 'Hey, they are alert'—but those who really want to come aboard will. The hoses I have will not impress the pirates." I am beginning to detect a change in his attitude toward piracy. Once he believed that it would be impossible to board his ship. Now, I think, he is not so sure.

Captain Postma will double the watch, have both radars switched on, required for the Malacca Straits anyway, and prepare a distress message to send (according to company requirements) in case of boarding. "How is anyone going to send a distress message if we are boarded by pirates?" he wonders.

Bill McKnight says that the ship company firmly adheres to the citadel concept and believes that creating a fortress within the ship is the best way to deal with piracy. If pirates do manage to get aboard, keep them out of the control areas. During passage through dangerous waters, company policy is that all personnel not required on the bridge remain behind double-locked doors.

The citadel concept, however, does not have much appeal to Captain Postma. In fact, he is not aware of it. He insists on doing things his way.

"This is SMS—ship management policy—my own ship's policy; we get together, the chief mate, chief engineer, and others and we discuss what we should do to prevent piracy. But this citadel, I don't know. It sounds like you are hiding in a bunker. We lock everything, of course, and the last opportunity to get in is through the bridge-wings. But they could get in other places." He cites the tempered glass windows on doors to the outside. "If they want to come in, they will. If pirates wanted to break the glass and enter the ship, they could take a fire ax that we have on the fo'c'scle and break the glass—that is what it is there for."

Captain Postma calls this bunker approach counterproductive. "If you lock yourself in, this bypasses the possibility of deterring pirates."

A lockdown may seem like a good plan to the ship company but not to Captain Donny Monteiro. "If someone throws a firebomb on deck and you are locked inside, then what do you do? You are trapped and the ship is on fire. At least some of my crew were able to put out the fires while the pirates were aboard. I think the citadel is a stupid idea."

There is one policy that is universally accepted: Don't fight the pirates. "That is the company policy that I know of," Captain Postma says. "Don't play the hero."

Captain Monteiro and Captain Hoare knew better than to resist. Homi Tarapore, the third mate on the *Valiant Carrier* with the karate black belt, fought back, and Donny believes his resistance so startled the pirates that it triggered the violence. Monteiro says he also was not pleased that his crew tried to rescue him.

"When I told the crew to back off, to go away, they didn't know whether I was forced to say that or whether I meant it. Had they left it alone, I could have given the pirates the money and they would have gotten off my ship without anyone getting hurt. It doesn't matter how many locks you have on the doors, if they have a knife at someone's throat, then it is all over," Captain Monteiro says. "They are aboard and they can kill; you give them anything they ask for."

Captain Postma will have crewmen patrolling the deck and they will be equipped with knives. "These are not for fighting but to cut the ropes of the pirates if they try to board."

Aboard the *Montrose*, Niko is indisputably our own wild hair. When the pirates come, I'll duck behind this big man.

"Pirates, ha! Thirty days against Serbians. I kill Serbians—I don't know how many I kill, but I kill," the lovable Croat says during dinner. "I handle. No worry."

"You're not supposed to resist. They might kill you."

"No worry. I handle."

This is one seafarer who has not got the message.

Each company vessel undergoes a security audit, an inspection carried out at random by former officers now working in the London office. The *Montrose* passed with flying colors. The audit showed that there were:

—No serious shadow sectors near boarding points or citadel entrances;

—Full lighting of overside poop deck area;

—Secure padlocks with anti–crowbar/bolt cropper features;

—Padlocks on a master key system rather than a high number of individual keys;

—Internal bridge door. Robust, ability to lock from either side;

—Bridge windows, rear windows, either armored glass and/or fitted with one-way film;

—Watertight doors on the lifeboat and sunken deck can be padlocked from the outside.

The audit is a well-intentioned report that seems to have been conceived by those who have been off the ship too long, created with the naval architect's blueprint in front of them. It is as if someone was scratching his head trying to remember what the weak points were when he was on such a ship. While some of these precautions might briefly slow down those who want to take over the *Montrose*, they do not turn the ship into an impregnable fortress. Nothing, for example, is mentioned about the windowed doors on the upper decks or the large meter-square windows that front the decks in cabins like mine. A fire ax could make quick work of them. But there are none in the industry who really think their vessels are invulnerable.

It is evening and the sky to the west is a splay of brilliant orange. The sea is marred by whitecaps and long, low swells from the south. A VLCC in ballast returning to somewhere in the Middle East for a refill passes us to starboard a few miles away. She is high out of the water; a bone in her teeth as her bow splits the breaking seas.

Captain Postma stands on the far end of the sunken deck looking out at our ship's long trailing wake, his hands clasped behind his back. He turns toward the passing tanker. Placing his hands on the railing, he leans over and looks down at the transom and at the sea. I don't know whether he is deep in far-reaching cosmic thought, or whether he is assessing the distance between the water and the deck. His body language tells me it is the latter and I join him.

"No, it is not difficult to board this ship," he now admits. "More difficult on that ship," he says, nodding toward the empty tanker riding high in the water. "But here, it is not so difficult."

We both lean over and look down at the sheer drop of our ship's black transom; the wake churns white and green, turbulent like the bottom of a waterfall. The deck here is very close to the surface.

"Yes, they could come up here."

I recall Captain Hoare of Stolt saying he was quite happy not to be in command of a VLCC on a delivery down the Malacca Straits.

"Don't let anybody tell you that size and speed is any kind of protection. If a VL is loaded," Brian said, "then it is a sitting duck. They have to watch their draft and their speed; too fast and they squat, and if they go too slow, they are in the pirate area for two periods of darkness.

"Those poor old VLs."

We will be in the Straits in a couple of days.

7

A Christian Approach

As our captain determines how best to protect the *Montrose* from an attack by pirates, there are masters at sea who don't need a refresher course on shipboard security. They run ships that are on full-time alert; it is not necessary to persuade the captains of these ships to be on guard.

The *Pacific Teal* and the *Pacific Pintail* each transports, in forged steel caskets, recycled radioactive waste—enough mixed-oxide reactor fuel to build fifty-six nuclear bombs. This is not a cargo that can fall into the wrong hands. According to scientists it is relatively easy to chemically separate the plutonium from MOX fuel to build a nuclear device.[17]

The handsome blue-hulled ships are part of the fleet of Pacific Nuclear Transport Ltd. The vessels are purposely built to carry 446 kilograms of MOX, plutonium separated from spent nuclear rubbish. That cargo is the by-product of nuclear fission inside reactor cores. It is not something that can be disposed of easily. It must either be buried for thousands of years deep within a geologic formation or reprocessed to recycle the plutonium and uranium into new fuel.

Once reprocessed it is returned to Japan as MOX and used by Japanese electric power companies in their commercial nuclear reactors.

There has been controversial two-way traffic in this toxic and unstable cargo since the 1980s, when Japan first shipped its spent fuel to England and France for recycling. The radioactive waste is shipped from Japan to the sprawling COGEMA–La Hague nuclear reprocessing plant near Cherbourg, France, on the English Channel. Security precautions at the site are extreme. The French government in October 2001 ringed the complex with antiaircraft missiles to prevent aerial attacks similar to the ones that destroyed the World Trade Center in New York City. The COGEMA site, like many other nuclear installations worldwide, is considered vulnerable.

The specific routes of these waste-carrying ships from Cherbourg to Japan are closely guarded secrets and are revealed only after the ships have departed. There are only so many ways to get from here to there, and some of the shipments necessarily have passed through narrow, constricted waterways—known pirate areas. One route takes the ships through the Malacca Straits and the South China Sea, some of the world's most dangerous waters, an area in which the Abu Sayaf, self-professed Filipino Islamic extremists, attacked ships with rocket-propelled grenades. Other routes eastbound include the west coast of Africa around Cape Town; a westward route under Cape Horn; another south of Australia; and another through the Panama Canal which occurred unnoticed in July 2001 to the belated protest of environmentalists. Passage planners are working out the feasibility of a route across the Arctic ice cap over the top of Russia. Pirates and maritime terrorists notwithstanding, these ships cross some of the wildest seas on the planet.

British Nuclear Fuels, one of the two companies that manufacture MOX, also owns the shipping company. It is convinced the security of its ships is as tight as the steel drums containing the cargo.

The British-flagged vessels usually travel together; one of them carries the cargo and the other acts as a decoy/watchdog. The vessels are equipped with an "automatic voyage monitoring system," similar to the ShipLoc tracking device advocated by the IMB. The AVMS reports the vessel's latitude and longitude, speed, and heading every two hours to the Emergency Control Center at Barrow, northeast of London.

Thirty members of the crack United Kingdom Atomic Energy Authority Constabulary, the force that guards British nuclear facilities, ride herd on the *Pacific Pintail* and the *Pacific Teal*. In addition to small arms the UKAEAC Marine Escort Group, reputed to be the toughest unit in the world, man three 30mm cannon.[18]

The ultimate in high-seas security was provided the *Akatsuki Maru* in 1992 as it transported 1.7 tons of plutonium oxide from Europe to Japan. The ship was accompanied by the *Shikishima*, a warship loaded with Japanese marines, heavy weapons, and helicopters. It was shadowed by a couple of U.S. nuclear submarines, one of which carried navy SEALS, and was tracked by spy-in-the-sky satellites. One source acknowledged that U.S. reconnaissance satellites constantly monitor the progress of the *Pintail* and the *Teal*, and the ships are shepherded by at least one U.S. or British nuclear sub. The threat of maritime terrorism, at least concerning the transport of weapons-grade nuclear fuel, is taken seriously, full-time.

A 1988 Pentagon threat assessment on plutonium shipments warned, however, that to "adequately deter theft or sabotage, it would be necessary to provide a dedicated surface combatant to escort the vessel throughout the trip." Even with an escort, it added, "no one could guarantee the safety of the shipment from a security incident, such as an attack on the vessel by small, fast craft, especially if armed with modern antiship missiles." Even these ships are vulnerable.[19]

Commercial vessels outside the nuclear sector must resort to more conventional methods of protection. The use of "heavies"—maritime SWAT teams—is getting greater play as piracy increases.

In 1718, when Royal Navy lieutenant Robert Maynard fought Blackbeard in hand-to-hand combat in North Carolina's Ocracoke Inlet, it was major news. It was one of the last great battles in the Golden Age of Piracy; Blackbeard was dead.[20]

Today, nearly three hundred years after piracy was consigned to the history books, more than a dozen private navies from Florida to Australia wait in the wings, hoping to be called to retrieve a vessel from the clutches of pirates or terrorists. The companies are usually created by enterprising retired soldiers—former British Special Air Service commandos or U.S. Special Forces, and government types from the intelligence communities. Many of these swashbuckling adventurers have retrieved ships, not from pirates but from shipowners who have defaulted on their bank payments.

Some of the marketing efforts for these seagoing SWAT teams do get the juices flowing. Coriolis Corporation of Arlington, Virginia, and San Diego, California, says:

> In troubled times it's good to know the best are there to help. Our operators are the best military counterterror, counterpiracy, and maritime security professionals there are in the private sector . . . period. With skills honed in the elite military units of the world—the U.S. Navy's SEAL Team Six, the U.S. Army Delta Force, the Royal Navy's SBS, and others, the Coriolis operations staff can ensure your government or company the quality and results it demands.

The blurb further boasts that their hired guns are "particularly adept at assisting governments [to] secure maritime facilities from terrorist or piratical assault" and "are skilled in lethal, less-than-lethal, and nonlethal methods of counterpiracy—whatever your need and prevailing law permits." As most sailors know, there is no enforceable law in international waters. Pirates beware.

One company offers submersible vessels to help locate and retrieve stolen ships and another offers ships and luxury yachts a device called "Covert"—a watertight package housing a .50-caliber machine gun and a chaff dispenser to repel aerial attacks.

Heavies are used rarely, and most seagoing masters think they serve little purpose. Captain John Swain of Vancouver was chief officer on the *Stolt Eagle*, a chemical carrier owned by Stolt Nielsen of Greenwich, Connecticut, when pirates attacked his ship in Brazil. He fought them in hand-to-hand combat, losing three fingers to a machete-wielding pirate. Still he is not convinced that the use of heavies is the way to go.

"We had an ex-SAS guy come to the office in Houston to talk to a group of captains and chief engineers about pirate attacks," Swain says. "The presentation was a bit too military oriented for our needs and would require us to train for weeks on guns and to purchase special and expensive equipment. It was not really the right direction for us sailors."

Since the terrorist attacks in September 2001, maritime security companies have scrambled for work. One, which successfully retrieved a hijacked ship off the Somali coast in East Africa, has put together a group to combat the terrorist threat against shipping. A security audit costing shipowners between $100,000 and $500,000 is aimed at the oil majors, cruise ship companies, and gas carriers, ships most vulnerable to an attack. The company says that while shipowners would be paying up-front for the service, they might be able to recoup their outlay through lower insurance premiums.

Captain Jayant Abhyankar, the IMB's deputy director, says these seagoing secret soldiers "are well intentioned, eager, dedicated, aggressive, and very sharp—but we tell them not to expect to make a living on it. Shipowners just cannot afford them. And if someone gets shot and killed, all hell would break loose; it's a nonstarter, except in extremely rare circumstances."

Those circumstances, however, do occur and they are not so rare. Underwater Security Consultants in London is the parent company of professional pirate fighters whose exploits startle all but those who hire them. Tapping into a network of former special forces commandos, Graham Shaw, an ex–Royal Navy commanding officer, can muster within minutes any number of eager, tough, battle-hardened men to fly to the far reaches of the globe to protect ships from attack.

"We have rules about opening fire. We shoot only when it is absolutely necessary," he says. "We really try not to kill them."

It was a strange statement from the man who sat behind the desk ("Let's just say I'm well past retirement age") with damaged hearing, thick glasses, a elderly kindness in his eyes, the director of one of the world's busiest antipiracy/antiterrorism outfits.

Appropriately, Graham's office is aboard the HQS *Wellington,* a decommissioned World War II frigate lying hard against the wharf on the Thames. It occupies some of the most expensive real estate in London. Graham seems surprised that anyone would be interested in his company's antipiracy protection force, and he speaks candidly of recent firefights with the casualness of a trader discussing pork belly futures.

Shaw started the company twenty-five years ago as an advisor to the "society" of underwriters within Lloyd's of London. He wrote assessments of risk and suggested ways to protect operations, personnel, and equipment in politically unstable regions, war zones, and other dangerous areas. When an insurance company needed to know if an operation could be accomplished without bloodshed or damage, they called Graham. In high-risk areas he often advised clients to hire security personnel. When he discovered there were few companies that could provide such support, he created his own security company.

Graham had the background. He is a highly decorated underwater demolitions expert, who concluded his navy career as head of the Royal Navy's bomb squad, the Fleet Clearance Diving Team, covering an area from the Red Sea to China; in his day he must have been one tough item. He had worked in enough theaters of war and had defused enough mines, bombs, and missiles to know how best to protect commercial interests in dangerous parts of the world. The company today, like its venerable creator, is well established. His commandos protect cruise ships, cable-laying and seismic vessels, cargo ships, and oil rigs in some of the most violent waters in the world.

Graham's company has chalked up some impressive credentials: It was involved in the recovery of the black box from the Air India 747 that was blown up by terrorists off the Canadian coast in 1985, killing 329 people; removed warheads from tankers attacked during the Iran-Iraq war; and recovered chemical weapons from the floor of the Black Sea.

"We're not security guards you can just hire around the corner," he says. "We won't do that kind of work. We answer to insurance companies. We are driven by the underwriters." USCL is the parent company—the hired guns work for its operations company, Wellington Offshore, Ltd.

"I wouldn't call my men mercenaries—that means they are working for foreign governments," he says. "No, they are working for my government, wearing our flag. They are working for a British organization, for British clients; sometimes these chaps do work for kicks but also to earn a living. They know they are being looked after back home."

As Graham speaks, his office rocks gently from the wake of a passing Thames barge or tour boat, the sound of river chop slapping against the metal hull. The headquarters of USCL is in the fantail of the ship. The office is brightly lit and loosely cluttered with nautical charts, ship engravings, hull blueprints, white boards, ship photos modern and ancient, and computers also modern and ancient; the windows are portholes and the view is the river. It has the smell of an old warship, of tarred hemp, of grease, paint, bunkers, and cordite; the hooks for the hammocks the men slept in still poke out of the low ceiling. Some of the original tin kerosene lanterns hang in the rooms.

"I am a strict disciplinarian. In the navy my ship was never 'as good as,' it was 'better than.' " He should be at home on this vessel; he was the commanding officer of the HMS *Redpole*, the sister ship of the *Wellington*.

There is a quiet, unassailable authority about the man. He doesn't command respect—it is simply there. He gets all that is due a retired naval captain but the salute. Graham is old school, Old World, all the qualities so often associated with the Empire. He is a spit-and-polish man and a proper gentleman. In the days I spend with him, I am never to hear him utter a profanity; the only expletive is a "Thank goodness" that he mutters into the telephone. It is when he learns that none of his men was injured in a shoot-out in West Africa.

It comes during a call from one of his commandos aboard a cable-laying ship off the coast of Nigeria. "Our boys just repulsed an attack," he announces after he hangs up. He looks thoughtful, smiles.

"They win?"

"They won. Communications with the field is the worst problem," he says. "Sometimes we don't know what is happening down there for a while; it worries the wives."

Nigeria is a dangerous place for seafarers. Piracy is common, so common that most assaults never are reported. In the year 2001 there were nineteen reported attacks on ships off the coast or in Nigerian harbors or rivers, double the number of the previous year. However, that figure hardly represents the severity of the problem; pirates attack or attempt to board a commercial vessel or oil installation about once a week. The Nigerian coast is notoriously lawless; the American, British, Dutch seamen manning oil rigs, support vessels, cargo ships, know that no one cares much about piracy in these waters, so what's the point in reporting an attack to some bureaucrats in London or Washington? And many attacks are not reported because the local police assigned to the vessels fear reprisals from villagers once they return to shore. The only recourse is to hire professional soldiers for protection and to keep your mouth shut. Who needs the paperwork when summary justice is available?

Graham says he has created three levels of alert on ships that he has been hired to protect: **Green**—low risk; the vessel can carry on normal operations. **Orange**—a higher state; the vessel is in a pirate-prone area, limited citadel; operations continue. **Red**—attack potentially imminent or imminent, everything should be locked shut within one minute.

"We have strict rules of engagement that all my boys follow. They can be broken by the men at the scene, but we'd prefer they follow them." Unlike the Malacca Straits, where knives are the most common weapons, in West Africa guns are almost always used in attacks against ships. "We have rules when my men can open fire and when they cannot. Of course, they can override those rules when need be. We do not shoot to kill. Only to wound—unless, of course, it is close range and our lives are in danger. When it is point-blank range, then often we use the rifle as a club.

"We take the Christian approach—they may not but we do; they are still human beings. If they are the walking wounded and they can get back into the boat, then that is their problem. We let them go and be done with it. But if they are seriously wounded, we render assistance and treat them on board."

Every one of his men is issued a pair of surgical gloves, and during patrol they are always worn. If there is blood to be spilled, AIDS can be as deadly as a bullet.

"We really try not to kill them. There are administrative problems."

"But don't they report that you shot them—or shot at them?" I ask.

"No. Do you think they would report that they were shot while trying to board?" Apparently only back in the village, where everyone knows they just tried to attack a nearby ship, is the truth known.

"Out beyond the high-water mark the strongest wins. We have never lost a man," he says with evident pride.

I would expect Graham's teams would tout the most sophisticated guns available. Hardly. His commandos use Mossberg pump-action shotguns filled with No. 6 shot.

"They will know they are not welcome aboard that ship once they feel the birdshot," he says.

"How about using rock salt instead? Maybe a little less lethal," I suggest.

I tell him that in my preteen years a friend and I sneaked into Bessie Smith's barn for a bite of her winter stash of apples; she was the old spinster who, as rumor had it, was a witch. Her high-pitched, quivery shout stopped us dead in our tracks. We turned to see that she had a gun in her hands. We raced out the back door. She hobbled after us, her wrinkled grimalkin face twisted with fury. I heard the shot and felt the sting on my bare legs. She shot me! I thought I was going to die, but dying could come later—I kept running. In the woods I examined my wounds. Blood trickled down my legs amid huge welts, worse than a hundred wasp stings. Old Bessie had laced me with rock salt. Hers was a persuasive argument.

"Salt?" Graham says.

"An old custom in the States when you want to convince someone not to trespass. Take the shot out of the shell and replace it with rock salt. Very effective."

"I'll investigate that," Graham says. "You should meet my 'tame booty,' our antipiracy specialist. He'll be here in a couple of days; he was involved in that last incident."

To attack a vessel before thoroughly checking it out is a stupid thing to do. But that is what six Nigerian pirates tried to do to the cable-laying vessel CS *Seaworker* one night in the spring of 2001. They met the Wellington commandos and some enthusiastic marine police who were prepared. The vessel was just off the coast, laying fiber optic cable for the French telecommunications company Alcatel—a project that extended from Oporto, Portugal, to Cape Town, South Africa. The ship was on a code red alert. Razor wire had been strung along much of the deck, and bright halogen lamps beamed a protective ring of light outboard; the crew had been ordered inside and the ship was locked down in the citadel. A Wellington commando patrolled the upper deck with handheld VHF radio, night vision glasses, and binoculars. Shotguns were within reach. Three Nigerian maritime police officers slept inside; their modern automatic rifles were propped against a table and a 9mm Beretta pistol on a bedside table next to the big one who snored.

The cable ship is the type of soft target that pirates look for. With a freeboard of only a few feet it is easy to hop aboard. No ladders, no ropes, no hooks, just a short jump. The *Seaworker* had been working the coast, slowly laying cable along the sea floor, steaming at about a knot and a half—about the speed of a fast crawl. At dusk it anchored close to its cable track about three and a half miles offshore. The wide white beach and the jungle beyond was shrouded in a thick tropic haze, the sky was overcast, and there was a pretty good ocean swell running—about three meters, which made life a little uncomfortable. It was going to be a very dark, very long night.

Brian Winchester is Graham Shaw's "tame booty," his antipiracy expert. A Special Air Services veteran with years of combat experience, Winchester had been very selective when he set up the *Seaworker* ship's security team. His commandos had trained with the ship's crew three times a week, preparing for an attack that they prayed would never occur. You wait and you prepare, Brian says, and you hope you got it down; a mistake could be fatal.

This is as close to the old Wild West as it gets. Brian and the other hired guns are the guys who protect the wagon train, the ones who ride shotgun on a stagecoach through ambush country. This is no fantasy. Perhaps armed guards never really did ride up on the buckboard of stagecoaches—I only saw it in the movies—but this team of commandos is their modern-day counterpart. As the tracks of the transcontinental railroad extended slowly, mile after mile, through the untamed hostile territory of the American West, so, too, is the communications cable being laid—just as slowly, mile after mile—along the wild coastline of West Africa. Moreover, like the wagon train, stagecoach, or railroad, the cable ship and its support vessels can expect to be attacked. And they are. Regularly. By the villagers on the coast who see the slow-moving cable ships as rich pickings. These pirate fighters are out there, and at this moment one of them is standing on a narrow deck looking out into the humid darkness, the ship rolling under his feet, and looking, and waiting, and wondering if anyone is going to get killed tonight.

At about 2300 hours one of Brian Winchester's men patrolling the deck noticed a motor canoe prowling just outside the ship's outboard floodlighting. He followed the boat with his night vision glasses, watching it move with the stealth of a water snake, drifting down the port side toward the stern. The little boat kept about twenty yards off, but the deckhand could see five coiled figures crouched low in the canoe while one in the back paddled. Except for the halogens that shone outboard, the *Seaworker* was unlit, and the pirates couldn't know anyone had spotted them. The little boat turned toward the cable ship. The guard shouted a sudden warning and a powerful lamp directed from the bridge snapped on, drilled in on the boat, spotlighting the pirates. The outboard engine on the little boat kicked in and the intruders fled. Because of the high seas the pirate boat had been invisible to radar.

A few hours later, at 0350 hours the next morning, the canoe returned. Again it crept up on the *Seaworker* from the port quarter, off the left-hand side of the stern. Because the quarterdeck was ringed with barbed wire, it was not illuminated and the pirates decided this was a good place to board. The deckhand followed the canoe with the image intensifier as it moved up to the rear of the ship. He shouted up to the bridge and the searchlight snapped on. The canoe kept coming.

"We had a hell of a time getting the Nigerian police to wake up and give us a hand—really had to light a fire under their arses," Brian

Winchester recalls. "When they got moving, they finally took some action."

The senior Nigerian officer, a big potbellied cop still half-asleep and clad only in his knickers, ran out onto the deck, cocking his pistol. He shouted at the pirates but still they kept coming. He fired his Beretta over their heads as a warning. Instead of retreating they charged the *Seaworker*. The pirates were going to try to take the ship, Brian says, in spite of the warning shot. Even if it killed them. The men of Wellington grabbed their shotguns and waited.

The pirates opened fire. The commandos ducked and the Nigerian police, armed with CAR-15s, a powerful assault rifle, shot back. "If we don't have to shoot, we won't," Graham adds. His policy is that if there are locals who will use their guns, then he tells his men to hold back. The men on the ship could see the muzzle flashes from the canoe, and it was anybody's guess how determined they were to take the ship. After a few more volleys the canoe made a sharp turn and retreated into the darkness, taking their wounded with them.

"The bloody Nigerian police opened fire too fast," Brian says. "They woke up, came out, and started shooting. We wanted to draw the pirates closer, and I thought we should let them board so we could capture them—dead or alive. I wanted to cuff them and hand them over to the local police and make an example of them. Then every one in the area would know to leave us alone. The police botched it."

Like anywhere else that piracy flourishes, pirates were after money, watches, televisions, equipment, food. And they were also after the vessel's synthetic mooring rope. Back in the village their women would peel it strand by strand to make fishing nets.

Brian Winchester is a fifteen-year veteran of the SAS. He served in combat intelligence in Northern Ireland, in Angola, on the front lines in the Falklands, in the Gulf War, and as a cop in the southwest of England. His immediate boss, Brian Phelan, the head of Wellington Offshore, calls Winchester "the pointy edge of what we do." There is an undeniable tone of pride in the statement.

"If we're doing our job, we won't get boarded," Winchester says. He describes it as hour after hour of boredom with about a minute or two of a dopamine rush. Sometimes, he admits, he'd rather not do the job so well; it gets pretty boring waiting to get shot at. There is no doubt he would love to have ambushed and captured the pirates that night.

Brian Winchester says that he is forty-seven, but he looks like he could be in his mid-thirties. His hair would be turning gray, that is, if you could find it—it is shorn so close that the top of his head looks as if it merely needs a shave. His eyebrows are sun bleached from patrolling the decks looking for pirates, and they are all but invisible.

He has a sense of humor. A little perverse, perhaps, but humor nonetheless. Before he and his boat troop of SAS commandos attacked a beachhead in the Falklands, he scratched his name on the brass jacket of a 5.56 Armalite bullet and stashed it in his locker on the ship. When asked why, he said, "that's the bullet that's got my name on it."

This is a professional soldier of fortune, and I begin to feel he possesses something special—a strength, an assurance, the likes of which I know I will never have. There is little question that he could kill, has killed. But he is not a cold-steel killing machine; he is not a hired killer, a hit man. In his current life he is a protector, a defender. It is apparent that he is well used to living on the edge.

"The locals, our security men, don't mess about with piracy," Brian says. "They deal out rough justice." The locals are guards who are hired to protect the small dive boats and the divers who work on the cables.

"You see bodies floating ashore regularly," Winchester says. "I'm in favor of rough justice"—and then, *sotto voce*,—"too much paperwork as it is. We try to be as humane as possible, but there is a degree of ruthlessness involved. If you have to teach somebody a lesson, it has to be something they will remember."

"What if you have to shoot someone?" I ask.

"What about it? We're there to protect the crew."

"You must have to rely on your buddies—have to trust them," I say.

"Usually we know the people we are working with—we've worked together before and they're all proven. It's a pretty close group of blokes. Have to be—we all have to sing from the same hymn sheet."

As a Wellington "security consultant" Winchester gets pretty good pay, but then maybe no pay is good enough for getting shot at. In addition to health, life, and—hard to believe—even accident insurance, he is paid £250 sterling a day—$375—plus all expenses.

Brian knows he is on a good wicket. He is an aging gunfighter in a young man's profession. The pirates he has faced and those who lie in wait are half his age, twice as agile. There is always a faster gun. Those he works with, those he relies on and those who rely on him, know that there will come a day when he'll have to step aside. His mates do not have his experience, have not seen what he has seen, have not been shot at quite so many times; he knows the risks not to take and when to keep his head down. He is a survivor, an expert at what he does. And despite the years he is no less gung-ho, no less brave. Still, he sees the twilight ahead, and, while fearing no man, he does fear the future. Age is evident: His leathery skin is beginning to wrinkle and the skin around his neck is a little loose. He has been lucky because he doesn't yet need reading glasses, or maybe he does and he just endures the strain. However, the day will come when he will have to admit he is no longer a twenty-five-year-old commando.

Brian is a member of Graham's collegial network of good old boys, recently retired combat veterans from the elite Special Air Service or Special Boat Services. "I don't employ people off the street; they have to be part of the Known Club," Graham says. The Known Club is run by a military headhunting outfit in Hereford, UK, close by the training headquarters of these elite special forces, and it provides him with his pirate fighters. Most of these guys served in the same units, fought side by side in the more conventional conflicts. "They must have a professional military approach to the job, discipline above all."

There is evidently an esprit de corps among his tame booties that goes right up to the top. Graham is the father figure; he oversees, he deals, he soothes, he makes peace, he checks on the welfare of the wives, he sends his men out on dangerous missions. The founding principals of the British special forces to which he adheres: "... all ranks in the SAS were to be one family and all ranks to possess a sense of humor and humility."

His thoughts return to the pirates. "Their lifeblood is piracy. If they received the money due them from the oil that is taken off their land by the oil companies, piracy in this area would be eliminated." His point was underscored in April 2002, when ten Shell employees, including an American, were taken hostage from their oil-rig supply ship off the swampy coastal village of Amatu. The forty youths, ethnic Ijaws, were apparently retaliating for the destruction by Nigerian security forces of their boats, thought to have been used in pirate attacks. Shell, which negotiated for their release, has often been the target of attacks by locals who claim they get little of the revenue from the resources.

Poverty is the driving force behind the increase in piracy, not just off the coast of Africa, but in the Caribbean, South America, India, Bangladesh, and Southeast Asia. Pirates go after targets of opportunity, ships at anchor, off-loading in ports, or passing offshore. Pirates are local boys who know that most things on a ship are worth more than anything they could ever hope to have in a lifetime of living in a coastal village. (Local girls have been pirates too. Recently twelve women with machetes attacked a ship off the Nigerian coast; they weren't going for the strongbox in the captain's cabin but the crew's laundry in the washing machines.) In the Malacca Straits and South China Sea the sharp increase in piracy coincided with the Asian economic crisis in the late nineties, which saw the precipitous fall in the value of regional currencies. One particular incident in the Straits during this period well represented the economic desperation of pirates. A gang of hijackers stole not only the cargo from a ship but nearly everything else that wasn't bolted down. They took bedding, books, magazines, even toothbrushes and soap. The crew was left unharmed. When the ship approached a Malaysian harbor, the captain asked shore authorities to bring enough clothes for twenty-one crew. The port officials thought it a joke, but when they arrived on board they found the captain behind the wheel—buck naked.

In many parts of the world it has become evident to hungry locals that attacking a ship is more lucrative than fishing or growing rice, and robbing an undefended ship is a lot easier than robbing a bank.

"Pirates have wives and children," Graham continues. "For about sixty percent of them it is a profession out of desperation—and they are shot, they bleed to death. They never go home."

8

But We've Got the Dummies

Montrose

There is no one shouting *Land Ho!* at the sight of the volcanic peak of Indonesia that has popped out of the early morning haze. No one seems particularly interested. We are not parched, out of victuals, dying of scurvy, tempted to bugger anything on two feet. There are no sailors running to the railing to gaze gratefully at the first sight of land, on their knees muttering grateful prayers of thanks that they didn't perish in a storm at sea or from food poisoning or from the lash. We have merely been part of the conveyor across an ocean and we have been out for nine days.

Over the land the thundery buildup is already beginning. The pyramidal peak of Gunung Suelawaih Agam, a silhouette of mucky blue, rises six thousand feet out of the sea, grasping at the thickening cloud above it. Building cumulonimbus brace the dormant volcano on either side. I will never get to see it, live it, know it, other than from this distance, but I imagine its volcanic slopes, the muddy little kampungs at the bottom, the rural industry of the barefoot natives. Land, hazy, shrouded, mysterious land.

We have turned the corner around the top end of Sumatra and are entering the northern entrance to the Straits—hardly a narrow channel, for it is three hundred miles from Indonesia across to the mainland of Malaysia. It is, however, the beginning of the long and difficult passage south.

This is another sea, a relatively flat sea, water of nervous little chop, tight little waves that go this way and that. Those languorous ocean swells are of a longitude left far behind. This blue-black sea is scratched by streaks of white that tear at the surface—confused and conflicting. An outflowing westerly current meets a west wind and stirs up tidal eddies and overfalls.

There is a different feeling to these waters. As if we are entering a new neighborhood. Each sea has its own characteristics, its own personality. Each seems to lie within its own atmosphere, a sensation she offers to those who traverse it and who can pause long enough to understand.

We are on the straight track of world trade, a waterborne truck route of lonely men and heartless steel and smoky machines, having left behind the solitude of an ocean where ships pass in the night. We are at the convergence, the area where ships from four continents merge into the procession down the Straits. We are joining the ranks of sixty thousand vessels a year that use this waterway.

Our radar picks up a small target a couple of miles ahead of us. It shows no movement. It is probably an Indonesian fishing boat anchored to its nets that hang suspended just above the seabed. Fishing boats seem plentiful here, scattered along the path of commercial shipping. There are probably just as many boats within the lanes as outside them; perhaps it is in the blood of every fisherman—when there is a NO TRESPASSING sign around a likely fishing hole, then he knows the fishing has got to be good; and he knows he might get caught. Perhaps this is the thinking with these fishermen—the fishing must be better where they are most likely to get run down.

A line of weather appears to be forming just about a mile or so to the windward of the fishing boat. We see it on the black radar screen as a thickening line of yellow splotches. Weather fronts during the monsoon in this area are rare, yet this seems to be forming into a solid frontal barrier of electrical storms, wind, and rain. Possibly a white line squall—nothing that could concern a ship like the *Montrose*, but one that could play hell with a small fishing boat or a sailboat with any cloth up.

This area is notorious for its sudden and unpredictable conditions.

The Admiralty Chart of the *Mariner's Routing Guide of the Malacca Straits* warns:

> *The most significant squalls in the Malacca Straits are those known as "Sumatras," which occur from April to November. These storms nearly always develop during the night, chiefly between Melaka and Singapore, and normally last from one to four hours. "Southwesterly" squalls occur in the north part of the Strait during the SW monsoon (May to October). These squalls usually last longer than the "Sumatras" and occur during the day or night.*

The electrical storms are severe in the area. More than one small yacht has been charbroiled by lightning in these waters, ruining thousands of dollars of equipment and, in once instance I recall, electrocuting the skipper of the boat.

The horizon before us is starting to glower, turn heavy, darker. We bull toward what appears to be a solid, impenetrable wall; it is approaching us as fast. Towering multilayered dark storm clouds, angry, turbulent, rise and curl and merge into a chaotic sky.

A ragged curtain knuckles over the surface; its claws rip across the sea with a fury we can only imagine. It is close now, no more than a mile or so ahead of us; lightning creases the upper clouds and is swallowed by roiling gray and black. At the surface, under the squall line, the sea is wild, the tops of its snarling white water torn and flung in the face of the wind. The ill-defined horizon, what is left of it, is close at hand, charging us, furious; it has become a wall of spume sucked out of the sea and thrown into the maelstrom above.

The blow hits us hard and we feel it. Or imagine we do. It is too powerful to think we have not been affected. It envelops us in darkness and suddenly there is no definition, no depth. The gusts whip the rain over the deck and blast the bridge windows. The radar screen, which had shown several small targets, has become a confusion of yellow smears; the ships that were once so clearly defined are now mixed in with the echoes of the front. That fishing boat has long vanished in the clutter.

The rain pounds the whipped-up waves with such force that it flattens them, punishes their confusion. Visibility is down to zero, and even the cargo deck below disappears to the point of dissolving. Our world, such as there was of it, is nowhere.

Wasim switches on the ship's foghorn; it is electrically operated and mounted on the masthead at the bow, facing forward, and it blows automatically every two minutes.

"There was a small fishing boat I was seeing off to the starboard," he says. "Maybe she will be hearing me." He tweaks the dial on the autopilot and the *Montrose* moves a little off its course.

The storm passes and a light blue fishing boat, boxy and top heavy, wallows crazily from side to side in the swells just off our starboard. Wet, shirtless fishermen haul up their precious net, unconcerned about the huge tanker that rumbles so close, so high above them. The boat apparently did not move, for it is still attached to its string of floating bamboo poles, which marks the end of its set. If Wasim had not adjusted our course, we would have run it down. I wonder if they would have died rather than lose their net and their catch?

⌒

After the front passed, the crew, in white boilersuits and hard hats, emerged onto the steamy deck and wrestled with the fittings for the fire hoses, tested the spotlights aft, got them unstuck and to swivel. Those lights were original equipment built to illuminate the corporate logo that was once emblazoned on the funnel. Now their purpose is to alert potential pirates that we have an antipiracy policy.

Captain Postma thought it important for me to attend the senior officers' weekly meeting, which, among other things, outlined our piracy defenses. He has admitted that he has caught up on his reading about piracy, dusted off some old files, opened a few ancient attachments in the ship's computer. I have told him of some of the events that I know about, of the ships attacked on our route. And Brian Ashdown has spoken at dinner of his experience with pirates on the VLCC *Litopia* in Singapore. Brian is too busy with the operations to dwell on the possibility of another attack, despite the fact that this ship passes through five hundred miles of pirate country and will anchor in the heart of it. Like others on this route he is convinced that one day a VLCC will be pirated and break up in the Straits, but he has his job and it is, after all, for him, for the captain, and for the ship company, a matter of risk assessment; it hasn't happened yet and the chances are when that day comes, it will happen to someone else and that is too bad. Nonetheless, we have this meeting and the manuals and instructions are on the shelf. Sitting informally around the ship's office, Viktor, the chief mate, suggests that we dress up like a French warship that was approached recently by pirates at night at the southern entrance to the Red Sea. "The ship turned on its lights and aimed their gun and the pirates ran!"

Apparently this is the first time the *Montrose* under this skipper has ever undergone such thorough preparations for an attack by pirates. The captain reads off a memo he has just created:

Piracy prevention forthcoming STS Karimun
"During dark hours Malacca strait one man on sunken deck in *moving mode.*

Position on sunken deck. Pirate deterrent.
    At least 4 hoses producing water
    Two dummies on watch
    Two fire hoses standby under pressure. (ready for action)

Pirated boarding prevention tools
    2 × Powder extinguisher standby
    Wire cutter standby

Crew should be in possession of knife to cut climb ropes. . . .

The whole piracy policy is based on boarding avoidance and deterrence. Once on board, to avoid blood shed, do not play the hero but resignation and try to make the best of it [sic].
                    Montrose 20 August 01

I wonder about the London office reaction to these instructions. The ship company's policy, and one echoed by every master I have spoken to, is the same: Do not ever fight back. Even Captain Postma's freshly created instruction sheet says don't play the hero. Yet he assigns two men, one armed with a fire extinguisher and another with a knife, to hold off armed intruders. With the *Valiant Carrier* in mind I wonder if he has any idea what a dozen panicky pirates could do. Yet the stories of pirate attacks that I relate are events that happened to other people.

"When you see a head coming over the side," the captain tells his officers, "you put the powder from the extinguisher in their faces. That will make them cough. And they will not be able to see. It is a little weapon but it might work."

I can see myself or Tony or Brian or one of the slight Filipino crewmen standing gallantly, Horatio at the Gate, as a swarm of pirates fly over the railing. The one who blasts a pirate in the face with a fire extinguisher will be one dead sailor. A pirate sees a crewman wielding a knife "to cut climb ropes," and it is all over.

"Where will he get a knife?" Brian asks.

"All seamen carry their own knives," Tony says.

"Ours don't. One of my boys had to ask the bosun to borrow a knife," another says.

"Well, see that he gets a knife," the captain says.

The captain is adhering to one company recommendation, strapping mannequins, clad in coveralls and hard hat, to the railing.

"Where do you want the dummies, Captain?"

"Next to the hoses. Not back out of the way where they can't be seen. Right next to the hoses on the railings."

The dolls, I had been informed in London, are supposed to replace the men on the deck. The crew is supposed to be hunkered down inside the citadel, not outside on the lower deck patrolling for pirates. Our captain is going to have dummies and a crew patrol. He is covering all bases.

The captain seems eager to contribute something else—a risibly plausible tale: a mannequin that the crew had forgotten to remove after they had left the Malacca Straits was still standing guard when the ship returned to Dubai. A supply vessel pulled up to the *Montrose*, and the ship's agent aboard shouted up to the figure on the deck to fetch the captain. He did it a dozen times and got no response. Finally, the official climbed up the gangway, stormed into the bridge. "He was very angry. He told me you have the most stupid crew on any ship I have ever seen."

"Four hoses?" Tony asks, reading the captain's instruction sheet. His comic what-me-worry face seems to swell and his eyes widen. He says later he has never heard of four hoses "all pissin' out at the same time."

"Sorry, Captain," Brian adds, a little puzzled, "but we don't have four hoses that can work at the same time on the sunken deck. If we try to hook four hoses aft, we are going to deplete our fire gear."

"Okay, then make two hoses shooting water, and two hoses on standby."

The pirate drill will take place this afternoon; the way things are going, it might provide entertainment comparable to an old Keystone Kops comedy. The general alarm will sound and the captain will announce, "Pirates on the poop deck! Pirates on the poop deck!"

"I want to see their reaction. Maybe they will lock themselves in their cabins. We will see," says Postma.

The *Montrose*, I am discovering, is pirate friendly, and climbing aboard, getting inside, and taking over the ship, despite our best efforts, would not be difficult. There is outside access to the elevator shaft from the bridgewing: the red-painted, heavy iron emergency escape hatch to the shaft is located next to the wheelhouse, and when it is opened, a micro switch stops the elevator automatically. It cannot be locked from the inside. Another point of ingress, Brian points out, is the little door of the lube oil tank that opens into the engine room. "But if they are going to enter the ship, they'll get in through our windows on deck. It is the easiest way to get in, I would have thought." Most of our crew and even most in London know that it is impossible to keep pirates out; the doors will be locked according to instructions, but there are many ways to get inside, as I discovered on other vessels. A ship was designed to carry cargo efficiently, not to resemble Fort Knox.

"Pirates! Pirates on board! Lock your doors and go to your muster station. Attention, pirates on board!"

Although the announcement has been expected, it sends shivers up my spine. The ship's booming horn and the piercing fire bells of the general alarm ring out over the empty sea and shatter the relative silence. As I head down to my cabin the captain runs by, taking the stairs two at a time.

It is not the comedy that I expected—the crew had been warned. They muster in the narrow hallway by the ship's office, standing at attention in their grease- and paint-stained boilersuits and hard hats, and face each other. There is a bit of good-natured banter. Viktor takes the roll call. Once all are accounted for, the captain paces up and down between them and proclaims in a strong voice:

"This is a drill—it was just a fake. We are going to Karimun, and that is a hot area where pirates are known to be attacking. Is there anybody with military experience?"

"Yah! Of course. Me!" Niko says, stepping forward. He tears off a bite from a green apple. "You need me!"

"Yes, good. Now, when pirates come aboard, they are here to take your money, your valuables," Postma tells his crew. "They will be fighting. They are violent and they can kill you."

The captain warns his men that pirates would come up the transom onto the sunken deck, the lowest point of the vessel. The fire hoses will be blasting outboard and the aft end of the ship will be guarded by our two dummies that he calls General Patton and General MacArthur.

"Our dummies may not help—but they might make pirates hesitate. When you are on watch, do not hide. Show yourself, move, and then maybe they will refrain from coming aboard. We will have the hoses to wet the guys and we will have extinguishers with powder. When they have powder in the face, that makes them cough and they can do nothing more. It is only a small weapon."

The bosun reports to the captain that all doors are sealed and padlocked or bolted from the inside. The captain sends Tony out to check all points of ingress, including hatches, manholes, and skylights, and I follow. Tony, his red plastic earmuffs atop his bald round head, says he bets he knows how to get in. Indeed, the first door, the starboard entrance to the sick bay, swings open easily. Someone forgot. The men in the hallways think they are locked safely within the citadel. We come up the back steps and Tony announces, "You've been pirated!"

The engineer gives them another ten minutes to get it right, to double-check the locks before we go on another inspection. The captain looks a little distraught.

Out on deck Tony and I lean on the railing and stare out at the sea and wait. Tony is dressed like all the engine room gang who spend their working days in the sweltering bowels of the ship—in greasy coveralls that are unzipped down to his hairy navel. He admits that he has never gone through a pirate drill before but that it is not a bad idea. "To be fair," he says, "there are desktop drills as part of the International Safety Management Code; we go through those a couple of times a year, but never something like this. There should be more of these."

We take the steps down to the sunken deck to check the engine room entrances. Two small padlocks secure the engine room door under the funnel. Tony jiggles the locks and pulls open the steel door; the locks are too small for the hasp. Those locks were slapped on the door without anyone giving the purpose much thought. It looked good and that was good enough.

I am reminded of the plaints of one captain who had been pirated: "We need a modern security system. These ships cost sixty to eighty million dollars to build. And we use domestic locks that are no good in a saltwater environment." He suggested that during passage through pirate waters ship companies use hotel-type key cards to access locked doors or automatic closing systems as used on modern warships.[21] The security of the crew, cargo, and ship is worth something more than a padlock no bigger than that used to lock a bicycle. The realization that piracy is a threat must come from the top down.

Having broken into the engine room, we run down the stairs into the elevator that opens up onto the line of men still waiting in the hall; they are startled that we have found a way inside, and I sense that perhaps this exercise is not a waste of time, that these men realize that they and their ship are indeed vulnerable. Pirate drill or not, we now know that we can't keep out anyone determined to get in.

⁓

Captain Postma has received word of his next passage on the conveyor of crude oil. Following discharge in Singapore, he will turn around and go to Kharg Island, Iran, for pickup and then into the Red Sea to off-load at a terminal in the Gulf of Suez just south of the canal. The *Montrose*, too big when laden to make it through the Suez Canal, will feed the crude into a pipeline that will carry it across the desert to a terminal on the Mediterranean Coast. There the oil will be loaded aboard another tanker and taken either to Europe or to the States.

That voyage will take the vessel through the Bab el Mandab, the treacherous rock- and reef-bound southern entrance to the Red Sea, just a few miles from Aden, where the *Cole* was blown up and where pirates, armed with heavy firepower, routinely attack ships. I wonder whether the *Montrose*'s antipiracy defenses will be in place for that passage?

The boys in London move and shuffle these VLCCs like pawns in a chess game. When there is a ship available and the price is right and the demand is there, they will move the crude wherever. The conveyor may change direction but it never stops. It is not unusual for one of these big M-class vessels to lift at Saudi, steam down the Gulf through the Straits of Hormuz, then hover off the Omani coast and wait until the charterer finds a buyer for the floating 300,000 tons of crude oil. Only then will the captain of that vessel know where on the globe he is heading. You don't plan to meet your loved one at a specific port in this business.

Many of the ship company executives are ex-seafarers, former captains, chief engineers, or chief officers. They are on the beach because they know their stuff and theoretically can relate to the men at sea. If one were to believe the shoptalk on the *Montrose*, however, they soon get land-bound and forget the frustrations of those they are shuffling.

The *Montrose* is monitored closely by the ship company officials in

London as it enters a known pirate area. Behind unmarked doors in the neon-lit office of the company's headquarters is the emergency nerve center. Normally unused except when meeting space is needed, it gets as busy as a rail station in rush hour when there is a problem— a collision, a terrorist threat, an oil spill, an attack by pirates.

The room is brightly lit, windowless, and functional to the extreme. There are no potted office plants in this place. Long rows of desks are packed with computers, high- and low-frequency satellite receivers, and telephones of various colors; the walls are paneled with whiteboards. The chamber's sterility, its lack of warmth, its bright harshness represent the seriousness of any situation critical enough to man it. When the call comes in, the particulars of the potential disaster are noted on the walls in stenciled red letters:

Name of the vessel	**Lat**	**Sunrise**
Ownership	**Long**	**Sunset**
Name of other ship	**Ship's heading**	**High Water**
Casualties	**Nature of seabed**	**Low Water**
Details	**Current Sea Temperature**	**Present Wx**
Logistics	**Soundings**	**Forcast Wx**
Personnel		**Contract**
Liability		

The categories represent all possible information to enable the Designated Person Ashore to formulate a management plan on disasters ranging from the breakup of an offshore oil rig in the North Sea to a piracy/terrorist attack on one of its vessels in some far distant port. The communications are direct to those on the scene, including to the captain of a stricken vessel, to politicians, to government agencies and to the press. An oil company these days has to be prepared for the worst, no matter where the event occurs.

The *Isomeria*, a Shell liquid petroleum gas carrier, was famously attacked in January 1998, while discharging its cargo of propane and butane in the port of Santos, Brazil. Deborah Harrison, an attractive young second officer with flaxen hair and lively green eyes, had just taken over the watch on the bridge when pirates armed with Uzis broke in through the wing and forced her to take them to the master's cabin.

With a gun in her back, she took them down to the captain's quarters where they demanded the captain open the strongbox.

"They became very agitated when they discovered there was no cash in the safe," she said. "We explained that there was no second safe but they were getting very angry and they grabbed a holdall and started taking anything valuable they could get."

Deborah said they seemed placated when she took the pirates to her cabin and gave them cash and her camera. On the way to the main deck level, they ran into a gun battle between police and the remaining pirates and a frightened cadet who had just seen one of the gang killed.

Using Deborah as a human shield, her captors also fired on the police.

"I pushed the cadet into an alcove so that we were well out of the line of the bullets," she said.

In the firefight that followed, she was shot. "I don't know at which point I was hit but I just remember looking down and seeing a large red stain starting to appear on my boiler suit. I remember being somewhat bemused at first. I was still moving and it was not like in the films where they are coughing and spluttering on the floor. I hadn't really felt anything other than it just being like a strained muscle."

The worst moments came when the pirates put a gun to her head. At least, she thought, it is going to be quick. "All the time I was thinking I should be scared—when you see this sort of thing on the TV, people are screaming."[22]

Deborah was awarded the Commendation for Bravery by Queen Elizabeth II for "maintaining her composure" and for saving the life of the cadet whom she had pushed out of the line of fire. She is now chief mate on another tanker.

As for the pirates, at least one of them was killed in the shootout. A few were captured and one or two jumped overboard and escaped into the night.

It does not go unnoticed among the ship company's executives that just a few miles down the Thames at Wapping, pirates of yesteryear also paid dearly for their crimes. Captain Kidd and other brigands swung on the gallows for attacking ships (after the pirate's body stopped twitching, the executioner cut it down and chained it to a piling and left it there until the tidal waters of the river ebbed and flowed over it three times).

⁓

Out at sea, five thousand miles away, we have prepared for battle. We have our fire hoses blasting out into the night, Captain Postma has his two blue twenty-pound fire extinguishers on standby next to the railing. "Of course they won't do any good if the pirates are already over the rail," he says.

Our life-size dummies, General Patton and General MacArthur, standing *in terrorem* under the bright deck lights, are in full kit. General Patton wears a yellow boilersuit, green hard hat, and a round head stuffed with rags that is a bit too small for the body; someone has sketched a sort of pumpkin grin on the white cloth face with repeated strokes of a ballpoint; he looks distinctly Filipino—scraggly mustache, Asiatic eyes, and a nice smile. General MacArthur was created by a different artist—while Asian in feature, he wears a decidedly infelicitous expression. From afar—and not so very far at that—both generals look like they could be human.

On the bridge young Wasim, the ever-pacing Pakistani third officer, is on watch. We are in blackout night conditions, and even in the dark I hear him shuffling from end to end. A string of lights dots the horizon some miles ahead, fishing boats standing by their nets. The supersensitive radar is on enhanced mode and should pick up objects as small as large fishing floats. It may not pick up wooden speedboats, but according to Captain Postma it does a fine job of detecting their wakes.

Wasim says he is not too concerned about pirates. "My main concern is safe navigation," he says. "If I am steering clear of all objects, then I am safe from piracy. Because what I am trying to do is to keep my ship away from another floating object, whatsoever it is."

There is the impression that someone who drives one of the world's biggest ships down one of the world's busiest channels would be an old experienced hand, a veteran of years of the high seas, a wizened spread-legged old salt with telescope and sextant and swashbuckling tales. This is not the case. Those at the helm of these greatest of all man-made objects, who merely tweak a dial just a little to avoid another ship or a fishing trawler, are basically young, bright men and women from several nations who have worked their way from mess boy to cadet to officer, via schooling, courses, intense training, and more schooling.

Deborah Harrison started her sea career as a cadet; she is one of those unusual seafarers with dual certification, qualifying as both an engineer and deck officer. She will soon qualify as captain.

Danny, the Filipino second officer, who unlike the other young officers always reports in his dress whites, will be the officer in charge of the watch from midnight to 0400 hours, responsible for the safety of the ship, its cargo, and the lives of those aboard. He was once a ship's "cleaner," the lowest in the chain, empowered to scrub toilets, make beds, and empty garbage.

The radar begins to beep quietly, flash a red CPA, the collision alarm. This indicates that another vessel has entered our guard zone and is headed toward us. In this case it is a couple of pair trawls dragging a net between them. Wasim reaches over and turns the dial of the autopilot, like fine-tuning a radio station, and our bow swings slowly a couple of degrees away. The alarm is silenced.

Out on the bridgewing the air is hot; plasma lightning streaks overhead across the roof of the heavens from Malaysia to Indonesia. It is quite a light show and good for visibility. There was a target just astern of us that we were watching and then the radar flashed a warning: LOST TARGET. It could be sea clutter or it could be something else. Out on the bridgewing I search the waters with binoculars—lightning illuminates the sea and I find nothing. Below, General Patton, with sclerotic glare, stands watch next to the blasting fire hose; his knees are a little bent, his hands in front of him on the railing. The crew has formed him so that it appears he is taking a leak. The crew has strapped Patton's colleague, the helmeted General MacArthur, to the stern under the flagstaff; his gloved right hand is raised in a sort of royal wave but it is no more than a sagging, limp-wristed salute. "They'll wonder what kind of ship this is," Tony joked during our earlier inspection of the guard.

We have entered the designated shipping lanes southbound— ships in front and ships behind and some, going faster, on either side. We are crossing over 04.33N–98.43E, a mere spot on the globe, the exact site of a little-known tragedy. On the bridgewing I look into the darkness. It had been a night like this in the summer of 1992, electrical storms in the area, the sea reported calm and visibility good. The *Nagasaki Spirit* was also southbound, also laden with Persian Gulf crude oil. The master of that big ship was, like our own captain, probably asleep in his cabin, content that his ship was in the capable hands of his crew on the bridge.

The sea, ever moving, changing, influenced by tide and wind, never permits a permanent monument or marker to the missing; there is no exact location on the sea as there is on land, merely the coordinates that mark a position. We toss flowers, wreaths, overboard to mark the spot where our loved ones perish, and like our memories, they drift away. As I look down into the black waters I feel that the remains of some of the crew might still lie below. But no one knows for sure; most of the men simply vanished. It is a modern-day mystery of the sea and has all the hallmarks of an old-fashioned ghost story. As we cross over the position, I devote a moment of respect to those who lost their lives.

9

Dead Men Tell No Tales

As master of an oceangoing salvage tug, Dave Betts gets as close to the blazes of hell as anyone on earth; he puts out the fires on the high seas. He has seen his share of horror and he has discussed his mortality with his Maker more times than he cares to recall. If there is a collision at sea, if a ship is on fire, breaking up, sinking, or people need to be rescued, he gets the call. Yet in his thirty-six years of salvaging vessels and rescuing survivors, he was not quite prepared for the two burning ghost ships he was called to save.

The first signs of the disaster were the twin swaths of dark smoke on the horizon that rose into the nacreous sky. Thick and oily, the smoke feathered into the high cirrus and formed a sooty blanket above. From the bridge of his salvage tug *Salveritas* Dave Betts knew that this was going to be one hell of a mess. Betts found the M/T *Nagasaki Spirit*, a 100,000-ton crude carrier, listing to port and down at the head; an explosion had peeled the deck back like a sardine can. Balls of flame belched out of a gaping rent in her midships tanks; rivers of molten fire poured into the sea. The tropic air was fouled— he could taste the fire; the sour-sweet tang of sulfur would stay in his mouth for days.

Close by, a large container ship burned furiously. Flames swept stem to stern, engulfing the more than five hundred boxcars that were stacked three high on her deck; the smoke and flame were so dense that it was difficult to tell it was actually a ship that was burning. Occasionally some of the cargo inside the steel containers exploded, sending muffled reports rumbling across the sea. The bow of the ship had broken off from the impact; as big as a five-story house, it floated among the burning oil and debris nearby. The dismembered section included a short stretch of torn deck that still supported rows of stacked containers, some ablaze, others twisted and distorted from the blistering heat. One forty-foot-long box slid off the edge of the broken deck and fell slowly into the burning sea. The radioed distress messages had left no doubt what had happened—the 27,000-ton container vessel *Ocean Blessing* had plowed full bore into the oil tanker *Nagasaki Spirit*, ramming her amidships and rupturing her number-six tank just forward of the ship's bridge. The tank had been filled with Persian Gulf crude oil.

The collision occurred at night on September 19, 1992, at the northern entrance of the Malacca Straits about thirty miles off the coast of Sumatra, the spot that we are now passing. The conditions were good at the time: good visibility, flat seas, no weather to speak of. Betts's partner, Kenneth Bales, commanded one of the salvage boats that had been sent to the scene to salvage the *Ocean Blessing*. Captain Bales blames the accident on the "vessel-on-my-starboard-bow syndrome and VHF-assisted collision"—a charitable way of saying that the master on the burdened vessel was either not adequately familiar with the rules of the road or used the radio to find out the intention of the other vessel. Relying on radio communications leads to miscommunication and is the cause of most ship collisions today. "Some of the crap you hear over the radio—well, then again, I wouldn't be in business if they followed the rules," Betts says.

Excepting the sinking of a cruise ship or a ferry with all passengers, the collision of two ships this big is about as serious as it gets at sea. To put the event into some perspective: Many of us have been involved in a car crash and we well remember what that was like. Think of a freight train pulling one thousand five hundred boxcars colliding with San Francisco's Transamerica Building. Consider the impact;

imagine being aboard. Captain Bales, who found the log repeater in the engine room of the *Ocean Blessing* stuck wide open at twenty-one knots, says it was "the unstoppable hitting the immovable." The facts are irrefutable—the *Ocean Blessing* had nearly sliced the *Nagasaki Spirit* in two. Investigators later concluded the tragedy could have been avoided if one or both of the vessels hadn't been attacked by pirates.

At least one of the ships had been steaming out of control through the busy waterway when they collided; perhaps one of the ships no longer had anyone aboard at all. Forty-four crew members aboard the two vessels never lived to tell the story.

Betts had to make a decision—which of the two ships would he attempt to save? The container ship looked to be a total loss, but he thought the tanker could be salvaged.

He had seen it before and the sight sickened him. He knew the agony, the terror, a person experiences when he jumps off his ship into a sea aflame with burning oil. One survivor of a tanker on fire and sinking during World War II described what the crew on these two ships must have lived through:

> Oil was ablaze. The heat was so intense. This was the hottest breath of air I ever breathed. I had to swim under the water. I was in the middle of an inferno. I reached a lifeboat, but the men were in this oil that was on fire; they were drenched in oil, trying to swim out of it. The skin on their faces was just falling off. This one was trying to reach up and try to get a hold of the gunwale—I tried to lift him up; his skin all came off. . . .

Captain Betts worked the salvage tug between the ghostly silhouettes of the smoldering containers that floated through smoke, steam, and flame, looking for survivors, signs of life, bodies.

As small explosions ripped through the *Nagasaki Spirit*, Betts eased his tug forward until it nearly touched the flames and the liquid black smoke that rolled off the surface. The twin-screw *Salveritas* looked small and ineffectual before these big crippled merchantmen, but it carried powerful and sophisticated fire-fighting equipment. Included in its weaponry was the American-built Hellbeater system, a self-contained fire cannon on the after port side of the tug's boat deck that accurately shot 650 cubic meters of seawater/foam mixture the length of a football field. So powerful was the gun that it required two men to control it. Despite the Hellbeater and the fire hoses Betts knew that he could not soon control the oil-fed fires. So wild were the flames that he worried that he might not carry enough fire retardant to quench the fires and enough dispersants, oil cleanup chemicals, to limit the spill. It was going to be a long haul.

The "casualty," as they call a stricken vessel in the salvage business, had suffered major structural damage. The *Ocean Blessing* had cleaved a deep gash in the side of the *Nagasaki Spirit* in the form of a *V*, a clear outline of its bow. Small explosions from within both ships, the grinding and moaning of rupturing steel plates, and the roar of the oil-fed fires made speech nearly impossible. Betts, dressed in yellow coveralls, banged-up white hard hat, and stout leather boots, stood behind the wheel out on the bridgewing and carefully eased the tug even closer to the fires that jetted out of the tanker's hull. He shouted to his crew manning the Hellbeater to aim the cannon into the jagged split in the ship's side. Suddenly he was thrown back by a rolling ball of thick liquid orange flame that leapt out of the smoke. "A flashover inside the tank caused a fireball to vent out of the split," Betts recalls. "It blew out with something like—what? Something like a loud *whoosh!* The heat was unbearable." He knew he had to get out of there in a hurry, and he threw the salvage tug into reverse, backing away from the inferno. The blaze, so hot that pieces of the ship's steel hull dripped molten into the sea, burned the hair off one of his firefighters; Betts himself had his hair singed so badly "that if my mother saw me, she'd tell me to come right home."

As Betts and his crew on the *Salveritas* fought the blaze on the *Nagasaki Spirit*, two other Semco tugs, the *Salvigour* and the *Salvenus*, arrived on the scene to help put out the fires on the *Ocean Blessing*. A Semco twin-engine aircraft flew overhead and radioed the conditions of both ships to Betts, whose vision was limited by smoke and the size of the ship he was trying to save. The *Nagasaki Spirit* carried a third less crude oil than does the *Montrose;* yet she was nearly as long and she dwarfed the tug. From the bridge Dave could see only fire and smoke that poured out of the giant ship's side.

"The *Nagasaki Spirit* burned for five days," he recalls later in his office on the Singapore docks. Outside his windows some of the Semco fleet of salvage tugs and towboats, capable of moving anything from oil rigs to floating hotels, lie in wait for the next job. His office, cluttered and small, is decked out with colorful photos of shipwrecks and vessels ablaze. A flinty sailor who tends toward the stocky, Dave went to sea in 1964 at sixteen and worked his way up through the ranks from deckhand on a tugboat to captain and finally senior salvage master of Semco Salvage and Marine Pte Ltd. of Singapore. It is in his blood; his father before him was a salvage master in the UK, as were his brothers.

Despite the fires on the tanker Betts and his men donned breathing apparatus and climbed aboard the ship. They groped their way through the oily smoke down the stairwell and along the corridors in search of whatever was left of the crew; the beams of their powerful flashlights pierced through the acrid smoke no more than a few feet ahead of them. It was an eerie scene: three bulky masked figures in hard hats with air bottles strapped to their backs, clad in wet soot- and oil-stained yellow coveralls, heavy fire-resistant gloves, and solid boots. The drifted like ghosts as they felt their way through the dark corridors.

"I was frightened," Dave says. "I'm always frightened. Anytime I get a call I'm frightened." His candor is surprising. Physically he looks like a man without the corruption of fear. Think of a pugnacious bull-dog with a smile, a good smile, and you have Dave Betts. Not someone you want to tangle with but a man you know you probably can trust with your life. Unlikely that the *Montrose* would ever suffer such a fate—though the crew of the *Nagasaki Spirit* assumed it would never happen to them either—but if it did, I would want this guy nearby.

I had met with him several times; the last time he was laid up. He had suffered the first mishap in his years of dangerous work; his foot, caught between his own salvage boat and the hull of a ship, had been crushed. But he was impatient to get back to sea. "Any day now," he says, although by the look of it, it would be longer than that.

"I am not a brave man by any means." That is debatable. Some years back Betts was master of the *Norman*, a tugboat in the North Sea, one of the most treacherous bodies of water in the world, where sudden winter gales spawned in the North Atlantic form without warning. On December 13, 1975, it lived up to its reputation. A storm blew in from the north. Heavy winds whipped the tops off the waves and pelted the boat with snow and ice. A rogue wave slammed into the big forty-six-meter tug and tossed it onto its beam-ends, and she began to founder. He sent out a mayday, and after he was certain his ten crewmen were off the ship and in life rafts, he jumped off the lee side into the frigid seas. He has the kind of personality that allows me to ask a smart-aleck question: "Think about going down with the ship?"

"Hell, no! I had no intention of going down with her. But I was going to be damn sure that I was the last man off." He grabs his throat for effect: "My balls were up to here."

Betts and his men found the cargo control room of the *Nagasaki Spirit* relatively undamaged; the computers looked in pretty good shape, papers still cluttered the work table, and the instrumentation on the control panel that measured pressures, flow rates, and tank capacity seemed intact. Some of the windows that faced the deck were blown out and smoke and sunlight poured through with competing intensity. Outside, his salvage tugs continued to shoot foam onto the fires that rose out of the gash in the deck. The men ducked instinctively as a fireball erupted and swelled toward the windows. They had to hurry. It would be close. The ship could blow.

They turned back to the smoky darkness of the unlit corridor to search the cabins, not knowing what they would discover; this was the worst part of the job, and he braced himself for the worst—the discovery of the remains. It was hard to imagine that those he might find had only a day or two before lived relatively normal lives, working the ship, with wives and children who still were awaiting their return. He kicked in a door and played the beam through the smoke from one part of the room to the other. Betts expected they would find the bodies of some of the crew, half hoped that they might find someone still alive. But this and every other cabin was empty, and none yielded any signs of life anywhere or even much indication that that there had ever been life.

Except for the captain's quarters. Captain Alan MacKereth, of

Fairvale, New Brunswick, Canada, was the master of this relatively new ship. The *Nagasaki Spirit* represented state of the art and there was little doubt that the master had been proud of the big crude oil carrier. What transpired in the moments before the collision and after—whether he had a gun to his head or was asleep—is conjecture. Dave could imagine MacKereth's terror at the moment of impact. MacKereth was probably thrown out of his bed when these two giants collided; the jarring crash, the explosion, the ringing of automatic alarms, the blasting horns—Betts felt it personally. And it bothers him to this day.

"On his desk were photos of his wife, his children. Letters were written to his wife that were waiting to be posted," Betts says, his voice getting sandy with the memory. "All his personal things were as he had left them. People think we're tough and rough, but believe me we're not. Seeing the photos of his wife and kids—that was the worst thing. I thought there but for the grace of God . . ." A helicopter from the American warship USNS *Niagara Falls* found MacKereth's body. Cause of his death was "inhalation of soot and fumes, burns over the entire face . . . the whole body including the face was covered by a thick tarry black viscous liquid."[23] It was the worst way to die.

"I suspect that the captain was the last man off the ship," Betts says quietly.

Dave and his men had walked onto a ghost ship. "There was not a single piece of evidence of any remains on the *Nagasaki Spirit*," he says. An Indonesian coroner days later searched the *Ocean Blessing* and was able to identify what were remnants of human beings—small heaps of ashes. "The men on that ship never had a chance. I had never seen a ship in such a mess in my life."

It is possible that the crew on the *Nagasaki Spirit* had abandoned ship, because the starboard lifeboat, a new bright orange self-enclosed model identical to those on the *Montrose* (which, because of its shape, Captain Postma jokingly calls the Orange Coffin) had been launched.[24] "What happened to the lifeboat or any people in the boat, nobody knows," he says. "But it should have been found—at the least pieces of it." The sea was calm, the weather clear. Yet, in this heavily trafficked waterway, the lifeboat, like the crew, vanished. So what happened to the crew?

Four months after the collision, workers at the breaker's yard of the Guangdong Shunde Shipwrecking Company in southern China were beginning to dismantle a 17,000-ton cargo vessel then called the *Hai Sin* when they noticed a putrid stench coming from somewhere down below. Cautiously they opened the heavy doors of the ship's long-idle walk-in refrigerators and found, piled in ashen, decomposed knots, ten charred corpses—many naked, none with any personal effects or identification. Their bodies had been doused with gasoline and torched.

Eric Ellen, a former chief constable of the Port of London, was the man who created the International Maritime Bureau. Until he retired, he had waged a twenty-year war against high seas piracy. The attack on the *Nagasaki Spirit* and *Ocean Blessing* and the discoveries of the corpses on the *Hai Sin* occurred on his watch. The *Hai Sin*, an investigation revealed, was the missing *Erria Inge*, an Australian-flagged bulk carrier pirated a year earlier.

Ellen believes that the bodies found in the reefer of the *Erria Inge* were some of the crew of the *Nagasaki Spirit*. How they got there is a mystery; theories abound, but Ellen and others think it could be evidence of murder.

Examination of the remains by a forensic pathologist led to conclusion that the bodies were probably Caucasian and not Chinese.

"The bodies had no sign of injury," Ellen says. "When found, they were badly burned and there was a smell of petrol. I can think of no other reason why the bodies should have been in the refrigerator room unless they had been picked up from the sea. That they might have been refugees can easily be discounted. They were not crew of the *Erria Inge*. There were no other reports of missing persons."

Perhaps more to the point is that no authority even to this day has investigated how ten corpses could be stashed in the cold stores of a stolen ship. Equally dismaying is that no investigative authority has looked into what happened to the forty-four missing crewmen from the collision.

"If ten rotting corpses were found in an apartment in New York or London," Ellen says, "police inquiries would be relentless. If a crime is committed in international waters, then life is a cheap commodity," a statement that pretty well covers the infrequent and usually futile efforts to track down and apprehend these sorts of pirates. "Nobody is interested in what happened to the crews—they are not even statistics."

The attack on the *Nagasaki Spirit* occurred sometime before midnight. The tanker had been taking some antipiracy precautions that frustrated Betts's efforts to search for survivors or remains. The ship was battened down in the citadel mode, and Dave and his crew had to force a number of padlocks on doors to gain access inside. Whether the ship had had its deck lights on, fire hoses on standby or firing off the side, and dummies strapped to the railings is unknown. Betts found no evidence that the fire hoses were in place when he went aboard.

During his search for survivors Betts discovered that most of the cabins were unlocked and some of the drawers and lockers had been flung open as if ransacked. It was impossible to tell whether this was a result of looting or whether the crew had removed some of their own personal effects before abandoning the vessel. Captain MacKereth, however, had concealed a camera in an electric locker, hidden presumably in case pirates boarded. Missing from the ship were all valuable personal belongings, including clothing, radios, cassette players, CDs, and the TV sets. When the crew abandoned their ship, they certainly did not take the televisions.

The ship's safe was missing. "There was an empty space in the captain's cabin where obviously the safe should have been," wrote Betts for the investigation.

Captain MacKereth's last message leaves little doubt of the cause of the collision:

> Have been fired upon and now have fire in Nos. 5 and 6 and central tanks. Abandoning vessel immediately into two 16-man liferafts and will activate EPIRB in Lat 04 33N, Long 98 43E, at 1623 GMT Sept 19. No time to report further as abandoning vessel.

It is believed that the *Ocean Blessing* also may have been pirated or was trying to escape the same gang that had just taken down the *Nagasaki Spirit*.

Ex–U.S. Navy captain William A. Chadwick, of Great Falls, Virginia, led the investigation into the affair for the Liberian government's Bureau of Maritime Affairs.

"Initially I dismissed the thought of piracy," he said. "However, gradually I came to the irrevocable conclusion that piracy was involved in this collision." The *Ocean Blessing* had been observed by another ship to move "in an erratic manner—changing speeds from 10 to 20 knots, from side to side as though the deck watch officer was trying to employ evasive maneuvers to avoid being boarded by pirates."[25]

Ellen says the captain of the *Ocean Blessing* was probably scared to death. "You see films in which the heroic captain stands on the bridge, brave, solid, calm. This doesn't happen in real life when a ship is about to be attacked. I believe the pirates could have attacked both ships."

The *Ocean Blessing* burned from stem to stern in what was the worst fire on any ship Betts had ever seen. It took three weeks to put out the blaze, and to the veteran firefighter this was not normal, not for a ship carrying general cargo. Some digging uncovered documented evidence that the container ship was carrying an illegal arms shipment from China to the Middle East, which, one source said, fed into the inferno.[26]

The *Ocean Blessing*, once a proud ship, today lies as a disintegrating hulk in the shallow waters off the west coast of India. Sometimes bunker fuel seeps out of her tanks and sullies the beach. At midtide twisted fingerlike muffler-steel frames of what is left of the containers on-deck claw agonizingly out of the water. It is a grisly monument to the remains of the crew who are inside.

Up to this point Captain Betts was primarily concerned with putting out the fires on the *Nagasaki Spirit* that raged across the deck and flared out of the side of the vessel. He knew, however, it would not be long before he had an even bigger job on his hands. And it came on the third day, when traces of unburned oil began escaping into the sea from the tanker's open wound.

The collision had the potential to become an environmental crisis. Few people involved with oil tankers have not learned a lesson or two from the grounding of the *Exxon Valdez*, the nation's greatest environmental disaster since Three Mile Island. Betts knew what a similar spill of crude oil would mean to the coral beaches of Thailand and Malaysia only a couple hundred miles to the east; when his office filled out the Lloyd Open Forms—the standard no-cure-no-pay salvage agreement with the vessels' owners to save both ships—he was committing his company legally to "use their best endeavors to prevent or minimize damage to the environment." Containing the oil was as important as putting out the fires.

The collision of the *Nagasaki Spirit* and the *Ocean Blessing* occurred 370 miles north of Singapore, and it took the Semco salvage crew steaming at full speed the following morning a little less than thirty-six hours to get to the scene. An estimated 12–14,000 tons of crude oil had that much time to float away from the stricken vessels and drift toward shore.

A major regional ecological disaster was averted for a number of reasons. Most of the oil had been consumed by the flames at the site of the collision. Also, oil spilled at sea will "weather" naturally and break up over time by spreading, evaporating, dispersing, emulsifying, dissolving, or sinking. In the case of the *Nagasaki Spirit* some credit goes to Betts and his crew, who fought a round-the-clock battle to contain the spill.

Because he was at sea, containment booms could not be effective; his only alternative was to use the dispersants he had aboard, solvents that would break down the spilled oil. But this was no simple task. To eliminate the oil from the surface he had to know the physical and chemical properties of the spilled crude: the rate this specific oil would evaporate, the viscosity of the oil as it evaporated, whether the oil was likely to sink or to float, what chemicals would disperse the spill, and the health hazards to his men from the detergents. Dispersants are virtually useless on very viscous floating oils, because they tend to run off the spill and into the water before they can penetrate. If not tackled within twenty-four hours, the properties of oil on water change drastically. After a couple of days you are wasting your time with dispersants. The viscosity changes because of evaporation and it becomes gooey, thick, and ugly.

Dispersants also are ineffective for dealing with heavy oils that have a high "pour point"—oils that will no longer flow below a fixed outside temperature. It is like changing oil in your car. If the oil is too cold, it will thicken and pour slowly. The properties of crude, including the pour point, vary according to its origin. Betts knew that the properties of the oil in the tanker might be different than stated in the manuals, because crude oil from the pipe is often blended. Even if it were pure from the wellhead, it still could be different than what he would expect to clean up. Like fine wine in which the grapes that grow on one side of the hill yield a different taste than those that grow on the other, the depth of the well and the year the oil was produced could change its properties. Fortunately for Betts and for the region, the 40,000 tons of crude carried in the tanks of the *Nagasaki Spirit* was Saudi Khafji Crude, relatively "light" oil; it had been blended with naphtha and it was easier to disperse.[27]

We on the *Montrose* are transporting three cargoes: 141,000 tons of Arabian Light, 84,700 tons of Omani Export Blend, and 38,218 tons of Abadan Straight Run Fuel Oil. The outside temperature on this bright sunlit day where the *Nagasaki Spirit* and the *Ocean Blessing* collided is 27°C, the water temperature about 25°. The pour point of the Omani Crude is −24°C, and the pour point of the Saudi Arabian Light a little lower. Our cargo has also been spiked with naphtha, a practice common among the oil companies. Thus our crude oil is light; were our precious cargo to spill out upon the sea, it would have to be very cold, such as in the Gulf of Alaska, before the type of crude we carry could solidify. Betts could use dispersants successfully to limit the damage. However, our Iranian Straight Run Fuel Oil is as thick as molasses, and its pour point is 10°C above, about 50°F. As soon as it hits any water, it would become an unmanageable sludge, and barring natural degradation and the sinking of the sludge to the bottom, it would be very difficult to clean up the mess until it reached the shore.

It is for an environmental nightmare such as this that the ship company's emergency nerve center in London was created. The information needed from the scene—current sea temperature, sound-ings, nature of seabed, among other facts, as well as ownership and liability—are all critical figures needed to manage such a disaster.

The *Montrose* carries two million barrels of crude, nearly ten times the amount spilled by the *Exxon Valdez* and about fifty times the amount of oil washed onto the Alaska coastline.[28] The devastation from a VLCC breaking up in the Straits would be inconceivable. Not accounting for natural degradation, evaporation, and containment ef-forts, were the oil that we carry to reach land, seventy-five thousand miles of coastline, the equivalent of nearly three times the circumfer-ence of the globe, could be affected. Using the formula for the dam-age caused by the *Exxon Valdez*, were the *Montrose* to spill all of her oil—84 million gallons of it—five-hundred thousand square miles, twice the size of the State of Texas, could be covered.

These figures are so outrageously monstrous that sometimes it is easier just not to consider the consequences of such a spill. Not only would this environmental catastrophe be one of the worst the planet has ever experienced, it would be crippling economically.

Michael Grey, of Lloyd's of London, editor of *Lloyd's List* and a re-spected expert on shipping casualties, is one of many concerned that a catastrophe in the Straits far greater than the spill from the *Nagasaki Spirit* is just around the corner. "What you can't forget is the menace to the environment. There have been cases where pirates boarded large merchant ships like in the middle of the Malacca Straits, and held the crew captive while the ship was steaming full speed [out of command] down the busy channel for eighteen to twenty minutes."[29]

It happened to the *Valiant Carrier*, it happened to the *Nagasaki Spirit*.

More astounding, it actually did happen to a VLCC—at a section of the Straits where the waterway is the narrowest, where the traffic is the thickest. The M/T *Chaumont* was en route from the Persian Gulf to the refinery at Limay, Philippines, laden with crude oil. She was at-tacked in the early morning hours on January 16, 1999, in the Phillip Channel, the narrow passage at the industrialized southern limits of the Straits.

The Phillip Channel in the best of times—daylight, clear weather, little traffic—is extremely difficult to navigate. It is a rubbish heap of mishaps. A month later the *Star Aquarius*, a cruise ship, collided with the fully laden VLCC M/T *Stresa*. That was an accident. Dave Betts and his crews were able to contain the spill. But it had the potential of being a major catastrophe.

It is also near this stretch of difficult water that gangs of pirates, minutes away by fast boat, lie in wait in the nearby mangrove swamps.

The *Chaumont* was a sitting duck. She was in an endless line of vessels, behind her and ahead of her. She had to slow down for oncoming traffic and had to delicately navigate a channel that was at this point only a half mile wide, pinned in on the port side by the rocks of Pulau Takong Kecil and on the other by the shallow waters cluttered with wrecks and reefs. This is the only channel for deep-draft vessels. A half-dozen VLCCs steam by here daily.

The inevitable happened. Pirates on small boats crept up from behind the *Chaumont*, keeping well inside the blind spot of the radar. This blind spot, called sector blanking, is an angular pie-shaped dead zone immediately behind a ship caused by the vessel's large funnel. On the *Montrose* it is an arc of about twenty degrees.

Pirates armed with long knives nimbly scampered up the transom of the VLCC, climbed onto the poop deck, and overwhelmed the deck patrol. Despite the crew's being locked down in the citadel, pirates quickly gained access to their quarters. Some of the gang assaulted a couple of the officers and tied them up in the officers' mess, while their confederates stormed the master's cabin and looted the safe. There are conflicting reports, but it is said this huge French-flagged tanker steamed down the constricted shipping lane out of command for thirty-five minutes. She should have run onto the rocks or collided another vessel. No one can explain why she didn't.[30] The stark reality, however, is that a VLCC has been taken down by pirates.

Dave Betts spends much of his life cleaning up the mess. "If a VL were pirated and broke up in the deepwater passage of the Malacca Straits, that channel would be closed," Betts says. "No VLs to Japan, no large bulk carriers, could get through." And worse, were it to occur a mile or so farther down the channel, the entire Straits, the gates to so much of world commerce, would be shut. Asia accounts for $500 billion worth of global two-way trade; every nation in Asia would suffer setbacks, and that would tip the delicate balance of the global economy.[31]

It was nothing short of a miracle that the *Chaumont* did not collide with another ship or slam into a reef. If an attack occurs again on that ten-mile section between Takong Kecil and Batu Berhanti where the channel is in places less than a mile wide—and five to six hundred ships a day thread this needle—the consequences could be disastrous.

10

To Hell and Gone

Montrose

Jumping off a burning tanker into the flaming sea is a horror never far from those who work these ships. All tankermen live with the fear of a possible collision, a solid bump, anything that can spark ignition. Despite the stringent safety precautions they know that their home is a potential floating bomb. It is dangerous enough work without the worry of an attack by a bunch of barefooted pirates with knives in their teeth. The notion of our ship steaming out of control in these busy waters while pirates loot the ship and we are locked below, unable to escape and certain we will collide with another or run onto a reef, is a nightmare no one wants to consider.

"It would be panic, panic, I can tell you," Captain Postma says quietly after I tell him about the *Nagasaki Spirit* and the *Ocean Blessing*. "No matter how many fire drills, no matter how prepared—the collision happens. And inside you there is silence." He stares down the long cargo deck in front of us that bulges with 300,000 tons of naphtha-laced crude. Possibly he is thinking of the fate of Alan MacKereth, master of the tanker. "What happened, you ask yourself?

You don't know what to do first—there is a moment of, of"—he searches for a word—"complete void. It is a nightmare."

The captain's eyes narrow and he taps his fingers nervously on the sill of the window. He shakes his head as if clearing away the horrific vision. "You know what you have on board and you know what will happen and you see death. I try to imagine but I cannot."

A red-hulled chemical carrier, the *Polar Belgica*, passes us a few hundred meters to starboard. She is a handsome ship with nice lines— a raised flared bow and cutaway deck. A phalanx of fire hoses, from the cargo deck to the stern, six of them, shoot water into the sea. It is midday—that captain is taking no chances. It's a safe bet that her master is one who once had a run-in with pirates and who does not need to be told that the threat in these waters is a fact.

Chief Officer Viktor Travnik, the young, muscular Croatian with wide, eager eyes and a fast wit, challenges me to join him and his junior officer on the inspection below of the water ballast tanks. I accept and he appears surprised.

The *Montrose* is a relatively new ship. Built in 1995, she was designed with the environment in mind. Unlike the *Nagasaki Spirit*, which had only a single sheet of steel separating its cargo from life outside, the *Montrose* has a double hull and a double bottom, and conforms to U.S. Oil Pollution Act of 1990. The legislation, hastily written following the *Exxon Valdez* disaster, required that all tankers calling in at American ports, in time, have double hulls and double bottoms.

The two-hull system is quite simple, and on paper it seems like an effective concept. The cargo tanks are built inside, suspended inside, the ship's hull. They are separated from the outer wall by empty spaces called the water ballast tanks that, when the ship is empty, are filled with seawater, providing stability. When the ship is laden, as it is now, that space—about twenty-five feet from the cargo tanks to the hull—is dead air. If another ship or a reef or an iceberg were to pierce the outer skin of the *Montrose*, it would have to travel through the water ballast tanks before penetrating the cargo tanks. Smart thinking. In theory.

"The *Ocean Blessing* cut right through the *Nagasaki Spirit*," Captain Betts says. "A double hull wouldn't have made much difference." He should know; he has been called to salvage more punctured oil tankers than many naval architects have ever boarded. When the unstoppable hits the unmovable, something has to give.

If one were to imagine a city skyscraper colliding with another, then double hulls separated by water ballast tanks are really little more than a gimcrack solution. A double hull limits the spill of oil only in a minor bang-up. Full speed for these ships is about sixteen knots, nearly twenty miles an hour. Even when steaming at three knots the inertia is enormous; the prospect of slamming these 300,000 tons into a reef or into another large ship even at that speed is beyond the ken of imagination.

Viktor is one of those with compelling good looks, flat mouth, well-trimmed dark mustache, who looks like he belongs in a movie or in command of one of these big ships. For him command may not be far off. Viktor "pays off" after this trip for his home leave. There he will wait for the telephone to ring, an invitation to go to London for The Interview—the grilling by psychologists to determine if he has the character to be master of a ship. It is, he says, a great time to be alive.

The mission down below is a monthly ritual that conscientious ship operators follow: a check of the condition of the zinc anodes welded to the floor that prevent electrolysis and a search for the first signs of corrosion inside the hull—peeling paint and rust—and for leaking hydraulic pipes and valves. It is a trip into an area few ever see, and the chief asks if I am sure I really want to go along.

Before descending Viktor attaches one end of a coil of quarter-inch rubber hose to a nipple on the "sniffer," a humming camera-sized box that detects poisonous gases in the holds. He feeds the bitter end down a vertical pipe into the bilge, the lowest part of the ship, and waits for the digital readings: 20.9 percent oxygen and .1 part per million of H_2S—lethal hydrogen sulfide. If we can trust the box, we will not be overcome with noxious or toxic gases while we are below. Viktor exhales into the hose. A bell on the box trills from the reading of his carbon dioxide. "Good, now we know it works."

This ship is overwhelming from the outside—looking up, looking long, looking down. I cannot begin to imagine what it is like inside its very bowels. Our muscular young Croat, whom I joined in the gym the other day—he can press weights I can't begin to consider—assures me that if he can handle it, anyone can. We step into a large uncapped tube in the deck and climb down a steel ladder, then down a metal stairway, and more metal ladders. Hand over hand we lower ourselves, the chief mate, a third mate, and myself. The protocol, I see, is to wait until the one below you is off the ladder before beginning the descent. I look up the tube, and silhouetted against the sky is one of the crew checking our progress—his head, his hard hat, has simply become a small round ball against the light. The deeper I go and the darker it gets, the more I wonder: Do I really want to do this?

No electric lights are permitted down here. Flashlights, intrinsically safe, rubberized and spark free, are issued. The one I have been given craps out only minutes after I turn it on. Viktor and his partner, with lights only a little more energetic than my dead one, lead the way and I follow, more by feel and instinct than sight. Viktor tosses over his shoulder that nobody goes down here if he doesn't have to.

We land on the bottom, or what I hope is the bottom—a long metal walkway that runs the thousand-foot length of the ship. If the ship's length seemed interminable when I stood on the deck outside, it is arguably endless from where I now stand. I have entered a cavern of deep shadows, gray-painted crossbeams and girders, and thick steel plates with limber holes. The outer hull is the wall on my left, and I press my hand against it; I feel the vibration of the sea running past on the other side. On my right, some distance away, the towering wall of the round-bottomed cargo tank looms above me. It contains part of the 84 million gallons of scalding crude, and I feel it is just busting to find a way out. The ship's real bottom, the bilge, is another ten feet below the grating. Water sloshes over the floor. I remember that this ship flexes and twists in a seaway. I don't feel it or see it, but I do hear it creaking.

The tarry Straight Run Fuel Oil had been heated to 51°C, about 125°F, to ease the flow into and out of the ship's tanks. The dead air between the cargo tanks and the outside hull in which we stand provides insulation that keeps the oil almost as hot as the day it was loaded. It is stifling down here.

I follow the two officers along the walkway. Viktor shines his light on the joins where the intercoastals, steel girders that form part of the ship's frame, are welded to the hull and the cargo tanks. These are solidly affixed to the floor of the ship. No rust or corrosion has been permitted to get ahold of the *Montrose*. Viktor spots a little paint that is peeling, a faint streak of rust. A ship this old should show signs of aging and structural deterioration, he says. From what I can see, the inside of the hull appears nearly as clean and as rust free as the day it slid down the ways. He is pleased.

The slow roll that we have felt topsides is not noticeable. We are well below the waterline and close to the center of gravity. In fact there is no sense of movement at all. We are inside a lightless pit of subtle horrors; our voices bounce off the walls and respond in short echoes of conspired whispers. Were it not for their lights, it would be pitch-black.

An odd raspy sound, like the scratch of sandpaper along a piece of hardwood, charges us from out of the shadows ahead. It builds to a crescendo, rising from a scratchy whisper to an instant guttural roar; no, two sounds, this roar commingled with a terrifying, ear-piercing wail—a jet plane just feet overhead and a thousand women screaming in terror.

This frightful noise, mechanical, human, fluid, colored with hysteria—agonizing cries of banshees with sharpened teeth, popping eyes, rising up from the very depths of hell itself, unmediated, discordant, shrill, charging from out of the darkness; and, by God! the darkness itself trembles. The metal walkway on which I stand begins to vibrate. I grip the handrail. I wonder if we are going to be crushed by tons of cold seawater. Tons of scalding crude oil. I am lost, the lights I had followed have vanished; the insanity of sound becomes the space into which I fall. Holding on, I work hard to peel away the darkness, find the answer to these painful laments that are rushing so quickly toward me. The roar, the shrieks, wash over me, rush by, move on, and subside into a whispered rasp, a sigh, and then silence.

A light flashes in my eyes. "Frightening, isn't it!" Viktor shouts. "I should have warned you! I never get used to it." My head pounds, my ears ring. It was a crossing swell that, with the power of a thousand freight trains, struck the bow and bullied its way aft along the hull. It was the communication between ship and its element, an animated sound of conflict as if the sea itself was in protest.

⌒

Sweat pours freely from under my hard hat into my eyes. I will have to peel my clothes off when this is over. And when will it end?

As if reading my thoughts Viktor says, "This will take about an hour. Then after lunch we do the port side. So far everything looks like new. You see those welds? That's good, no?" It looks good to me, but I know that he'll not get me to go on the port-side inspection.

"Okay, now we go more below. To the bottom."

We descend yet another ladder into the ankle-deep waters of the bilge. This is the remains of ballast water that fills these tanks when the ship is running without cargo; when the ship arrives in a port to pick up cargo, these water ballast tanks are emptied. It is poison water that carries bacteria, disease, virus, amoebae, sea life, parasites, and strange foreign matter. It is not uncommon for a crab that was sucked into the tanks in its infancy in the Philippines be spit out as full grown into another harbor after the passage, ten thousand miles away.[32] Many nations are creating regulations that prohibit changing water ballast within two hundred miles of their coast. Viktor, who spends some of his life down here, thinks it should have been done long ago. "But now it is too late. You have creatures that grow in Africa now growing in America."

I duck under the cargo tanks; 300,000 tons of crude oil is on my head. And I start to think about it. The heat, the dark, the unexpected. I am not known to be claustrophobic, but then you don't have to be down here. I know it is psychological. If you wonder if you could be claustrophobic, then a voyage into the stygian depths of a VLCC will certainly confirm it. On one side the ocean speeds by at fifteen knots; we are seventy feet below its surface. Down here you have to control your mind.

I wipe the sweat from my eyes and hurry after the distant figures that I can no longer see nor hear. A light flickers through one of the manholes cut out of the girders, and because the bottom is symmetrical, I can figure how to get there. Hopping over the crossbeams of the ship is slippery business; a thin layer of mud covers the floor, sediment that had been sucked in with the water the last time the ship was in ballast.

The suppressed paranoia and the shortness of breath are not helped by the overwhelming heat. An hour down in the hellhole fully clothed is comparable to being trapped in a runaway sauna. The loss of a few pounds is not this important.

The ship takes another thumping and this time I know what to expect, but it is nonetheless frightening; the banshees begin their tormented screams, erasing our senses with a deafening roar, charge past us, and fade off into something like an exhausted sigh. I am now interested in getting back topsides.

"You see? The anodes are not wasted, also like new," Viktor says as I catch up. "That is good, very good. Now we are finished." He shines his light in my face. "What? Are you hot?"

I once competed in a marathon, but I don't think I ran any faster then than I do this day back to my cabin to pry off the sweat-soaked boilersuit and jeans and sink into a chair to crack open a cold beer.

⌒

Zamir, a lanky, intelligent lad, stands before the bridge windows, his hands clasped behind his back, staring out at the traffic. It is a posture of command and one day, with practice, he will be the master of his own ship. When not standing like Admiral Lord Nelson, he paces. Why do these officers pace? Zamir and the other pacer, Wasim, are nearly inseparable, and I suspect Zamir may not have been much of a pacer before he met Wasim on this trip. They appear to have become instant friends. Wasim often arrives an hour early to relieve Zamir and Zamir stays an hour later, and they spend their extra hour on the bridge pacing together. They are a pair; not quite Laurel and Hardy but close to it. Zamir is a tall, lighter-skinned youth with bright, unhappy eyes on either side of a rather predatory nose, curly dark hair, and innocent face, and Wasim counters as the darker, shorter, more muscled, intense new father. The two charge back and forth from one end of the bridge to the other, hands clasped behind their backs, bodies angled forward, speaking quietly, earnestly, to each other in incomprehensible Urdu while the big ship plows though the sea on autopilot.

They pace to the door of the bridgewing and, like plinking targets in a shooting gallery, straighten and then, in near mechanized precision, swing around and pace back toward the other side, unconcerned with the next shooter. I have seen the captain eye these two, not sure how to deal with their nervous and distracting locomotion. He frowns, shakes his head, and decides to let it go. It is Zamir's evening watch and he polishes the floor with his shuffling pace. "I have been pirated three times. Two of the pirates I captured," Zamir offers, slowing. I see that he wonders whether to put on the brakes. He does.

Zamir was a young cadet on watch aboard a ship at anchor in Mongla, India. At three in the morning a half-dozen men scaled the side of his ship and disappeared down into the open cargo hold. As a youngster from the streets of Karachi he feared nothing, and he ran down the deck and tackled one of the thieves, who was struggling with a fifty-kilo bag of rice. He hauled him back to the crew's mess, tied him up, and woke up the captain. The captain barked at him to keep the guy tied up and not to bother him until morning. The thief eventually escaped overboard.

Event number two occurred in Surabaya, Indonesia, when he spotted machete-wielding pirates leaving his ship with their arms full of loot. He chased one pirate toward the front of the ship, and just as the thief mounted the wide lip of the bow and was about to jump overboard, Zamir grabbed him. The pirate fell forward and Zamir held on to his legs, dangling him over the side, upside-down, until the thief's loincloth fell off, exposing his genitals. Zamir decided to drop him.

In the anchorage at Chittagong, Bangladesh, Zamir returned from shore leave to find that his cabin had been ransacked by someone who had squeezed in through the porthole. Among the items stolen were his brand new pair of "joggers." When walking through the market section of town the next day he saw his stolen shoes hanging by their laces in a stall. He tried them on, bargained with the stallkeeper, and bought them back.

"You call them pirates, Zamir. I thought pirates attacked ships at sea."

"No! Pirates attack ships—at sea, at anchor, or in port. It does not matter, you know, where they come from. If they come on your ship and they steal from you or hurt you, they are pirates. Many times they are the same people. I do not know why you would call them one thing because the crime was committed at sea and call them something other because their crime was committed at anchor. They are pirates."

Whether committed on the high seas or close to shore, piracy has taken place since the earliest hunter-gatherers hopped on a log raft with a prized piece of meat and floated down some wilderness river. Homer first recorded an act of piracy around 1000 B.C. in *The Odyssey*, and the imperial barge carrying Julius Caesar was reported hijacked during a Mediterranean crossing in about 75 B.C.

In many parts of the world today the culture of piracy dates back many generations; robbing ships is considered an acceptable part of local tradition and is a normal if illegal way of making money. And certain recent influences conspired to make modern piracy so much easier to commit, whether on the high seas or in a harbor. The end of the Cold War is one of them. No more superpower navies patrolled vital waterways; the age of international indifference settled in and local nations were left to deal with problems that had been heretofore international in nature. Piracy also was made easier with the availability of gadgetry. Pirates no longer had to rely on cotton sails, oars, sextants, and dead reckoning to mount an attack. Easily available were mobile phones, handheld satellite navigation systems, handheld VHF ship-to-ship/shore radios, and mass-produced fiberglass and inflatable dinghies that took larger, faster, inexpensive Japanese outboard motors. The shipping industry, too, provided unwitting assistance. The automation of vessels reduced manning levels from around forty-four to seventeen, making it easier to take control of a ship. The increased cost of fuel necessitated the reduction of speed from twenty-two to a more economical fourteen to eighteen knots, and

that also made it easier for pirates to board. Ultimately, word got
around how easy piracy really was. A good day's work netted up to
$40,000 for only twenty or thirty minutes of effort. With the excep-
tion of a few notable hijackings in Southeast Asia, few pirates were
ever caught alive. The crime had become easier, more profitable, than
pulling up a disappointingly empty fishing net. And anyone could be
a pirate.

The crime of "piracy" in legal terms had been a crime committed
on the high seas in international waters. It had never been a local
crime for local investigations in the historic sense. Yet in the twenty-
first century, because it was occurring increasingly in local territorial
waters with such violence and cost, something had to be done. Label-
ing an attack on international shipping in one of the world's most important waterways merely a local robbery minimized the crime and
left it up to local officials to investigate. But, justifiably, there is little
faith in the ability of many local officials to investigate crimes that
they would prefer to ignore or in which they are indirectly or directly
implicated.

Defining the crime had become something of a political football.
When piracy takes place in the waters of one nation—no matter the
national origin of ship, crew, or cargo—that country wants to call it a
robbery at sea and they expect to handle it. This was and still is part
of the problem: Many piratical events today under the law are territorial matters.

The 1982 United Nations Convention on the Law of the Sea
(UNCLOS) definition is very specific:

> Any illegal acts of violence or detention, or any act of
> depredation, committed for private ends by the crew or the
> passengers of a private ship or a private aircraft and directed: On
> the high seas, against another ship or aircraft, or against persons
> or property on board such a ship or aircraft, or against a ship,
> aircraft, persons or property in a place outside the jurisdiction of
> any State; any act of voluntary participation in the operation of a
> ship or of an aircraft with knowledge of facts making it a pirate ship
> or aircraft . . .

This was adequate for the time it was written, and it included the notorious attacks on the Vietnamese "boat people" in the late seventies and early eighties. (In 1981, for example, of the 455 refugee boats that made it to Thailand, more than three quarters of them had been pirated. An estimated 571 persons were killed, 599 women and girls raped, and 243 persons kidnapped in that one year alone.)

Because of the ease with which attacks were being carried out, close to land as well as far offshore, the reality of the day demanded something other, a definition that would account for the increasingly common vicious attacks on ships that occurred in territorial waters, at anchor or tied to a pier. These horrific territorial crimes had to be internationalized.

When Eric Ellen created the IMB, he investigated maritime fraud, which included piracy. Attacks by pirates were not much of an issue in 1981; maritime fraud, theft of cargo, insurance scams, were. Eric was told at the time that there was no more piracy, just muggings at sea. But when a tanker the size of the *Valiant Carrier* was attacked in Indonesian waters and careered down the sea lanes on fire and out of control, there had to be some changes.

The first step to stopping piracy was to redefine it, make it easier to report and more identifiable to the industry and to the public at large. Eric's definition of the crime, written hastily on the inside of a wrapper of a pack of cigarettes, is generally now accepted by the international community:

> An act of boarding or attempting to board any ship with the intent to commit theft or any other crime with the intent or capability to use force in the furtherance of that act.

The definition covers actual or attempted attacks, whether the ship is berthed, at anchor, or at sea, but it excludes petty theft unless the thieves are armed. It certainly includes two of Zamir's experiences, as well as my own. While not possessing the regulatory and legal clout of law, there is strong sentiment in the shipping industry to adopt the IMB definition of the crime universally.

In addition to the jurisdictional problems, not only is it difficult to get someone to investigate, but it is also difficult to get someone to request an investigation. Consider a typical case: A ship built in Japan, owned by a brass-plate company in Malta, controlled by an Italian, managed by a company in Cyprus, chartered by the French, skippered by a Norwegian, crewed by Indians, registered in Panama, financed by a British bank, carrying a cargo owned by a multinational oil company, is attacked while transiting an international waterway in Indonesian territory and arrested in the Philippines. Such a Byzantine paperwork trail entangles an investigation and leaves the hapless ship even more vulnerable, an even softer target for those suited pillars of organized crime who hire gangs of pirates to hijack ships. The syndicates are well aware that they can get away with murder. Literally. The futility and lack of such investigations is one reason why so few pirates are ever apprehended. It is also why only ten to thirty percent of the attacks are reported; tying up ship and crew at the cost to the shipowner of tens of thousands of dollars a day while somebody figures out where to start, if at all, is not worth it.

Despite the problems of jurisdiction and definition, those who have suffered at the hands of pirates don't give damn what it's called. And, I was to discover, neither did those who go out gunning for them.

11

The Lost Command

Montrose

Zamir is relieved by Wasim and, after a few minutes of studied pacing, disappears below, leaving the two of us on the darkened bridge. The fishing fleets continue to work their nets in the deep-water channel and the radar screen is a litter of small echoes. The sound of the young Pakistani officer shuffling across the floor is broken by one of the radios. The voice is hard to understand—it is either Malaysian or Indonesian.

"Mike Juliet Romeo November Two, this is the Royal Malaysian Marine Police—*Papa Zulu Four*. What is name of your vessel, please?"

"*Papa Zulu Four.* This is the *Montrose.*"

"Good evening, *Montrose*—what is your cargo?"

"*Papa Zulu*, we are carrying crude oil from the Persian Gulf."

"Roger, *Montrose*, what is your destination?"

"*Papa Zulu*, destination is Karimun Island lightening anchorage."

"*Montrose*, how many aboard including yourself?"

"*Papa Zulu*, twenty-two on board."

"Thank you, *Montrose*, we wish you a very pleasant voyage. *Papa Zulu* out."

"That was highly unusual," Wasim says in his singsong voice. "We have never before been hearing from the Malaysian police. I did not know they were out here."

A flashing blue light winks from off the starboard quarter. "I do believe that is the police boat."

Papa Zulu Four

Such communications with the *Montrose* may be unusual, but the Royal Malaysian Marine Police are out there patrolling the Straits twenty-four hours a day looking for trouble. Sometimes they catch a few pirates. Before I joined the *Montrose*, I spent time on the *Papa Zulu Four*, one of fifty-two vessels that patrol the Malaysian side of the channel. About 110 feet long, she is "mother vessel" to a fleet of smaller high-speed "strike vessels" that guard this three-hundred-mile stretch of marshy coast.

The small wheelhouse of the "*P-Zed-4*" this night is crowded. A dim light on the chart table and the glow from the radar screen are enough to make out the young officers intent on the instruments before them and on the lights of the passing ships ahead. These are perfect conditions for pirates—no wind, little moonlight, and the never-ending parade of fat and laden cargo vessels. Two men stand over the outsized radar screen and watch the iridescent green arm sweep over every object within twelve nautical miles. Opposing columns of bright little echoes extend right off the screen: A ragged line of targets, cautiously navigating merchant vessels, heading southbound toward Singapore and to the rest of Asia, forms one column; the string of northbound ships destined for Europe, the Persian Gulf, India, or the States forms a line of echoes moving slowly in the opposite direction. On the screen the columns seem alarmingly close. The largest radar echoes within the columns are the *Montrose*-size VLCCs.

The officers at the radar are not interested in the nearly stationary fishing boats but in a fast-moving blip—likely a speedboat—that might be closing in on one of the targets in the procession. If the echo keeps going and cuts across the shipping lanes, it is either intending to attack smaller ships closer to the coast or smuggling illegal immigrants.

Assistant Superintendent of Police Jamaludin Kassim, standing at the screen, reaches over to the console and switches off the blue strobe light. "That should do it—we have to let them know we are here, especially the big oil tankers," he says in heavily accented but perfect English. "We don't contact all the ships in the area, but one or two; all of them hear our communication—or should."

Jamal is the head of the Southern Command's marine police anti-piracy operations. He is not in command of this ship but he tells the captain where he wants to go and, during an operation, how to go about it. Were it not for his uniform, which he seldom wears, he could never be made as a cop. A veteran of wars against the Abu Sayaf and the Moro Liberation Front in the Philippines and against gangs of Indonesian pirates and smugglers here in the Malacca Straits, he has been shot at and wounded during bloody battles at sea that make the fanciful tales of cutlass-swinging brigands of yesteryear pale in comparison. Yet there is little hardness evident, no ice-cold killer eyes, none of the stereotypical Hollywood stuff that feeds our images of a combat-scarred pirate fighter; his relaxed manner belies the Rambo-like zeal that drives him.

The *Papa Zulu Four*—Mother vessel has no other name, no affectionate or diminutive handle, it is strictly a stoutly armed patrol boat—bucks through the southerly chop at twenty-eight knots. Spray flies up and over the wheelhouse; often it reaches as high as the raised open deck behind the bridge, where a young officer, usually a cadet, sits with binoculars in a mounted fishing chair, scanning the black seas ahead; he is the eyes and ears of the patrol boat, and he can find pirates better in the dark than those behind the windows in the wheelhouse. The helmsman down below can see little more than the compass; his vision to the outside is blocked by the large turret of the ancient 40mm Bofors gun mounted on the deck. In the daytime it is the watchman above who can spot a small two-man fishing canoe lying in the patrol boat's path or floating rain forest trees washed down a nearby river that could poke a hole in the patrol boat's fragile skin. He alerts the bridge through a voice tube that terminates just above the helmsman in an oversized trumpet.

P-Zed-4 is an old girl, and she is no longer the swiftest boat on the Straits. Built twenty years ago, she is past her sell-by date. Unless she is at the right spot at the right time with guns unsheathed, she can do little more than show the flag and serve as a support vessel for her sleek strike craft. She is hardly as fast as the pirates she chases.

It was with some pride that the Malaysian marine police announced it had just upgraded its forces with the purchase of small fast boats, jet-powered shallow-draft vessels to chase pirates right back to their lairs deep inside the mangrove swamps. They also purchased a number of black RIBs, rigid inflatable boats, and strapped on twin two-hundred-horsepower engines to rocket the craft to nearly fifty miles an hour.

"I wanted boats, boats that were quicker than those of the sea robbers. And now we have them," the head of the Malaysian marine police had said earlier in his office in Kuala Lumpur.

In a briefing before I joined the *P-Zed-4*, Commander Muhamad Bin Muda had told me that while "sea robbers" had fast boats, his teams finally, after much scraping for funds, had faster ones. Pirates can hide, he had said, but they cannot run. That superiority, however, would last only for a few weeks. Local gangs, most of whom were known to Muda's men, got wind of the police escalation and built sleeker fiberglass and wood boats; and they added two more engines that gave them eight hundred horses. Muda said he was not too concerned; his stealthy little RIBs could put up a good chase and were far more maneuverable.

Who are the pirates that Muda's men are chasing? The Malaysian police do not often battle Malaysian pirates. They stalk, ambush, fight, and bloody gangs from Indonesia, gangs who sneak into Malaysian waters on speedboats, attack and hijack ships, then scurry back to the safety of their territorial waters just a few miles on the other side of the Straits. The police have their hands full. In 2000 there were sixty-six reported pirates attacks in Malaysian waters alone and twenty-eight attempted attacks. In the first six months of 2001 as many ships were hijacked in the Straits as in the whole of the year before. These are IMB figures and they are misleading. They do not include unreported attacks on passing ships or actual hijackings, which the Piracy Reporting Center in Kuala Lumpur says could double or triple the figure. They also do not include Malaysian fishing boats or local coastal "barter trade" cargo boats, which are frequently robbed and looted. Indonesians, the industry knows, figure in nearly every assault.

The governments of Malaysia and Indonesia have cordial ties—these two nations have much in common and are nearly brothers; their languages, food, traditions, and cultures are similar. Indonesia was colonized by the Dutch, the Malays by the British, both subjugated by the Japanese in World War II. But Indonesia today is in a shambles, the result of years of mismanagement and political upheaval; its economy is in trouble and its politics and particularly its military are riven by graft and corruption. Anarchy in many places of the island chain seems daily just around the corner. Malaysia, on the other hand, once a backwater of rubber plantations and rice paddies, is one of the shining lights of Asian enterprise: a technologically advanced nation with smooth-working transportation and communication networks, a relatively stable society, a people that, on the surface at least, appear content; it even boasts the world's tallest building, for whatever that is worth. To hard-pressed Indonesians just across the usually placid Straits, eight miles away at the narrowest, Malaysia is the Promised Land.[33]

Indonesian pirates strike at passing vessels in the Straits at will, frequently on the east side in Malaysian waters. So emboldened were pirates in November of 2000 that they attacked a tanker at the northern entrance to the Straits in broad daylight, the first such daytime attack; after robbing the crew they fled back to their island village on white speedboats marked by distinctive red stripes—easily identifiable—safe from all, including their own accommodating officials.

One of Commander Muda's fears is that these loose-knit gangs of village thieves will one day "unionize" with other gangs along the coast, that they will syndicate, form an alliance of hit squads with bases from top to bottom of the Malacca Straits along the Indonesian coast. Syndicates, Muda says, mean organization and outside foreign money. Syndicates mean a different modus operandi; instead of wielding homemade long knives made out of car-spring steel, pirates will have access to more sophisticated weaponry. Captain Choong, director of the Piracy Reporting Center in Kuala Lumpur, warns that unionizing would indicate that organized crime is becoming involved: "If they do get organized, they will bring in guns, and then who can stop them?" Except for terrorist-sponsored groups, guns among local villagers had been very difficult to come by in Indonesia.

The picture of the future for shipping in the Straits is bleak. Syndicating pirate activities will give gangs more muscle than were they to remain disparate groups of opportunists. It will be far easier to buy the authorities and to bribe local Indonesian navy commanders to look the other way. Of the six hundred ships that transit the Straits every twenty-four hours, Choong thinks that pirates, underwritten by organized crime, could hit as many as "four or five ships a day. That would net them a lot of money. And if they are smart—and they are—they will confine their activities to the Indonesian side where the Malaysian police can't go."

Piracy in the Straits took an even more menacing turn one night recently when an armed Malaysian SWAT team nabbed pirates at work within three miles of their coast. The pirates were caught in the act of robbing a "barter trade boat," one of the Indonesian cargo vessels that cross the Straits daily to trade with Malaysian coastal communities.[34]

However, these pirates were not local kampung boys with meat cleavers who decided to do something different on a Saturday night. These were six freelancing commandos from the Indonesian navy who, like their Malaysian counterparts, were helmeted and armed with assault rifles, and wore government-issue black uniforms and bulletproof vests; they were using a craft typical of the Malacca Straits pirates, a low-slung speedboat powered by two big outboards.

The Malaysian and Indonesian SWAT teams, commandos trained to kill, stood facing each other, muzzle-to-muzzle.

"They resisted a little," Muda says leaning back in his office chair in K-L, lacing his fingers across his stomach, grinning like the cat who had caught the mouse. "They were surprised by my boys— 'What the hell you doing here?' they asked. They claimed they were just 'checking out' the barter boat, but we know they had come across to rob it and the others in the area. Yes, they were very surprised to see us."

"These were not sea robbers," I offer.

"No, these were a lost command."

Although the Indonesians hotly deny it, the word is that the local commanders of the Indonesian navy send out these rogue patrols with orders to bring back at least a million rupiah, either in goods or in cash. Not much for a night's work—that's about ninety-five dollars. But then a million rupiah goes a long way in this part of the world. These lost commands dart into the Straits to rob a passing ship or, failing in that attempt, take after the barter trade boats. The next morning, according to one informant, the navy commandos are back at their base with cash in hand, earning commendations for promotion.

This is a far cry from the significant, modern Indonesian navy of ten years earlier. Those I knew well who served in the navy in the east Java port of Surabaya often boasted they had one of the finest forces in Asia. Yet even then the naval commands in remote locations in the sprawling Indonesian archipelago—Sumatra, Irian Jaya, the Celebes—were known to be loose cannons; under international pressure during the Suharto regime the problem was held in check. That was yesterday. Today, under a fragile political and economic climate, the ingredients are all there. An Indonesian navy lieutenant is paid about ten dollars a month wages. His house and food are subsidized by the government. Still he nets only about ten bucks; freelancing, for the once proud sailors of the Indonesian navy, is the only way to go.

Muda says this particular lost command almost certainly had been involved in several assaults on ships in the Straits. His investigators found a spent cartridge on the bridge of one tanker that had been pirated, a 5.56 casing that could only have come from the Indonesian military.

The rogue SWAT team was handed over to the embarrassed Indonesian navy, who said they would be severely punished. From

Muda's expression it was obvious he expected the same lost command to return to Malaysian waters to rob ships and loot local fishing and cargo boats.

There are legal limits to what Muda and Jamal and their men can do to capture the pirate gangs. There is a strict but disputed boundary between Indonesia and Malaysia. The twelve-mile territorial limit cuts the Malacca Straits in half and where it is wider than twenty-four miles, the conflicting Exclusive Economic Zone reaching out two hundred miles from all the world's littoral nations applies. It is understood between the two neighbors that their boats may patrol only their own territorial seas, chase pirates only in international waters, and never enter the sovereign waters of the other. After attacking a ship the gangs turn west and escape back into Indonesia, where they know that under International law, codified in the United Nations Convention on the Law of the Sea, that same convention which defines the crime of piracy, the right of hot pursuit is not permitted without specific authorization, thus far never granted.[35]

"They are our neighbors and we must be correct," Muda says. It is apparent he would love to go in and privately kick some Indonesian butt. However, it is an open secret that as the gangs enter and carry out activities in Malaysian waters, the Malaysian police have chased them back into Indonesian waters.

In a recent speech for public consumption Muda played very much the diplomat. "Fortunately, the Royal Malaysian Marine Police have been working closely with our neighbors." There are frequent meetings with Indonesian officials but there is little or no cooperation.

"We are very angry—not just the authorities but the locals as well," Muda admits. "We don't want them here. They are intruders, invaders." In the fight against Indonesian pirates in the international waterway, it is war.

The *Papa Zulu Four* has concluded its patrol of the shipping lanes and is back at station, anchored about a mile off a long, winding river that weaves through the mangroves up to the town of Batu Pahat. It was here that a Japanese invasion force landed during the capture of the Malay Peninsula and Singapore in the early days of the Second World War. The marine police have a "forward base" up this river. It is not much more than a rotting wood jetty with some slats missing, but it is here that the formidable strike craft are based. The SWAT teams will soon board their attack boats and motor down river in the dark and out to sea and raft up to us for Jamal's nightly antipiracy briefing before they patrol the Straits.

"Ninety percent of the time pirates come out after ten Thursday night and work through Sunday," Jamal says, staring out at the sparkling lights on shore. "It's a weekend thing." The pirate gangs are also constrained by the tides. During springs, a few days after the moon is full or is new, tides in this part of the world become enormous, ranging more than ten feet. Pirates can't get out of their river kampungs during low water, when their boats sit high and dry in the mud; their high-speed assault has to wait until the tide is high enough for them to float their boats out of the mangroves. Tonight it is Thursday and the moon, despite the heavy cloud, is nearly full and a spring tide is on its way in.

A father of three boys and three girls, Jamal's almost personal crusade against the pirates on the Malacca Straits does not allow much time for a homelife. Most of his nights are spent on board these police boats on the prowl; when he is not on the bridge, he lies on his back in the officers' mess below in more of a slumber than a sleep, his arm draped over his eyes. When beckoned to the bridge he springs to his feet like a cat, and you are never sure he was ever asleep.

Much of Jamal's intelligence is provided by local coastal Malaysian fishermen who trawl or set their nets just up to the edge of Indonesian territorial seas. They don't use the traditional VHF radios to tip off the police. They call on their cell phones. "We keep very close to the fishermen. They can recognize the sound of an engine in the darkest nights. They know if a boat going through the fleet is one of ours or one of theirs."

Jamal is a quiet and modest man, almost to the point of being shy. His boss, Southern Command superintendent Aziz Yusof, thinks that

Jamal might be the world's most successful pirate catcher and personally credits him with the capture of more than thirty suspects. Fluent in Tagalog, the language of the Philippines, Jamal had infiltrated the communities of the Abu Sayaf on the Malaysian-Philippine border until his luck ran out and he was ambushed. He points to his groin. "The pirates shot me here. Within one inch of my balls. I was lucky."

The Malaysian government brought him back across the South China Sea to the Malacca Straits, where it was hoped that his no-nonsense approach to terrorists and pirates—interchangeable terms, according to those on the line—will help put an end to attacks on international shipping. It was a wise move.

Soon after his arrival Jamal learned many of the dialects of the area and went covert in Indonesia—up the rivers, through the mangrove swamps, and into the hideouts of the gangs. One such foray took his men, posed as fishermen, miles up the Selat Asam along Pulau Karimun into the town of Selat Panjang, headquarters of one of the more active groups.

"I slip in, and I slip out," Jamal says, speaking quietly. "I study the local politics, the local community, and I live with the people. I must learn what is going on, who is in charge, and the local way of thinking. I understand them. Then I can do my work."

Jamal and his men captured pirates in at least three major operations in the Straits in the first six months of 2001, all of which had been carefully planned and executed by ambush. He won't say how many pirates/smugglers in the Malacca Straits area have ended their careers floating facedown in the murky waters.[36]

We are finger-eating dinner in the tiny officers' mess in *Papa Zulu Four*—boiled fish and rice and something similar to collard greens. The standard drink is not coffee or tea but a glass of hot water. Tea and coffee come at the end. A gilded-framed photo of the sultan of Malaysia, dressed in a black suit ornamented with gold stitching and medallions, looks down upon us from the wall opposite.

"We do not want the ships in the Straits attacked. If a VLCC is attacked and blows up, it would be chaos, havoc. If it happened in the south where the Straits are narrow near Karimun, it would be a catastrophe," Jamal says.

He admits that if he were notified that a VLCC was being attacked on the Indonesian side of the shipping lanes, he would go to the rescue and maybe nab a pirate or two. "That would be the right thing to do," he says.

In the days I was to spend with Jamal, I was to see this was not a very complex man but a very efficient one. He is no tougher, no stronger, than most of us, just more fearless. He is not reluctant to pull the trigger. There is no outward bravura, no commanding voice, no bullish notice he is about to take charge. He has a presence that quietly expects and receives obedience and loyalty.

At the marine police base in Jahore Baru, Malaysia's southernmost city just on the other side of the causeway from Singapore, Jamal had proudly shown me some of their booty, boats taken from the pirates. The reigning speed champion of the Straits sat on cinder blocks under a tin roof, a thirty-foot open polyester pencil-shaped craft with a wide transom that had been designed to carry four 200-horsepower engines. Until recently there had been no faster boat in the shipping lanes. It had been caught ferrying illegal immigrants. The plan was to turn the captured boat into a police strike craft, "but we've run out of money." He says it with such resignation that it is obvious this problem is not unusual. "The pirates, you see, are rich."

A large boxy wood fishing boat, similar to the one the *Montrose* almost ran down in the squall, tugged at her lashings to the pier as if impatient to get back to work. "This is one of our decoys. We act like fisherman to get close to their coast. Easier to pick up intelligence." In one such operation they picked up information that led to the capture of three pirates who the police said were responsible for the attacks on about thirty vessels in the past year, including nineteen merchant ships.

That incident was particularly bloody and perhaps more than any other illustrates the intensity with which Malaysia is going after the gangs. A mob of pirates, Jamal had been informed, was going to make a major hit within a three-day period, possibly on a supertanker or on a cruise ship. The marine police were not going to let that happen in their waters. Or in any waters they could reach, no matter what the diplomatic consequences; piracy in the Straits was giving Malaysia a bad name. (Why did they have to name it the Malacca Straits? one government official lamented. Why did they have to name it after one of our cities? Why couldn't it have been the Sumatra Straits?)

Informing Indonesian authorities of the pirate plans would be useless, even counterproductive. The information would be fed back to the gangs, who would rearrange or postpone. No, these cops wanted the pirates badly and the ambush was kept under wraps. Even today Jamal is hesitant to reveal where he got his information—this would not be the last operation of its kind. After days of planning and waiting Jamal received a call on his little Nokia "handy" from a fisherman at about seven in the evening. A fast-moving boat had just flashed through the fishing fleet and was headed for the shipping lanes. Jamal, on the bridge of *Papa Zulu Four*, ordered the patrol boat to the south at flank speed; he knew he could never intercept the pirates, but he might catch them in the act of raiding a ship. His strike craft were already on standby. He would have to play it smart—he couldn't afford gunfire around a liquid petroleum gas carrier or a tanker carrying jet fuel, or around any ship for that matter. "We knew they were going to hit a ship. We knew that they had left their base and their operation was beginning. We were able to figure out the route they were taking."

Finding the old *P-Zed-4* too slow, he called one of the nearby strike boats to rendezvous. At top speed *P-Zed-4* had been able to get close enough for Jamal to track on radar the pirate boat as it shot toward the ship traffic.

Jamal watched the speedboat slow down at the southbound lane, circle one large radar target, make another pass, then creep up close to the stern of the ship until both merged as one target. Jamal knew he was about to witness the attack on a VLCC. As he was making plans to rescue the big ship, the tiny echo darted away and sped on a straight course toward the mainland. The attack on the tanker, for whatever reason, had failed. He strapped on his Kevlar vest, unlocked an M16 from the gun rack in the corridor, slipped a ski cap over his face, and joined five other members of his SWAT team in the rigid inflatable gun boat. Even better, he was thinking, they are going to attack the barter trade boats.

One of his commandos sat in the front seat behind a panel of recessed green, yellow, and red instrument lights while the others strapped themselves in the small padded seats facing the front. The little boat, all but invisible, flew across the waves. Jamal had radioed three other strike craft to form a cordon around where they suspected the pirate boat to go. They hadn't attacked a passing merchant ship and he didn't think they were carting immigrants. But what were they up to? What was Plan B?

Jamal's strike craft cut its engines and now drifted silently. Through his night vision glasses Jamal watched the pirate boat motor slowly up to a deserted beach and nose onto the sand. Although he was too far offshore to figure it out, it appeared they were loading something into the boat.

For a half hour he and his men nervously coddled their rifles, straightened and restraightened their ski masks, readjusted their bullet-proof vests, and tried not to make a sound. At last the faint sounds of outboards; the pirates were coming out.

The shadowy image of the pirate boat leapt suddenly forward, a bow wave spread outward. Its course should take them right into his hands. He fired a white parachute flare, lighting up the area. Go! Go! Jamal muttered to his driver; if he timed it just right, he could swing his strike craft around in a semicircle, pull up, and arrest them. The strike craft swung alongside the pirates, close enough to see a couple dozen motorbikes crammed into the boat, stolen off Malaysian streets and apparently kept hidden near the beach as Plan B. His strike boat maneuvered so close to the pirates that he considered reaching over and pulling one of them out. He counted eight of them, all wearing ski masks. Bullhorn in hand he ordered them to surrender, but instead they veered sharply away. The police boat turned and parried. It was something like a waterborne dogfight; one boat twisted and spun around while the other stayed hot on its tail. An outcropping of headland rose out of the darkness and the pirates saw they were trapped.

"They kept coming. We had a spotlight on them but they turned at us—they never stopped. They were going to ram us." It would have been an uneven match; the wooden pirate boat, three times the length, three times the weight, and just as fast, would have chopped up the agile little strike craft. "We turned away and they missed us and we came back behind them. They turned again and got behind us and tried to ram us again. We had no alternative. I had to immobilize them. I shot at the engine, but it was unfortunate that—uh—some stray bullets must have hit the pirates." Jamal tells the story with his boss, Superintendent Aziz, listening in. "We didn't want to kill them." They exchange a private, almost vulpine glance. "Yes, I had to immobilize them. The engines—that was what I was shooting at."

"Were they armed?"

"They had parangs. And Rambo knives—you know the ones with the notches on the back of the blade." U.S. Special Forces knives.

"Guns?"

"Yes. Maybe they threw them in the water."

I privately wonder how he could have shot at the engines mounted on the back if the boat was trying to ram him.

He sees my disbelief. "I have to defend myself and my crew. They were going to ram us. And—there were only two shot. If we wanted to kill all of them, we could."

A pirate fell overboard during the skirmish and was run over by the propeller of his own boat and two were shot in the chest. All recovered to plead guilty to theft. One was an ex-con who had served time in a Malaysian jail for a bank robbery. Under interrogation they admitted to pirating a number of merchant ships.

I wanted to know which ships.

"They don't know the name of the ships they attack—it is not important to them. They just want the ship's safe and to get off the ship as fast as possible and get back into their boats," Aziz offers.

The Malaysian cops are quite convinced they don't have to apologize for their lethal methods. Publicly they say the Indonesians are intruders; privately they say they are invaders and they will not allow foreign invaders to attack ships in their waters.

"We have a message to send to them," Jamal says. "If you come out [into Malaysian waters], we shoot you. That is very simple." In the latter part of the year 2001 piracy in Malaysia's Southern Command coverage area had been more than halved. The Malaysian marine police are proud of their success, no matter how summary the justice.

Sometime later I had a chance to inspect the high-speed pirate boat that Jamal and his crew had shot up. There were bloodstains on the seats under the cuddy. And there were two bullet holes in the engine block.

12

Where Are the Americans?

Papa Zulu Four

A two-tiered rack of rifles stands sentinel and ready for instant use within inches of the door to the deck outside; it is an impressive and intimidating display of firepower. I don't know much about military weapons; I once worked in Somalia for the United Nations as an aide worker and there I found that nearly every male over eight years old had his own AK-47 Kalashnikov, the distinctive assault rifle with the curved magazine. These guns are smooth, hard, and mean looking. Like a kid I'm fascinated. There is a gun that looks like it shoots grenades. There is a row of black steel automatic rifles, some with folding wire stocks, others with stocks of black plastic. Peering closer: Heckler & Koch 9mm. The row of guns on the lower rack looks uncomfortably familiar. A young officer walks up the stairs and sees me staring at the rifles—I straighten, I'm a little embarrassed, gawking at these things. What kind? I ask him, pointing to the lower rack. "M16. American," he says, then bids me good-night. Now it comes to me— it is the same kind that the punk kid used when he clubbed me over the head on my boat near Horsburgh Reef.

I wander down to the officer's mess for a cup of coffee; there is an hour to kill before the SWAT teams arrive for their assignments. Curious, that a boat this small should have a mess for officers and a separate mess for ratings. I might expect it on the *Montrose* but *Papa Zulu Four* is minuscule compared to the VLCC and yet there are just as many people aboard—where do they fit them all?

There always seems to be a pot of sweet milky coffee ready. As I pour, I notice movement in the corner of my eye. Something resembling half an orange remains on the sideboard, smothered by a few dozen German browns, large cockroaches with wings, digging in. Not surprising; in the tropics and on most boats, ships, and yachts in the world there is an infestation to one degree or another. They are brought on board with vegetables and especially in cardboard boxes. They lay their eggs among the voids in the paper and eat the glue that binds the boxes. German browns also fly, crawl, and even swim from boat to boat, from shore to boat. Cockroaches are not necessarily a reflection on the housekeeping, but the swarm on this orange does seem to indicate something else.

Food is always at hand on the *Papa Zulu Four*, but that is true on most ships at sea. There are a lot of overweight seafarers throughout the world, but if the food were not so plentiful, you'd find a lot of unhappy crews; it is one of the basic lessons learned by every navy the hard way—you don't skimp on food or you will have a recipe for a collective anger that feeds a mutiny. It is nearly 2200 hours and the small delicate-looking Malaysian chef has placed before me a pot of sweetened shrimp fritters and sambal, hot chili sauce. I can't get enough of them.

Even with the sinister reminder of the guns standing at attention just outside, it is difficult to realize—as dreamlike we ride the gentle swells—that this ship can spring to life, become a ship of war, in seconds, as I am told it has in the past. We are primed for battle, armed with grenade launchers, various small arms, machine guns, a big gun mounted on a turret, and a crew that is honed to kill. But this is not a warship; it is a police boat. Many of the crew are lounging in a state of casual alert on the top deck, feet up, smoking, relaxing in the warm tropic night breeze, waiting for the alarm. Some talk to their families on their mobiles, not to a far-off homeland but, for many, just across the water, a mile or so away on shore. There is no declared war out here and no declared enemy. It is not easy to imagine these man-boys as soldiers fighting what one shipowner calls a guerrilla war at sea, a battle against maritime terrorists. Down below on the bridge an officer watches the radar closely, searching for an invasion of one. Perhaps two.

Jamal joins me. He is dressed in a dark blue coverall—his commando outfit? He notices the cockroaches. Without comment he flicks his forefinger against the orange, sending them flying around the room.

"We have fifty boats in the marine police," Jamal says, "but we will never have enough to cover the coast." Singapore, not wanting a repeat of the attack that occurred on the VLCC *Litopia*, rings itself with a police boat every mile and a half, twenty-four hours of the day. The rich little city-state has the resources and doesn't have a thousand miles of coastline—east and west—to protect.[37]

I ask him how many boats he thinks he needs.

He shrugs. More than he could imagine.

"You get outside help? From the Americans? From the Russians?"

"The Americans? We don't get their help. Where are the Americans? The Straits are important to them too. Maybe they will help when one of their ships is terrorized. I don't know—they help Singapore and Singapore does not need help. Singapore is rich. No, we are alone out here."

This is as much a political statement as it is a fact. These sentiments are not unusual among those on the front line. Complaints about off-again, on-again American friendship toward Southeast Asia have been frequent in the past ten years. American policy in the area is a study in strategic neglect, a friendship polished up when it suited U.S. interests. Following the end of the Vietnam War successive American administrations displayed a woeful indifference to the nations of the region. Protecting the Straits through which a third of world commerce passes was never high on the agenda.

After the September 11 terrorist attacks Southeast Asia finally attracted some interest in Washington. Indonesia, Malaysia, and the Philippines have large Muslim populations that could not be ignored, and while Islam in these countries has a tradition of tolerance under secular rule, the United States finally began to realize that it needed the nations in the area to play a vital role in the campaign against terrorism.[38]

And the Japanese? There has been talk for years that the Japanese have wanted to send their warships to patrol the Straits against pirates. Since eighty percent of their oil comes this way, it is understandable.

His face clouds. He reluctantly admits that the Japanese have put most of the navigational buoys and channel markers in the Straits. "We don't want the Japanese." In Asia memories are long, history is short.

Despite the resentment of Jamal and others *realpolitik* has overridden the traditional hostility toward a Japanese presence. At least temporarily. In November 2001 Japan sent a small fleet of warships from the Sasebo Naval Base into the Indian Ocean through the Malacca Straits to support the U.S. war effort in Afghanistan. It was the first such foray through the region since the Second World War. The role of the Japanese Self-Defense Force was to patrol the sea lanes between Japan and Diego Garcia, a British Island in the Indian Ocean used as a staging point for allied forces. Those sea lanes include the Malacca and Singapore Straits, which flow through the territory of nations with long memories of Japanese activities in the war. It is not known whether the Japanese presence in the area will have any effect on the increasing number of pirate attacks. It is believed not. There is little doubt, however, that if pirates attacked a Japanese ship or a ship carrying Japanese oil in the Straits, their ships would go after the culprits, presuming they were in the area.[39]

Tonight, however, Jamal and his squads of commandos are alone fighting the battle against piracy.

Jamal seems a little tense—quick, ready, sharper than the somewhat sleepy pirate fighter of the daytime. He says he gets about two hours of sleep a night and many catnaps. He is used to it, doubts he could ever again sleep like a normal person. I know how that is—after sailing alone across oceans, it took me years before I stopped waking up every twenty minutes (a habit from looking out to see if I was going to be run down by a passing ship). And I still sleep like a cat; the slightest noise and I'm up like a shot.

The television, mounted on the wall next to the picture of the grandfatherly sultan, concludes its official broadcast day; it had been showing some early Discovery but now offers a video advertisement that it repeats every five minutes: "the Perfect Woman Natural Breast Enhancement System" featuring some buxom Californians with flawless skin, baring pearly whites, slinking in and out of a swimming pool. Jamal has lost his train of thought and he is now glued to the tube. This is as close to public pornography as the strict Muslim government will allow. I make some crass comment and Jamal pushes a button on the remote and settles for white noise. I didn't mean to embarrass him; I meant that it was unfortunate that this is what represented America to many in this part of the world.

I tell Jamal about the Indonesians who boarded my boat off Horsburgh. He listens impassively, does not seem surprised. "A lost command," he confirms, "on patrol." With the state of the Indonesian economy it is even more common today.

The years have been kind to the bastards who jumped my little boat. I had come to terms. I no longer awoke in the night seeing the snarling kid's face that I so badly wanted to flatten; and I was able to forget the lights-out pain of the crack to the back of my head—although when I recall it, I swear I can feel it still. I remember more the boys' father and his gentleness, and I had been able to replace each of their mugs with the faces of those Indonesians I worked with/for in Jakarta, for whom I had developed such a long-standing affection. But this investigation of piracy is not without its price: I speak to those who have had similar experiences with or without the violence; the memories, the images of that night, have slowly reemerged from under the covers into clear and distinct reality. And it seems more terrifying today.

⟶

Jamal complains that the Malaysian police are seldom able to prosecute pirates for attacks on international shipping in the Straits. Unless pirates are caught in the act, and they never are, it is impossible to charge them with the crime. Occasionally hijackers are caught when they stumble into the waiting hands of the authorities who have been tipped off, but local gangs who plunder a random ship are not.

"We can catch them committing another crime and then they will admit they attacked ships. The IMB has a report and we can know which ships have been attacked. However, the captains of ships don't testify that they were attacked. Our investigations take time, and by then the captains are in another part of the world." Shipowners would rather not report the incident and would rather such attacks be forgotten; cooperating with local officials forces them to remove the officers from their ship and take their ship off the run. Reporting a boarding also might reveal that the captain took no proper antipiracy precautions (hardly appreciated by the head office or the underwriters), casting a poor reflection on the management of the company and its staff. The fight against piracy is no-win.

"It makes our job nearly impossible."

There are an unknown number of gangs working out of the hundreds of islands scattered along the southern edge of the Straits. Many are loose groups with no real plans or strategy—hey, it's the weekend, let's go knock off a ship? Their successes have caused other unemployed Indonesian men, who lie around their coastal kampung wasting their lives waiting for the sun to set, for the sun to rise, for something, anything, to take notice. Fishing is still pretty good on the Indonesian side, but it is the trespassing Malaysian fishing fleet that reaps the harvest. The Malaysians have a market for their fish. But not so the Indonesians; except for local fish markets there is often no way of getting the fish to the bigger towns; there is no money for nets, or fuel for fishing boats or trucks to take the fish, or for the consumer to buy the fish. However, the piracy industry is thriving.

The success of one gang is the envy of the other, and the number of gangs is increasing faster than Jamal and his men can eliminate them; when the police put one out of business, another crops up. They know the police can't cover the entire Malacca Straits all the time and that there is no hot pursuit. It has become a deadly game.

"There are more gangs and they are getting bigger and more professional," Jamal says. "We can't keep up."

The gangs' successes are the villages' windfall. Villagers know who is heading out of the coves on their fast boats and going after a ship; when the local boys return with cash from a ship's safe, then much of it is distributed in the village, which assures protection.

This Robin Hood–style piracy is so important to the kampung

that the Indonesian military is not about to go into some village to stop it. The region has a history of volatility; the Free Aceh Movement, the fundamentalist separatist movement linked to Al-Qaeda, which recently claimed responsibility for hijackings, has been a thorn in the Indonesian foot since 1976. "This makes it very difficult to stop their activities," one source in Jakarta told me. "We have enough on our hands without starting riots in the [coastal] kampungs."

Jamal disputes this, doesn't think villagers protect the gangs. "No, they are not Robin Hoods. They are just criminals." The source in Jakarta was unimpeachable and I lean toward him.

Commander Muda once put the activity into some perspective: "They rob to survive. Indonesia is in a bad way today; when they attack our fishermen, they steal rice, flour, cigarettes, fishing hooks. When they rob a ship in the Straits, they steal the safe, cameras, watches, anything they can carry away. The money they get from the safe pays for fuel and another attack."

The more established gangs are the ones that worry Jamal and his teams. Run by local businessmen, the Order of Battle—ORBAT, as the Malaysians call them—are divided into groups of twenty men each. There is a roster of who goes where and does what on which night. Those who can climb coconut trees are selected to attack a ship; they are the wiry ones with strong arms who, with knives literally clenched in their teeth, can shinny up the thick bamboo pole ladders and scale the transom of a VLCC without breaking a sweat. A ship's vertical anchor chain is even easier; they can scamper up a ship at anchor in less time than it takes to wait for a streetlight to change.

There is no shortage of manpower, and recruitment is made to order. The businessmen who run pirate operations are the same as those who smuggle illegal immigrants to Malaysia. While many in the pirate gangs are local boys from the coast without work, others of them have never seen the sea before. They have arrived from as far away as the cities, or from some of the dried-up rice towns in the interior of Java; they are more accustomed to steering a water buffalo through the paddy fields than a small boat propelled by 800 horsepower. These men have left their traditional homes and come to these central Sumatra coastal towns to get passage across the Straits to the Promised Land where there is work. Once settled in the cities of Malaysia, they send some of the money they earn back to their families. But getting across the dangerous Straits, past men like Jamal, is costly. The dream is often more than they can afford, and they are forced to work for their passage.

Some of these hopeful pilgrims have never seen a violent moment in their lives. Suddenly they find themselves on board a ship like the *Valiant Carrier*, long knives in hand, confronted by an angry crew, scared for their lives. This is not what they dreamed about when they said good-bye to their wives and children to find a better life.

The squawk box in the officers' mess blurts out something unintelligible and Jamal jumps up, announces the strike boats are arriving. "You have a jacket? It gets cold out there." I don't. These are the tropics.

The meeting under the canvas awning on the upper deck is relaxed. It could be a bunch of the guys getting together for the weekly poker game. The three strike craft are rafted alongside and bang against the hull—two jet-powered boats and, farthest out, the smaller black-painted RIB (rigged inflatable boat) the tip of the spear. If I were on a pleasure boat minding my own business and this little batboat suddenly roared out of the night, I'd have a heart attack. There is only one use for this boat and its occupants—attack and combat. Showing the flag, warning invaders, are for the others. When this one is called out, it is usually too late for talk. The other strike craft are no less serious, just less terrifying. Low to the water, powered by jet engines, they are painted a midnight-blue. Manned also by the marine police SWAT teams equipped with Kevlar vests, helmets, assault rifles, and grenade launchers, these larger speedboats give the impression that at least there is room for discussion.

Jamal reclines in one of the flimsy garden chairs around a card table as the commanders of the strike force take their places. The other SWAT members balance atop the railings swinging their feet, or squat on their heels on the deck smoking, just passing the time while their leaders draw up the night's battle plans. Most, like Jamal, wear dark blue one-piece coveralls. Some of the boys just wear black slacks and black T-shirts; no commando uniforms this night. Perhaps they are worn only during a planned ambush. One wears a fake once-trendy World War II leather aviator's jacket with wool collar and colorful theater patches. It looks silly, but the big man who wears it could wear anything he wanted without anyone daring to comment.

These commandos have shot and killed and will again in a lick, and I can't help but regard them with the skepticism of a growing child seeing Santa Claus in a department store, not quite sure he's real or not. These guys don't look like battle-tested commandos. Brian Winchester of Wellington looked like a commando—tonsured head, cold green eyes, and tattoos. These soldiers look like soft kids. There is one, his ski mask rolled atop his head, with a baby-fat face. Were it not for the M16 by his side and his bulletproof vest that perforce gives him a cocky, tough appearance, he would simply look like a spoiled fat kid. A gun-toting commando? Probably, for this guy looks gormless enough to be effective.

There is a quiet discussion between Jamal and the SWAT leader on his left. Jamal's usual implacable manner seems to darken. His response, on the other hand, is casual and dismissive. He translates, says that one of the new Mercury 200-horsepower engines on the black RIB has a problem and won't be working tonight. The boys in that boat aren't disappointed. They get to go home. But Jamal is not pleased.

The discussion continues, furtive with undertone. Another glitch? Jamal mutters something sharp, unpleasant; here is the tough guy in him. He is not happy about this news either. He is wondering whether to tell me:

Indonesian fishermen have told Malaysian fishermen that the pirate/smuggling gang operating out of Pulau Karimun, the island where the *Montrose* will discharge its Omani Light Crude, has just purchased some three-liter 300-horsepower engines, Formula One type, and are fitting three of them on the back of one of their boats; 900 horsepower, capable of pushing a pirate boat beyond the ability to hold on—to a speed of about sixty knots. Such speed is not necessary to attack a slow-moving passing ship but to outrun the Malaysian police back to Indonesian waters.

And still more bad news. The same gang at Karimun is joining forces with several well-known lost commands.

"It will be different now. Very dangerous," Jamal says. "The lost commands will give them the guns."

That pirate gang will be a very powerful enemy indeed, equipped with boats that could never be caught, and tying in with the military that uses modern weapons instead of long knives. It will be an escalation neither the Malaysian police nor the international community can afford. The Malacca Straits are about to become far more dangerous.[40]

Jamal believes that this new regional alliance, the "unionizing" they so feared, eventually will become part of more powerful organized crime syndicates run from Hong Kong, mainland China, Singapore, Bangkok, and Jakarta, the international organizations responsible for hijacking ships, drug running, and transporting illegal immigrants. Jamal and the others feel they are out on the battlefield alone, and there is a sense that they are waiting for the rest of the world to take notice and step up. The United States and its allies have gotten involved before; they patrolled the Vietnamese coast during that conflict, secured the shipping lanes to and from the Persian Gulf during the Iran-Iraq War, and currently interdict drug trafficking in the Americas. A show of force is all it would take.

There is no intel that any of the Karimun, or other, pirates are out here tonight. Jamal looks up at the night sky; the moon shines weakly through the high clouds like ground glass and casts a dim light on a flat sea. These are perfect conditions, he says. For us? For the pirates?

Jamal and I and four of the SWAT team pile into one of the low-riding fiberglass strike boats. This is not a comfortable way to spend a night, but then sleep is not an option in an undeclared guerrilla war. With the propellerless jet engines fully open, we have to hold on in the sudden acceleration. He motions the driver, a big quiet man with blue coveralls, army boots, and a closely shorn head, to patrol the coast. I realize that Jamal is not now concerned about protecting shipping, he is itching to stumble on some freelancing Indonesian commandos.

The darkness is not quite complete, and the low hillocks on the coast rise as rolling black shadows sprinkled with a twinkling light or two. We slow as we near the delta of the river leading to Batu Pahat. The heady smells are conflicting and overpowering: exposed sticky mud, decaying vegetation, sewage outflow from the river, unidentified jungle night flowers, and the syrupy sweetness of roasting mangrove wood in charcoal kilns. Just above us, against the pallid light of the moon, a foxbat, the size of a small dog, flaps effortlessly toward the trees.

Jamal scans the waters with his night vision glasses, taps the driver on the shoulder, and jerks his forefinger off to the left. In the dim light something glides across the water, low and unheard above the low rumble of our own engines. The men unstrap their guns, pull their ski masks down over their faces. The strike craft cuts a wide, cautious circle around the boat ahead. Jamal aims a spotlight with a pistol grip. It is a barter trader riding low in the water with cargo. Two young men in ragged T-shirts and shorts appear to get immediately industrious under the cuddy; one is either taking out some papers or hiding them. The other grasps the metal pipe of the tiller handle between his legs and, ignoring us, steers the boat straight ahead as if he doesn't notice us. Jamal barks something over the bullhorn and we bump up alongside, none too gently, tossing the young sailors on their butts.

Jamal orders one of them to bring their papers over and the other to unstrap a plastic blue-and-white tarp that covers their cargo. A shoeless Indonesian in his early twenties clambers aboard our boat and hands over their documents. As Jamal inspects his Indonesian passport, another of our crew offers the youth a cigarette. "Look," Jamal says, "they have made the trip across twice today already." There is a tone of respect in his voice. He hands me their passports. They are filled with the proper stamps; there is one from early this morning. Which means these guys have been working steadily for about twenty hours carting goods back and forth across the Straits—on a leaky wooden boat that barely reaches above the surface of the water. On each trip they run the gauntlet of pirates, cross busy shipping lanes, suffer the bureaucratic hassles of customs and immigration inspections, off-load upriver, and return to sea. A number of these barter boats are lost each month from overloading and capsizing, sudden storms, or from being run over by merchant ships. They are never heard from again. On the bridge of the *Montrose* I know we could never see these boats, had never seen them even in daylight unless we were virtually on top of them. There are hundreds of them plying this route every day, crossing in front of us, day and night.

It is evident by their sullen cooperation that these Indonesians just simply do not like cops, or probably anyone in authority, but it is apparent, too, that they are happy to have the marine police close at hand. They know they don't have to be warned that they are fair game for robbers, lost commands, and sharks. The boy's companion pulls back the tarp and uncovers a stack of fifteen-foot-long mahogany timbers, each a foot square, cut out from some Sumatra rain forest. In the West the cargo of this boat would be worth a small fortune.

"He says that there was a lost command here two days ago," Jamal says apologetically. "We hadn't heard about that." The incursions into enemy territory by the lost commands must be more frequent than I realized. Jamal tosses the other Indonesian a cigarette and sends them on their way.

Within minutes we are slamming out to the middle of the Straits, and it takes only minutes to get among the endless string of merchant vessels. We cut the engines and drift, and when the roar of our engines recedes from memory the world around us becomes still. A warm breeze has replaced the blast of wind in our faces and carries the smell of wood fires, pervasive and irritating; it is the season of burning on the Indonesian side.

There is no delineation between the black sea upon which we float and the black heavens above. We feel suspended, and were it not for the slow and easy movement from the sea that forces us to hold on, that gives us some reference, we could be space-walking somewhere out in the universe.

The slow steady *thunk, thunk, thunk* from the engines of the parade of merchant ships vibrates across the water. Lumbering beasts— like cattle—stupid, slow, vulnerable, following each other single-file toward the barn at sunset, or to the slaughterhouse. The ships are darker silhouettes against the dark, barely visible save for the single green starboard light amidships on a ship heading north and the faint range light on the mast above the bridge and the lower light on the forward mast. Those that are concerned about pirates have brightly lighted their decks aft as if there were a party in progress, a card game on the poop deck. However, there is no party and there is no other sign of life. A large chemical carrier motors by us. Its dark hull takes on color, a deep night-red; its aft deck is flooded with light, and hoses fire into the darkness. No mannequins cling to the railings. There is no evidence of a deck patrol or any other life aboard; it just looks like everyone has gone home and somebody forgot to turn off the lights. These precautions are all that the captain of this ship feels are necessary. Maybe he's right—as long as someone is keeping a close eye on the radar. Our engines rumble to life, we are thrown back as the boat flies toward the next ship in the procession. It is a midsized tanker, about the size of the *Valiant Carrier*. There is no sign of any antipiracy precautions at all on this one. The ship looms as a dark shadow, blacker than the night that surrounds it. We close on the tanker's stern and position ourselves in the center of the slow-moving ship's wake. I am worried. This is how a pirate would attack her, from behind, in the blind spot of its radar. We are sneaking up on the ship and I am beginning to feel like a pirate. This is not a game; I don't want to be mistaken for a pirate.

We are a few hundred yards behind the ship. Her aft lights suddenly snap on one after the other. The ship's horn shrills over the sound of our own engines, an urgent call to emergency stations. The metallic ring of the fire bells inside the accommodation block pierce the night—these are the desperate cries of a frightened ship. She springs to life, the crew is convinced that it is under attack. There is confusion aboard. Figures scurry out on deck under the glare of the lights, slapping on their hard hats, rushing for the hoses. It looks like some are still pulling on their trousers. I feel their fear and I want to hide my eyes. I feel almost ashamed. They have been awakened by one of life's most frightful sounds, a general alarm, and they believe they are about to fight for their lives. This is a mistake. Didn't mean to. Sorry. Sorry. Sorry.

Jamal radios the ship, tells them that we are a Malaysia marine police patrol, sorry for the disturbance, and to have a pleasant voyage.

"This happens sometimes. Then they will report an attempted boarding to the IMB but they are really mistaking us for pirates," Jamal says.

13

Into the Breach

Montrose

We should arrive at Pulau Karimun to deliver the first part of our payload sometime after midnight. Captain Postma finds an indication in his marching orders that the anchorage at the island may have a problem or two.

The telex received from the ship's agent in Singapore: "While Karimun is a safe anchorage, it is best for your crew to be vigilant and keep a watch out and also keep the gangway raised at all times."

We are to be "mother ship," the telex states, and transfer the Omani Light Crude into "daughter ship," the tanker *Pacific Aquarius*. While the discharge operations will occur in Indonesian waters, Indonesia is not getting any of the oil, just payment for the use of its territory. The *Pacific Aquarius* then will take the oil to the refinery at Port Dickson, Malaysia, a few miles back up the Straits.

The *Pacific Aquarius* has been waiting for us for two days and we have not heard that it has had any security problems. I don't know that we would. Would they report the theft of some rope or paint or some "joggers" if they were waiting to pick up a cargo owned by this oil major? What would that tell you about their procedures?

The transshipment anchorage, however, has become safe for the Stolt Nielsen Company.

"We used to get boarded at Karimun frequently," said Brian Hoare, the captain of a Stolt chemical tanker who was attacked while in the loo. "We'd get fatalistic. Here we go, we'd say—another transit [through the Straits]. Part of our planning is the piracy factor."

The attacks on Stolt ships inexplicably stopped, a relief and a puzzlement to the masters. "When I asked the agent, he told me, 'Don't worry about it, Captain. It's being taken care of.' Rumor is that we are bribing the pirates—we're paying them off to leave us alone," Hoare said. Whether or not this is actually the case, paying protection money to pirates, especially when you are anchoring in their backyard, may be an effective way to avoid an attack. Eric Ellen, creator of the IMB, revealed that cruise ship companies also pay off not to get attacked. "It saves lives. It is cheaper in the long run." The U.S. Navy paid protection money to the North African states of the Barbary pirates in the eighteenth century; it should be no surprise that unarmed ships are doing the same today.

We are in a new neighborhood at sea; the shallower depths of the channel this close to Karimun have turned the water a coffee color. There is little wind, hardly enough to ripple the surface. Land lies on both sides, thunder squalls rest heavily on the Malaysian hills to the left and over the low-lying islands of Indonesia to the right. The channel these days is well outlined by markers, lights, and radar beacons. The last time I sailed through here the navigation aids, relics of the days of the old British Empire, were in a sorry state—lights extinguished, shifted positions—and one buoy was found on a beach. Things have changed in ten years; the nav aids have been up-graded or replaced by funds from the Nippon Foundation of Tokyo, a quasi-government charitable organization that has spent more than $100 million to beef up the navigational system. A good investment in light of Japan's commerce with Europe and the Middle East. But reliable nav aids don't guarantee security; during the past five years piracy in the Malacca Straits has cost Japanese industry close to $24 million.

The Straits here are crowded with fishing boats, *Prahaus* and sampans, coastal freighters and barges. The little barter trade boats, so small they sometimes don't show up on radar, chug across our path followed by a line of their smoky exhaust. From the bridge they are toy boats with flat cabin roofs and cargo holds strapped down tight with blue-and-white checkered tarpaulin. I think of those two indefatigable Indonesians that Jamal and his team stopped—tough but exhausted youths who routinely cross the lanes in front of giants like the *Montrose*, trusting that they won't get run over.

Just ahead is the notorious One Fathom Bank about halfway to Singapore, a section of the passage that has caused more than a few headaches. This is where many worry about pirates. This is where a VLCC must necessarily creep along. At the One Fathom Bank the sea bottom rises abruptly in the middle of the shipping lane over which hundreds of ships a day must pass. There is only room for one vessel through the mile-wide deepwater channel—a single-lane bridge. At night during a tropic downpour, when it is difficult to tell the difference on radar between clutter, rain clouds, small boats, and navigation buoys, passage through the slot is a challenge. Our draft, the depth of our ship under the water, is twenty-one meters. Under way, our "squat" adds another eighty centimeters—nearly three feet. A VLCC can not bump along a sandbar—this is the kind of thing that can break her despite her double bottom. We can cross over the sandbank only when the tide is high and our speed is low.

Captain Postma says he is doubling the pirate watch tonight. Our remaining hours will be in Indonesian waters, beyond the help of Jamal and his teams. The seas, protected by land on either side, are flat; not even the turbulence from our wake is more than disturbed water. All ideal conditions for an unwelcome boarding. Even during daylight many ships are taking no chances. Several ships fire their hoses outboard like that little red chemical carrier we passed earlier. Some of the hoses are aimed not out but down toward the water. This appears more effective than aimlessly firing into space; climbing up the hull would be like scaling a waterfall.

The conversation at dinner swings back to piracy. While this was a week or so before the terrorist attack on the U.S., Brian Ashdown does voice what many who serve upon these ships have long considered.

"What I can't understand is why terrorists haven't taken a VLCC and held it for ransom. Threaten to blow it up in Rotterdam. Or Houston or New York."

"Or English Channel. Or here in the Straits." Niko adds.

"If they want to get people to take notice, that's where they should do it, I would have thought. The environmental damage it could cause . . ."

"Then we get pirate bonus, I think."

". . . A few charges along the side of the hull. Wouldn't take a great deal more than that. . . ."

The talk is not as flippant as it seems. In June 2002, Moroccan authorities announced that they had broken up a plot by three Saudi nationals who were Al-Qaeda operatives preparing to attack U.S. and British ships in the Straits of Gibraltar with explosive-packed dinghies. Even before September 11 there were few who worked these ships unaware of the targets they presented to terrorists. Piracy is a threat because their vessels transit known pirate waters. However, not far removed is the knowledge that 300,000 tons of highly volatile cargo is also formidable political booty.

"I am afraid sometimes," Angela says, pointing to the big windows that face out onto the deck. "Look at them; could they stop a gun or even a sledge hammer? Once in the Straits, we were surrounded by some Indonesian patrol boats. They circled us and circled us—it was scary. You don't know who they are, really. You don't know what they want. I went back in and locked my door."

I have passed around a photo of one of the sleek speedboats Jamal and his crew captured from pirates near Karimun. The boat, so low to the water that from a distance it could be mistaken for a floating log, is painted black with a short dark-red deck; there is no windshield, no lights, no registration numbers, and no seats. Twin 200-horsepower engines are mounted on the back. Some tattered polystyrene mattresses that the pirates sat on are heaped in a discarded waterlogged pile inside the lethal little runabout. The boat is wood, nearly impossible to notice on radar.

"Don't think we could outrun it," Brian says.

⌒

We are in the thick of it now; eighty percent of the attacks on ships in the Malacca Straits occur between here and Singapore. At 2000 hours sharp our lights snapped on, our hoses fired into the night, and the bosun went from deck to deck, door to door, locking us down in the citadel. Generals Patton and MacArthur seemed to take on a somewhat menacing air—this ship means business. Except I would imagine that dolls are good for one pass only.

General MacArthur, especially in the dark, could fool me. At least from afar. The captain had ordered that whoever patrolled the deck should "look active, keep awake and walk around." Our Filipino bo- sun deserves an Oscar. I am admiring the lifelike dummy from a deck above when the bosun walks out of the shadows and joins the old sol- dier at the railing. The bosun, dressed in spanking white coveralls, hard hat, and a walkie-talkie strapped across his chest, throws his arm over the general's shoulder and, in the manner of one drunk leaning on another, starts talking. It is a real honest-to-God conversation. They gaze out into the dark, two old Filipino mates on the sauce; one seems to be saying, *Damn, ain't this beautiful—we sure got it made working on this here big beautiful ship, buddy. . . .* I wonder—is the bo- sun just following his instructions or has he started to lose his mind? Or has he been at sea too long? Or have I?

The captain will be on the bridge all night; his concern is not just pirates but navigation through the narrow channel. It is very black out there. A large container ship is bearing down on us. It apparently wants to pass. We are showing three vertical red lights on our mast, indicating that we are restricted in our ability to maneuver. The ship behind us switches on a red light, indicating he is carrying dangerous cargo. Severe little Wasim offers, "I'm thinking maybe he will be showing four lights. Then maybe we will be showing five. . . ." He will pass but he will have to come very close to us to do so, and in these waters it is a dicey maneuver.

One of the deck crew on his own initiative has added another fire hose and apparently, following the lead of the chemical carrier, the hose is aimed straight down the transom. I hope for the sake of the crew of the *Montrose* that after I am gone, and my tales of horror will not have dissolved into mere legend and rumor, that they continue to take the threat of piracy seriously.

As we pass abeam one of the islands off Karimun, the watch stander hurries out to the starboard bridgewing, turns on the big spotlight mounted at the far end, and sweeps over the surface. Leaving the light beaming down on the water, he returns and stands over the radar screen. "I had a small target, moving at eighteen knots. I lost it."

The captain radios the deck patrol. "Dumlao, this is the bridge, do you see anything?"

There is no response. "Dumlao, there is a small craft on the radar that is near us. Did you see something?"

"I see nothing, sir."

"Keep a sharp lookout, please. *God Verdaam het!* It is almost like wartime."

The chatter on the radio is getting irritating and rides over other traffic: An Indonesian is saying in his language that he is going south of some island, then adds conversationally in the same breath in English, "—and fuck you." Another responds in Indonesian that he will be happy to meet him there and in English "—and I fuck *you.*"

"No, man, I *fuck* you." They repeat this litany with different emphasis on the same line. It is both humorous and offensive.

Our ship weaves through sand barges and fishing boats yet maintains its designated course through the lanes. Captain Postma sits before one of the radar screens, his pale face complexioned by its orange and yellow lights. He whistles "Dixie" and taps his fingers to another beat. This, I have learned, means it is a nervous time. "Wasim, that ship off behind us; it wants to pass us, I think. Give me a couple of degrees to starboard and give him a little room." Then he adds, "Maybe there is a ship named the *Fuck You.* Then I could understand it."

~~~

Karimun

We were not vulnerable last night. It took until daylight for the *Pacific Aquarius* to raft up to the *Montrose*, and most of the crew was involved. The tide was changing when the tanker attempted to come alongside. As the tide turned, *Montrose* at anchor swung with it, making it difficult and dangerous to tie up. The activity aboard both ships would have been evident to anyone who was thinking about sneaking aboard.

Brian says that just before dawn, however, a small boat circled the ships and then hovered off our stern. "I turned the bridgewing light on them. They didn't seem to like that too much. Can't think of what they were doing there hanging off us—don't think they were up to any good. They went away eventually. But I am beginning to see what they say about this place."

Pulau Karimun rises out of the morning haze with monolithic defiance. It is a big island, takes up nearly the entire horizon. Rugged volcanic hills in the north fronting the Straits slope gradually toward the island's main town of Tanjung Balai. Like the island of Ocracoke that provided safe haven for Blackbeard and his gangs, Karimun is one of the centers of piracy in the Straits. And like Ocracoke the activities on Karimun are also beyond the reach of the law.

In a small village too insignificant to warrant a mark on most maps, not far from Balai, there is a whitewashed cement two-story house, quite common in this region, with a sundry shop located on the ground floor. The shop is a popular place that offers warm soft drinks, hammered tin pots, machetes, prayer rugs, detergents, instant coffee, and tinned milk. The top floor of the house is the family home of a man I'll call Bhudi Sunil, a wealthy local entrepreneur. It is also the operations center of one of the area's most notorious criminal gangs.

Downstairs behind the shop is a large open room with a cement floor that at times is home to as many as fifty people. Fifty people crammed into a room where they sleep, eat, and live waiting for a boat to smuggle them to Malaysia. The illegals are indentured to Bhudi; those without contact on the Malaysian side have to pay him up front for passage to the Promised Land. Those who haven't enough money work for Bhudi. Some of the men join the ORBAT of the Malacca Straits pirates. Their women are farmed out as household help on the island; the younger ones are ferried to Batam, the large tourist island to the east, where they serve as prostitutes for weekending Singapore businessmen.

Bhudi is one of the movers and shakers on Karimun; he is said to influence much of the commerce on the island, which includes banking, construction, and even shipping agents, one of whom might have told Captain Hoare that the piracy situation in the island's transshipment anchorage, for him at least, had been taken care of. It is Bhudi's organization that purchased those screaming three-liter engines to outrun the police and that was teaming up with the rogue military units. Blackbeard was captured and beheaded after a bounty of £100 sterling was put on his head. It will take a lot more than that to bring down Bhudi Sunil.

General Patton continues to get raves. Two young fishermen inside a small motor canoe off our stern are shouting at our cataleptic guardian. It appears they are trying to sell him some fish. I cannot imagine what the general looks like to them from down there. It is apparent that from far below they do not understand our crewman's fixed silence. Can't they see he is only a doll? The general, with his rigid Raggedy Ann smile, has become the object of their increasing frustration. The youth steering the outboard now appears to be shouting obscenities. He reaches for a stick in the bottom of the boat and shakes it threateningly. His companion has just dropped his shorts and is mooning him! He turns to his companion and shares a laugh at the poor general's expense, and with a Parthian volley of derision they motor away. I suppose that now word will get out that the big tanker out in the anchorage is crewed by a bunch of dummies.

A liquid natural gas carrier, anchored not far astern of us, still has its hoses firing out over the side. I wonder if the master of that vessel forgot to turn off his pressure water. Perhaps not. While the threat of piracy here at anchor is perhaps even greater than under way, it is still daylight. Yet, it is in this anchorage that so many assaults have been recorded; and Bhudi Sunil and his gang are just on the other side of those hills.

The chances are random that we would get boarded. A dozen ships are anchored here; a VLCC a few miles closer to the island is also discharging into another ship. Pirates have any number of vessels to choose from. The softest targets are those without obvious defenses in place, those with a lower freeboard, and those sitting out alone distant from other vessels. Are these little motorized canoes that circle us, then speed away to circle another ship, casing the anchorage? Perhaps they only hope to sell some fish.

It is natural to develop a sense of complacency when the passage is over. Land offers a false sense of security. It is a misconception that many sailors have; when a storm approaches, it is natural to seek shelter in a harbor, when in fact far offshore in a well-founded craft is often the safest place to be. In piracy the misanthropic have the right idea; it is safer far out at sea.

This attraction to land and the complacency it breeds invites trouble, especially in a place like this. Some ships neglect to turn on their hoses; many hatches, lockers, stores, and entranceways are left unlocked. Some even forget to raise their gangplanks after the pilot has disembarked, offering easy access to pirates or stowaways. Pirates have learned from history that a ship at anchor or in port is at its lowest state of alert.

One day antipiracy measures will be taken as routine. One day this captain and all masters on ships at sea, at anchor or in port, will regard a proper defense not as another nettlesome chore but as normal and as critical as every other safety measure.

Because of the extended rafting maneuvers the threat of piracy was not a concern to us last night; up to the point of tying up alongside the other ship, the *Montrose* had taken all the necessary precautions: lights, hoses, and deck patrol. Yet being rafted to another ship is also no guarantee of safety. If there is an attack, those on the *Pacific Aquarius* could not help us, nor could we help them. The vessels are separated by twenty-foot-wide Yokohama fenders. There is no way to jump across to help, no ladder from one ship to the other, no bridge. We are as vulnerable rafted together as if each ship were swinging on its hook out in the anchorage alone.

We should add a few precautions to our defenses tonight: the hawse pipes through which the anchor chain is passed will be covered, the gangway lashed well above the water, in addition to the standard antipirate routine.

It is well past 2000 hours and there are no antipirate precautions; none of the hoses is turned on; I walk to the bow and find no hawse covers to stop anyone from climbing up the anchor chain and in; no one patrols the sunken deck and no one has secured any of the outside doors. The captain's night orders, the official directions from the captain to the officers on the night watch, do not include instructions for a piracy watch; indeed, thumbing through the pages of previous voyages to and from Singapore over the past six months I find only one mention of maintaining nighttime piracy defenses, and that was during an approach to the northern entrance of the Straits. Three days ago. Evidently antipiracy measures are not yet commonplace aboard the *Montrose*. It does not mean that this captain has not taken antipiracy precautions in the past, but night orders are usually a definitive indication of the way a master wants his ship run when he is normally asleep. Tonight the ship is open, unprotected, and vulnerable. It seems as wise as leaving your car unlocked.

14

Dangerous Waters

Phillip Channel

We are on the home stretch. Our Omani Light Crude is aboard the *Pacific Aquarius* en route to the Malaysian refinery. It is near nighttime. We have weighed anchor and are carving a slow, wide circle away from Karimun to weave into the procession of vessels in the shipping lane. It looks like it might be difficult; the haze and smoke prevent us from seeing more than a couple ships in the column. Yet the conditions don't make much difference; in thick smoke, in the dark, during a tropic downpour, keeping a visual on the traffic is not very important. It is the big radar that gives us the information we need to make our move. We roll the trackball on the console and direct the cursor over a target, push a button, and the other ship's bearing, course, speed, distance from us, and its ETA to where we want to enter the channel is superimposed on the screen. The bridge windows could be painted black and we could see most of what is out there.

We duck into the main channel, taking position behind a fast-moving cruise ship garishly lit with festive multicolored bulbs. Some of the passengers line the railings and take videos of the *Montrose;* this is about as close as they will ever get to a machine this size.

There is only moderate traffic so far, no rain, no wind, and a dog moon of useless light overhead. The glow of Singapore City looms across the eastern horizon behind the twinkling lamps of refinery towers. An airplane snaps on its landing lights as it enters the final approach to Changi International Airport. I feel the familiar excitement of arrival, of returning to land. I have spent much of my adult life at sea, on fishing boats, merchant ships, even tugboats. I sailed away from San Francisco in 1983 on the *Unicorn* and kept going for seventeen years. I prefer the sea to land. Yet even for an eremitic waterborne vagrant there is the undeniable attraction to land and people. Bernard Moitissier, the famous solo yachtsmen, was in a single-handed race around the world, and when he reached the finishing line he didn't stop—just kept on going. I can understand. Arriving at a port after a long ocean passage is bittersweet. You can't wait to get there, and yet you fear your arrival. On a sailboat at least, six months at sea alone, even thirty days without seeing another human being, is for some of us enough to wonder why we have to stop.

This final leg to Singapore, a distance of about six hours, is the most difficult of the passage. This is the beginning of the Phillip Channel, the narrow, heavily trafficked entrance. A smaller tanker, low in the water, passes us, and like others her deck is brightly lighted and her hoses are firing. We, on the other hand, are not taking such precautions. We have this attitude—we are on the home stretch, we are a little higher out of the water after discharging a third of our cargo, it is still before midnight, and the possibilities of attack, especially with so many ships nearby, are very slight. There is a certain admissible arrogance. We are one of the biggest ships in the world and we are transporting crude for the world's second-largest oil company. Who would dare?

A ship on our starboard is bearing down from behind, intending to pass. It seems a wrong time and place to do so. We are plodding down the channel at a doddering pace and this ship is coming on at 14.6 knots according to our radar, faster than is permitted in these waters. There is no communication between the captains of the two vessels.

"I think we will give him a little room. He seems to be in a hurry," Captain Postma says. He orders a course change that aligns us along the northern side of the deepwater route. From out on the bridge-wing the overtaking vessel is a large dark hulk that gets closer, grows bigger.

Our adjusted course puts us close to the clutter of reef and rock of Pulau Takong Kecil, just outside the channel. A small flashing light on a buoy far below, just this side of the rocks, marks the edge of the shipping lane. I could hit it with a baseball. The rocks of the little island, silhouetted in black against the night, and which have claimed not just a few ships, seem very close. The ship overtaking us passes on the other side of the midchannel marker; there is not a lot of room here. Indeed, the distance between the two buoys through which we pass is about three tenths of a mile. I'm not sure how comfortable I would be squeezing through here even on a smaller ship at night. It is not difficult to understand why there are so many accidents on this stretch.

We are passing 01:05.7N–103:44.00E, the precise spot just off Pulau Takong Kecil where the *Chaumont* was attacked. The night is humid and sticky and as I watch the passing ships, the shore lights in the distance, the blinking and flashing navigational aids, I imagine the terror the crew must have felt when they realized that their ship was barreling down these choked waters with no one at the wheel. What I cannot imagine is how it could have threaded these narrow waters without hitting anything.

More pressing is how ships the size of the *Chaumont* and the *Montrose* can be boarded. It still seems improbable. The *Chaumont* was even bigger than we are. We carry 345,040.8 cubic meters in our cargo and slop tanks. The *Chaumont* carried two thousand cubic meters more. We are 332 meters long overall, the *Chaumont* six meters longer than that. If pirates could board the *Chaumont*, there is no reason to think that they could not board us.

Before I had joined the *Montrose* in the Persian Gulf, I wanted to find out how a bunch of barefooted armed pirates could board a ship our size under way, so I looked up some experts.

A British-American company that specializes in teaching maritime counterterrorism methods to foreign armed forces and police SWAT teams was based in Dubai. Run by retired commandos from the U.S. Special Forces and the British Special Air Service Regiment, BritAm Defense Ltd. had an impressive list of credentials: It had trained the armed forces of the United Arab Emirates and had just completed training the Singapore marine police in the latest antiterrorism, antipiracy techniques.

With attacks by pirates and hostage-taking increasing in Malacca Straits, Singapore was concerned that terrorists and pirates would one day take over one of the many cruise ships, passenger ferries, and VLCCs that operate out of its harbors. It contracted BritAm to upgrade its land and sea commando teams of the Special Tactics and Rescue Unit to make sure this would never occur.

BritAm's compact disc of the training of the STAR force is dramatic. Men in gray battle gear, helmets, flak jackets, snub-nosed assault rifles, gas masks dangling from their belts, scale the vertical wall of a ship in minutes. They make it look easy.

"You see it can be done. That is how the pirates do it. We have taken a page from their book. VLCC, cruise ship, passenger ferry—there is not a ship afloat that cannot be boarded. No matter how big, no matter how protected."

The speaker is not a grizzled, steely-eyed soldier of fortune but a lanky, middle-aged English businessman with a public-school manner and graying temples. Phil Doughty is an ex–SAS commando with a list of engagements that would be a credit to any combat veteran: Falklands, Northern Ireland, the Gulf War. He conceived BritAm Defense after training the UAE commando units in counterterrorism. It was there he met Scott Chapel, of Abilene, Texas, a former captain with the U.S. 5th Special Forces Group. Together they teamed up to create the commando training company, and while they have been called out on operations, they prefer to tap into the network of American and British special forces and concentrate on combating terrorism at sea.

Phil speaks of the tools of his trade—the Heckler & Koch 53 lays down good suppressing fire; the snub-nosed M5, a close-quarters submachine gun, is the weapon of choice; the M16 is a good all-round rifle; PE-4 is best for explosive method of entry—as a mechanic might discuss his Snap-on wrenches.

"Basically the only difference between terrorists and pirates is the motivation. Terrorists attack for political purposes; pirates attack for robbery. Taking back a ship from terrorists and pirates is the same," Doughty says.

BritAm taught the Singapore SWAT teams to board ships using pirates' own tried and proven techniques, with a little modern technology thrown in. There is the Plumett system, a shoulder-fired grappling hook with a line connected to a nylon ladder, ideal, Phil says, for scurrying up the side of a ship. And there is a series of four small, powerful magnets that a commando uses to walk up a hull: "Rather Batman-like, but effective."

One method is taken from the book of modern piracy: a long titanium pole with a grappling hook on the end, extendable to thirty-five feet. However, a length of stout bamboo, says Doughty, is just as good for boarding all but the loftiest hulls. It is what pirates use and, he says, it is a lot simpler—no moving parts. And considerably cheaper. The titanium pole costs in the neighborhood of $30,000. Doughty admits, however, that few can match the skill and agility of those half-naked local Asian boys with knives clenched in their teeth who have spent so much of their lives climbing coconut trees.

Phil Doughty is concerned that the shipping industry is not taking piracy and maritime terrorism seriously. "Hijacking airplanes now is so expected; it is so difficult to do. Terrorists are going to choose more vulnerable targets than airplanes. It is just a matter of time before they terrorize a cruise ship or take over a big crude oil carrier. And at the end of the day," he says, "a well-trained team can get aboard a VLCC that is under way within minutes. It is not difficult at all," he says.

As we pass the position where pirates scaled and took over the *Chaumont*, and keeping in mind that our sunken deck is so low to the water, I realize BritAm wouldn't need one of their space-age titanium poles to scale this ship. Just one of the many bamboo sticks found washed up on a local a beach would do it.

"VTIS West, this is the *Montrose*," Wasim announces on the radio. "Now I am shifting to VTIS Central and I will be having pilot shortly."

"Okay, *Montrose*, that's fine. Go VHF 14. Thank you and good night."

Wasim switches frequencies. "VTIS Central, this is Mike Juliet Romeo November Two VLCC *Montrose* calling."

"*Montrose*, good evening, sir."

"Yes, good evening. We have entered VTIS Central and I will be calling pilot and taking to Bukom."

"Roger, *Montrose*. Thank you. Stand by this channel 14 and keep me informed when pilot is on board. Over."

"Okay. Standby 14."

We are approaching the Southern Boarding Ground, where we will pick up the pilot to guide us to the Bukom refinery. The traffic is thicker here; not just merchant ships in opposing lines but crossing traffic of sand barges, fishing boats, warships, tugboats, ferries, and anything else that floats. Our peremptory attitude is not founded on vainglory. We are special and we get the treatment. We cannot move far out of anyone's way when the channel is this narrow. The rules of the road are specific: All others are the burdened vessels when we are restricted in our ability to maneuver. In these waters we are on a straight track. This is where Dave Betts predicts he will be scraping out the bodies from a pirated VLCC. "It's the most dangerous stretch in the Straits," he says. Eight out of ten accidents occur within a couple miles of here.

According to Betts the *Star Aquarius* plowed into the VLCC *Stresa* just a few miles down the channel. The tanker was making its way through the deepwater Traffic Separation Scheme. The rocks of Batu Berhanti were close by on her starboard and oncoming traffic to her port. She was hemmed in, had no room to maneuver, and could not avoid the passenger ship that charged at her from the left. She was trapped. The Vessel Traffic Information Service warns all ships that a VLCC is in the channel and they are advised to give way. The *Star Aquarius* apparently did not, though the captain may have a different explanation.

Captain Postma taps his fingers and whistles quietly, but he is in control and despite the recognizable signs, there is little question of his competence. Nevertheless, you do feel that you are riding by the seat of your pants.

"Starboard five," he orders.

Wasim, who has just relieved the Filipino bosun, repeats the order.

I am struck by an outrageously perverse thought. I have been investigating the potential of an attack by pirates, of an attack that would cause a catastrophe. On the bridge this night I realize suddenly that if some suicidal nutcase were at the helm and wanted to cause holy hell in these waters, to close the Straits for his moment of glory, then it would be done right here. It would be so easy to do. It would take no more than a nudge, a slight turn of the wheel, to put this thing and its precious crude oil onto the rocks; a slight course change minutes before Takong Kecil and we'd be on top of them; or a sudden turn of the wheel and we would wrap around them in seconds. If I were at the helm, I could do worse; I could steer this ship into another, into that container ship coming toward us in the opposite lane. Or another VLCC with a crazy at the helm—in ballast quite like a floating bomb because of the explosive gases still within its tanks—could be driven into us.

A small launch motors up to the lowered gangway, and minutes later a figure in white emerges on the steps from below and makes his way down the deck toward the accommodation block.

"VTIS, VTIS, this is the *Montrose*. We have the pilot on board."

"*Montrose*, VTIS. Thank you. Please be informed that there is a container ship, the *Singapore Bay*, coming from the east currently bearing from you zero four five degrees, three decimal nine nautical miles, approximate speed one-one knots—the *Singapore Bay*, over."

The captain responds. "Yes, we see him, thank you."

"Are you going to cross his bow?"

"We will go around his stern, thank you."

"Okay, *Montrose*. *Singapore Bay*? *Singapore Bay*?"

"VTIS, this is *Singapore Bay*. I copy that. The VLCC is going to cross my stern."

The pilot enters the lighted chartroom behind the bridge; he is a big man, a Singapore Indian, clad in a white safari jacket, white slacks, white shoes, and white gloves, carrying a black computer bag. He has a great white Tartar mustache and goatee, and curly silver hair rests upon his shoulders. He looks like he should be sweeping down the Khyber Pass on horseback, swinging a saber.

On the darkened bridge he begins directing the flight across the busy shipping lane.

"All stop!" His hand flies up with the conviction of a baseball umpire calling a runner out at the plate; we are slowing down to let the container ship pass.

"Port ten," he says, throwing his hand out to the left. He has flair.

"Aye, port ten, sir."

We start the crossing just before the *Singapore Bay* is abreast of us, aiming at its midships. Another unidentified vessel appears from behind the *Singapore Bay* and seems intent on passing the container ship. On the radar it is going 14.2 knots, breaking the speed limit.

"It should be no problem," the captain says lightly to no one in particular. When he speaks lightly it means he is very aware. These are tense moments; we are cutting across the shipping lanes, across oncoming traffic; it takes about twenty tensed-up minutes to cross this freeway to the Southern Boarding Ground.

The Bukom oil refinery, our final destination and the end of this section of the petroleum conveyor, lies just off the starboard bow. Burning gases flare out of long, narrow stacks, bright white lights by the hundreds outline vertical and horizontal pipes, towers, and storage tanks. Futuristic skyscrapers of the city poke out of an orange gloom from behind the island refinery. We nose up to the SBM, the tugboats take our lines and secure us to the mooring, the captain throws the telegraph into full stop, and the voyage is completed.

"So." He turns to me, grins, and disappears below.

Within a couple of hours we are pumping the Saudi Arab Light and the Iranian Straight Run Fuel Oil into the floating pipelines that run to the tank farm ashore. It was here at this mooring that pirates attacked the *Litopia*. Such an event could not happen tonight. A Singapore police boat motors by, lit up by the reflection of the halogen lights of our cargo deck. An unsheathed general purpose machine gun is mounted on its foredeck. It took only one incident against a

VLCC years ago to guarantee that here, at least, it would never happen again.

The discharge of the crude will take about twenty-four hours and then the *Montrose*, with its water ballast tanks full of seawater and cargo tanks empty of crude, will turn back to the Persian Gulf for a refill.

———

The parting with the captain is a little stiff. At sea—even on a ship this size—you are part of a tight little community. Twenty-two people is not a large crowd, no bigger than a cocktail party. Then you sign off and it's over. Gerrit hands me a bottle of fine Filipino dark rum, a farewell gesture that is well appreciated, and I collect my gear and head down to the cargo deck. Standing atop the gangway steps, looking down from this nearly empty ship and now so much higher off the water, I feel like a ski jumper staring down the chute; the way down is steep and long.

On the launch below I pause and look up the sheer steel wall of this ship now disgorging the last of its crude. There is a tiny figure looking down over the tip of the bridgewing. He is too far away to identify positively, but I'm pretty sure it's the captain who tosses a final little wave.

Wasim and Zamir sit together on the outside seat on the fantail of the agency's smoky launch as it motors across the harbor into town; they speak quietly about their plans for their day of shore leave; some of the Filipino crew sit next to them, laughing, excited about their time off; every one is pretty well scrubbed up—for some it is the first time ashore in two or three months. Brian and Angie, the captain, and Viktor, the chief officer, never get off; discharging the crude oil is their responsibility.

Big Niko was one of the lucky few, and he says he is going to buy a small television for his cabin and knock back a few cheap beers at People's Park. It is Friday and the Pakistanis say they are going to do some shopping after prayers at a mosque. The Filipinos say they will shop, drink a few beers, and sight-see, happy to be off the ship.

The launch winds through the ships at Western Petroleum Anchorage, past smaller tankers waiting for a berth at the refineries or waiting for a delivery contract. Behind us the *Montrose* is no more than a thick black scar that rests upon the horizon in the distance.

"Look!" Niko says suddenly, raising his fist victoriously. "You see, no pirate! Still got watch. Hey, maybe on way back, who knows?"

15

Ghost Ships of the High Seas

Kuala Lumpur

There are different ways to stop pirates. One is Jamal's method: just blow 'em out of the water. Another is more sophisticated but no less effective: organize an intelligence network that gets deep into the boardrooms of organized crime, follow the planning of a hijack, and then ambush the pirates red-handed on the ship they are stealing. It is a toss-up which is more dangerous; risking your life in a firefight or half expecting that someone has planted a bomb in your car.

"I warn my informants that if anything happens to me, if they kill me, someone else is going to take my place. I think this gets back to the syndicates." Captain Noel Choong, director of the IMB's Piracy Reporting Center in Kuala Lumpur, doesn't hide what he does. Except to his mother, who still doesn't know how her son earns a living and certainly doesn't know that there probably is a price on his head.

I have flown up the Straits to Kuala Lumpur, the capital of Malaysia, to see firsthand the progress in the war against piracy. It is in Noel's offices that news of attacks on ships is first received—frequently as the attacks are taking place, the ships are being taken over, the crews are being beaten, the ship's safe is being looted, or worse, as a ship is being hijacked.

Noel and I are sitting over a spread of dim sum served in a classy Chinese restaurant near his office. Noel hasn't chosen a table with his back against the wall, but with what he knows, perhaps he should have. The plaited bamboo pots of shrimp and fish balls, braised duck, sticky rice, chicken feet, and a cold Tiger beer lie enticingly in front of us; for the moment they go untouched. "I am nervous every time I meet one of these informants," he says.

Noel has a stunning record of catching pirates and retrieving hijacked ships. In the past twelve months he has been involved with the capture of nine out of ten ships; nine ships that the crime bosses, with cunning and meticulous precision, had their pirates hijack. If the organizations had counted on the sale of the stolen cargo from these ships and the subsequent use of the ships to meet their annual budgetary projections, then their expected revenue for the year from this branch of the business was disappointingly low.

A handsome, well-spoken Chinese Malay with long coal-black hair, Noel has an energetic, youthful manner and a disarming air of fatalism. But I look at Noel, who I have known for some time, with quiet incredulity and unconcealed admiration. How can he not fear for his life? He hides it very well.

Noel is proud of his record, but he does admit that he is cautious. Noel never permits his face or those of his staff to be captured on film, not by television cameras or by any photographer; he did appear in the Videotel antipiracy training film, but the features of his face had been rubbed out. He does change his route into work. But not often.

The syndicates, he admits, know who he is, know what he does. But he is something like a policeman; he tells the gangs that there is always another one behind him ready to do his job. "If the syndicates want to kill me, they can easily enough," he says. "They could plant a bomb outside my office door or set up a meeting like I have with my informants. There is nothing I can do."

He jokes that he has never been directly threatened, probably because his phones have been too busy. But the threat has been implied a number of times. Recently one of his informants boasted that he could have anyone killed for $500 and asked Noel if he had any candidates.

He stares at his chopsticks for a moment, then looks up. "To think you can end a life for five hundred dollars. I think he wanted to scare me. And he did."

While Noel does occasionally look over his shoulder, he gives the impression that he is impervious to danger. Perhaps it is because the International Maritime Bureau for which he works is part of the influential Paris-based International Chamber of Commerce, or because his work is mandated by the United Nations. Perhaps it is because he is on the side of Right.

Noel is one of the crime syndicates' greatest headaches. Organized crime bosses, with offices on most continents, work with impunity with the connivance and cooperation of top government officials. They buy the complicity of navies, government ministers, port, customs, and immigration officials, agents, bankers, and even shipowners. No one can buy Noel Choong.

Noel owes his success to his well-developed and complex network of informants. He persuades his sources, many of whom are connected by blood or marriage to crime bosses, corrupt government officials, and even to royal families, that his need-to-know is strictly limited. He wants no details of the organizations for whom they work, he wants no names of their leaders, no information about their other activities such as running drugs or smuggling illegal immigrants. While some may fear he is a walking *Who's Who* of the crime world, Noel tells his informants he wants only to know where the pirates are taking a specific hijacked ship, where it is at the moment, and where it will be in about twelve hours time. He is stirring the pot enough without getting involved in their other criminal activities. "It is not my concern. Any of that other information is in the safe in the office. It will never be known." Keeping the information under lock and key may keep him from getting killed.

"I don't have the authority to make arrests, to go after the syndicates. I just hunt pirated ships. The police make the arrests."

In his mid-forties, Noel could be mistaken for being many years younger; he is a modest, self-effacing man, a dedicated, churchgoing Catholic who doesn't drink and doesn't smoke. A former master of oil tankers, he has traded his epaulettes for a blue business suit, white shirt, and tie. He gives the impression he is just doing a job.

Officially his Piracy Reporting Center, the industry's early warning system, was created to alert ships at sea to the most recent attacks through the daily situation reports. While ships are not able to avoid piracy areas, their crews are at least warned of high-risk areas in advance.

His office is on the thirty-fifth floor of a central Kuala Lumpur office building with a view through the smog of the bristly Petronas Twin Towers, the world's tallest buildings. It is not far from the American embassy, where one visiting U.S. military official remarked that from here, it would be no big deal to lob a shell into the embassy compound—it seems people are always looking over their shoulders these days. It is a small office, filled with computers and radios and the lone safe stuck in a nook in the back by the office storeroom. He has no secretary, no assistant, he answers the phone himself, writes all his correspondence, and, despite the impassive Chinese face, admits he is very tired. The wall of the reception area is covered with maps of the world; red pins mark the year's history of reported pirate attacks. A tall dead acacia tree in a ceramic pot, its lifeless leaves a symbol perhaps of the futility of his one-man fight to stop piracy, stands next to the wall.

When Noel gets a call that a vessel has gone missing, presumably hijacked, he asks the ship's owners and underwriters if they are willing to put up a reward for its recovery. They usually agree to a price of about $100,000 to $200,000. If the ship is carrying $2.5 million in diesel fuel, then a couple hundred thousand for the return of cargo, ship, and—if not already dead—the crew, is worth it. Sadly, this is the priority of retrieval: cargo, ship, and the crew; if the seafarers aren't Western they are seldom a high priority for underwriter or shipowner. In the Philippines a shipowner pays up to $50,000 to the family of a seafarer killed during a pirate attack. And the book is closed. It is cheaper than keeping a ship in port for weeks while local authorities, prodded by a seaman's family, investigate the crime.

In one instance, during the early days of the Piracy Reporting Center, reward money was posted, and through Noel's efforts a ship was recovered. The insurance company, however, thought that Noel had paid too much and it reneged. Noel found himself with a near empty bag frantically scratching for the rest of the reward money. Had he not paid the informant what he had promised—and that was below the official reward offered—he would have been murdered. Never again. "Once I say I agree with the amount I negotiated, then I have to pay it. If they don't pay it, then the IMB has to pay. Today we get the money deposited up front so I'm not afraid to negotiate. I always keep my word and my informants trust me. If I don't—well, that could get me killed. Why should I risk my life?"

Noel calls his informants on their mobile phones in Bangkok, Ho Chi Minh City, Hong Kong, Manila, Singapore, Jakarta, and down the street here in K-L. First he gets their attention, says a reward is offered. Then he gives them the name of the ship and its registry, the destination, and the cargo aboard. And he waits. Within hours someone usually calls and wants to get together.

"I try to avoid meeting them, but sometimes they say they won't deal unless they meet me personally. The reward is a lot of money and they know we are going to negotiate. They want to meet me face-to-face—they don't want to talk about it over the telephone. I know that if a syndicate wants to kill me, it would set up a meeting like that."

Noel says it is always the same, whether over the telephone or in person: head-butting negotiation.

An informant called recently, told him he knew the location of a pirated ship and that he would meet him in Bangkok to discuss the details. Bangkok is a two-hour flight from Kuala Lumpur. It was the last place he wanted to go; nowhere would be more vulnerable. "Then I was really afraid."

The informant wouldn't budge. Noel agreed but insisted they meet at the airport hotel. It could not have been better suited for the purpose. The main arrivals terminal is connected to the lobby of the five-star Amari Hotel by a long covered walkway over the highway to Bangkok City. Noel took a seat in the cockpit lounge, drank his mango-and-papaya-juice mix, and waited. A middle-aged Thai, with his slinky girlfriend in tow, pulled up a chair and ordered a setup of ice and a half bottle of Sang Thip, the local hooch. The negotiations for the information that would lead to the recovery of the stolen ship, the cargo, and the lives of two dozen men were under way.

"The girl was very pretty. She said nothing, she just stared at the wall. I kept looking at her. He was saying he expected the entire hundred-thousand-dollar reward," Noel recalls.

The girl was compelling, like a statue, he says. Never moved, just kept staring at something across the room. He laughs at the memory. "I kept looking at the girl, but I was thinking—*I have to pay this person something. I think he really does know where the ship is.*

"It is like I'm buying fruit at the market. Do I want to pay a hundred thousand dollars for this fruit? This fruit really is not very ripe and it is not very sweet. No, maybe the information is worth only thirty thousand." In the Asian practice of dickering you offer the lowest, they counter with the highest, and you meet somewhere in the middle. Both of you save face, very important in this part of the world.

"An informant gives me the information, I check it out. If the ship is found where I was told it is and it is arrested, I deposit the money in his bank account. If the ship is not where he said it was, he gets nothing." There are variations; if the ship is found in the general area and it is arrested, he will show good faith and pay something; his sources are too important lock out.

Noel took the Bangkok information to the Chinese authorities, who captured the ship just where he said it was, anchored off the Dangan Islands in the South China Sea. The vessel had been given a new name, a new paint job, and a bogus new registration.

His informant set up an account under a false name ironically in one of the Asian banks influenced by the syndicate itself. Noel deposited $100,000. "The account was not in his real name, of course, and the account was closed after the money was deposited. How he did it is not my concern. We had the ship." His informant was now a very rich man. If he lived.

"Some disappear—they have made big money." Noel, pauses, shakes his head sadly. "But I think that man was murdered. I am not sure but that is what I heard."

The *Inabukwa* was transporting tin ingots, zinc, and white pepper when it was hijacked in the South China Sea in the spring of 2001. The ship was worth less than $100,000. Its cargo was valued at $2.1 million. Pirates wearing balaclavas and armed with pistols and parangs, stormed the ship, forced the captain and the twenty-two crew into a speedboat, motored through the night, then ordered the crew to jump overboard. The captain, bound and blindfolded, was convinced he was being thrown to the sharks. When he felt sharp pains in the soles of his bare feet, he knew he was standing on a coral reef. It was still dark when they managed to untie their hands and remove their blindfolds; with water up to their chests somewhere in the South China Sea, they dared not move. At first light they discovered they were within yards of a deserted island. Two days later the crew was found by fishermen, dehydrated and hungry.

"The *Inabukwa* was our fastest catch—four days after we issued the alert, the ship and the pirates were caught," Noel says proudly. But it was not without some sleuthing on his part. An informant who had proven reliable in the past told him the stolen vessel was being taken to Vietnam. He believed it was solid information because the informant provided details that Noel had withheld—the number of crew aboard and the names of the crewmen. "The information seemed legitimate, of high quality. But it was a wild goose chase. We were being fed false information by the syndicates."

While authorities scoured the Vietnamese coast searching for the hijacked ship, another informant, less well tuned in, told Noel he had heard that the ship was being taken to the Philippines. Noel alerted the Philippine coast guard and within hours they found a ship called the M/V *Chugsin* matching the description of the *Inabukwa* in the northern port of Salumagi, a remote town in Ilocos Sur province known to be a favorite place for smugglers to land with motorcycles and electronic goods. The vessel's new name had been hastily splashed over the original embossed on the hull. The syndicates had arranged for the cargo to be off-loaded into another ship and it apparently had been standing by for the transfer, but, according to Noel, the bungling pirates either didn't know how to open the hatches of the cargo holds or had jammed them. Desperate, they brought the ship into Salumagi and went ashore looking for some tools to open the hatches. The Filipino coast guard surrounded the ship and notified the IMB. The saga didn't end there. The cargo was so valuable, and the crime connections within the Philippines so secure, that another group of thugs tried to break the ship out of custody. The attempt was thwarted by Philippine navy SEALS.

The owner of the cargo had offered a reward of $50,000 for information leading to the recovery of the cargo.

Noel paid the Philippine government $40,000 for its role in the capture of the vessel ("I wanted to establish a relationship with the Philippine coast guard for the future"). The informant who had heard the ship was bound for the Philippines received $10,000. "Still the cargo, the information, and the capture was worth a lot more," he says.

Noel took a quick trip to the Philippines on behalf of the owners. "I saw the ship; there was a lot of damage, as if the pirates had ransacked it." The captain, Ade Sumarlin, claimed he was not involved, that he was just hired to deliver the ship. Noel knew this was a load of rubbish, that no captain would permit his ship to sail in such a wretched condition. "But it is not my job to interfere like that; if I press too hard, they'll come for me." Noel took photographs of the hijackers. Sumarlin is a heavyset, baby-faced Indonesian in tattered blue T-shirt and jeans; he doesn't look like a pirate, but few of them do. No one wears eye patches and walks on peg legs these days. The others are a hard-looking lot; the "cook" is a tough, pockmarked youngster with stringy black hair past his shoulders; another of the gang wears a long-sleeved shirt cut out of an American flag; the other kampung boys each looks like he needs a hot bath and a solid meal. The pirates, Noel says, stared him down with such hatred, such malice, such threat, that he will be haunted for some time to come. It was one of the times Noel asked himself whether risking his life was worth it.

The pirates were extradited to Indonesia but unless convicted, which is unlikely, they probably will be back at sea within the next few months, working for the same syndicate. "I don't think I'll be going to Jakarta in the near future. I can't forget those eyes." Noel says.

"I hope my informants get the message," he repeats, "if anything happens to me, there is going to be another one to do my job. Hopefully the syndicate won't destroy our office, put a bomb here."

~

While there are few seas worldwide where pirates don't operate, ship hijacking occurs most frequently in waters from the Bay of Bengal to the Pacific Ocean. Ships are not just passing targets of opportunity for rapine gangs, barefoot and poverty stricken, but, like the *Inabukwa*, targets of well-planned operations. At sea slow-moving merchant vessels, the lowest hanging fruit of world commerce, are ripe for the picking. Pirates working for organized crime strike in these international waters and often with impunity.

A ship is hijacked primarily for its cargo. Syndicates look for vessels carrying high-value commodities such as refined palm oil, kerosene and diesel fuel, rubber, steel, copper and aluminum concentrates, goods easily sold on the black market. They send their gangs out to hijack it, sell the original cargo, then use this phantom ship to run drugs or smuggle immigrants, or for cargo scams. In the latter an organization locates a shipper who is in a hurry to move his goods and who has a letter of credit about to expire; the stolen ship loads his cargo and then vanishes, sailing to a different port under another name, where it sells the cargo. After pulling off the heist the phantom ship again changes identities and goes to another port to find another cargo to steal.

Organized crime syndicates, with bases throughout Asia, North America, and Europe, operate with the efficiency of any multinational corporation. Many of their enterprises are legitimate and form a cover for drug running, cargo theft, immigrant smuggling, and hijackings. Some investigating officials are convinced that money from these activities has funneled down to various militant organizations in the region, including the Abu Sayaf in the Philippines, and to GAM, the fundamentalist separatist movement on Sumatra, and to the Jamaah Islamiah in Malaysia.[41]

Four loosely connected multinational crime organizations control four areas: The Singapore syndicate controls the southern part of the South China Sea and Malacca Straits; Bangkok controls the An-

daman Sea, bordered by Thailand, Burma, and Malaysia; triads in
Hong Kong control the northern part of the South China Sea;
Jakarta controls the Java Sea and parts of the South China Sea to Borneo. There are syndicate branches in Vietnam, Malaysia, Sumatra,
Cambodia, the Philippines, Burma, and mainland China. Targeted
cargo vessels steaming from one turf to another provide the syndicates with a movable feast and often the spoils are divided.

Eric Ellen, a lawyer by education and a cop by temperament, had
been asked to form the IMB because of his expertise in terrorism and
maritime crime. His wife, Lin Kuo, worked with the INTERPOL office in Taiwan and became the assistant director of the International
Chamber of Commerce's Commercial Crime Bureau. They were a
formidable team and became experts in tracing smuggling routes of
illegal immigrants aboard phantom ships.[42]

If not used in cargo fraud, phantom ships are often used to transport human cargo into the U.S., Middle East, Europe, or Australia.
"Once in the United States those [immigrants] on board ask for political asylum," Ellen says. "The crews of the phantom ships, including the captain, are not sent to prison, they are simply sent back
home to do it over and over again." Indeed, smuggling people is as
lucrative as smuggling drugs, and safer. There is not the worldwide
concern for the transportation of illegal immigrants as there is for
shipping narcotics, and in the unlikely event the organizers are
caught, the penalties are much lighter.

She-tou, the Snakeheads, so called because of the creative smuggling routes that snake from country to country before entering the
United States, have bases in Hong Kong, Fujian Province on the
southern Chinese mainland, Europe, the U.S., and Canada. They
have successfully smuggled several hundred thousand illegal immigrants into the United States and Canada over the past ten years, either by air or by sea aboard previously pirated ships.

Many of the illegal immigrants pay the Snakehead organizations
in Hong Kong and Fujian up to $35,000 for the passage. If a vessel
founders or is arrested, it is of little concern to the syndicates; money
for the passage already has been collected or pledged by the families
who remain back in China. If the would-be immigrants make it to
the promised land alive, they are bought or rented by Asian-owned

businesses in the U.S. and Canada as indentured labor; they will spend the rest of their lives working in sweatshops like those in Little Fuzhou, on East Broadway, New York City, earning a couple dollars a day for piecework.

One would suppose that the fare for passage and false documentation to the U.S.—it is $27,000 to Britain—would buy them luxury accommodations, cabins on a cruise ship with a sea view. Instead it buys them a voyage from hell, cramped space in the dingy holds of small, leaking freighters, phantom ships often pirated years before.

The *Golden Venture* was such a vessel. A small coastal ship with another name, she plied Southeast Asian waters until it was hijacked; she and her crew just disappeared off the radar. She was next seen on a roundabout voyage hauling illegal immigrants from densely populated Fujian Province. On the night of June 7, 1993, she arrived at her ultimate destination. The excitement rose to a fever pitch among the would-be immigrants on deck when the lights of the skyscrapers of Manhattan appeared on the horizon; after thousands of miles at sea in conditions comparable to those of a long-haul cattle truck and with the New World only hours away, the little ship ran hard aground just outside New York City; 10 of the 277 passengers died trying to swim ashore. Many who survived were jailed in federal penitentiaries. After their release many ended up slaving in the sweatshops paying off the cost of that ill-fated voyage.

It was no less a nightmare for 58 Chinese immigrants who suffocated in a truckload of tomatoes at the English Channel port of Dover on June 18, 2000. The syndicate that had organized the passage on the *Golden Venture* was responsible for smuggling these migrants. They had come from Changle in Fujian by phantom ship to Europe.

"Before they stole cargo to order, now it is human cargo," Lin Kuo, Ellen's wife, says. "The same gang is responsible. The owner of the ship charges per person just like he does to transport freight. Instead of how much a ton, it is how much a head."

Ten ships a month leave Hong Kong or other transshipment points. Each vessel carries about two hundred men, women, and children. Twenty minders on board each ship make certain there are enough eggs, instant noodles, toilet rolls, and water for the passage.

Ellen says the Snakehead organization responsible for organizing the shipment to Dover, in which only 2 out of 60 survived, "is the same one they have been tracking for years. There are two brothers in Singapore. They don't need headquarters, just a place to feel comfortable. It is there that they arrange the vessel and the payment. They always go by way of nicknames—it is informal but it is deadly serious."

Ellen identified a Mr. Huang in Fuzhou as the money behind the operation. Further investigation indicates that Huang runs the multinational underground banking system that finances the triad activities of drug and immigrant smuggling and to a lesser degree ship hijacking.

"There are three Americans of Chinese origin involved in these activities. They have American passports and they commute between Los Angeles, Hong Kong, and Singapore," Ellen says. "They are known." Their connections with officials in the U.S. government and with senior government officials on mainland China keep their operations well protected.

Ellen says they report to Cheng Chui Ping, whom he calls simply Sister Ping. Ellen's description conjures a mysterious and powerful ruler of the Chinese underworld who ruthlessly controls her international operations from the halls of her spacious ($3 million at last count) villa in Canton. "The business has become so lucrative that Sister Ping, who left Fujian about ten years ago, may have earned more than thirty million dollars in the smuggling business. She is still running it today," Ellen maintains.

Sister Ping, Ellen says, is the target of an investigation by the Office of Naval Intelligence in Washington and he has given them what information he has—names, contacts, addresses. "She is the one leader behind all this—they had her bugged. They still do.

"Your navy offered me a lot of money to give to my informant— they really want her." Ellen's informant now lives in Los Angeles. "If I identified him, he'd be killed. I offered but he didn't want to deal— he was certainly involved and he has been making a good living out of it."

Ellen's revelations were corroborated in testimony before an appeals court in the Netherlands in January 2002. It identified a Chinese woman—"Sister P"—as the ringleader behind the human smuggling operations that included the death of the immigrants in the truckload of tomatoes at Dover.

According to Ellen the U.S. Navy wants to interdict the ships carrying illegal immigrants while still out on the high seas, outside U.S. territorial waters. "Or send somebody into China to do the job." Once a ship reaches American waters, these high-paying migrants would have to be regarded as possible asylum seekers.

An entire volume could be devoted to organized crime and to the tangled networks of legitimate and illegitimate businesses, the names of the triads and their members, their locations, the government officials involved, and the revelations of past and ongoing investigations. Noel Choong keeps his information closely guarded in his office safe, but admits he has passed on a few things to Hong Kong's Organized Crime and Triad Bureau. Eric Ellen and Lin Kuo also have more information, as do the investigating authorities. Despite such details, unless the nations in which these syndicates operate crack down on top-level corruption within their own ranks, crime at sea will continue to flourish: ships hijacked, seafarers killed, cargo stolen, immigrants and drugs smuggled.

"In order to stop piracy and the hijackings," Ellen says, "there has to be the political climate or there has to be a major, major disaster, a huge environmental problem such as the one we nearly got with the *Nagasaki Spirit* and *Ocean Blessing;* either that or a cruise ship attacked and many lives lost. Then somebody will sit up and take notice."

According to legend the captain of the *Flying Dutchman* was accursed for uttering a blasphemous oath; he and his crew were sentenced to roam the seas for an eternity without ever stopping, without ever touching land. Anyone who set eyes upon the phantom vessel was also doomed.

The story of the *Fu Tai* is the stuff of modern-day legend. She was a new ship with nice lines, clean gray hull, and yellow funnel; she sat handsome at anchor off Batam Island, across the Straits from Singapore. On the night of August 5, 1998, armed pirates clambered aboard the ship, mustered the crew, and ordered them to jump overboard and swim; many didn't know how and they drowned. Those who made it ashore reported that their chief engineer had been kidnapped and was still aboard when pirates sailed the ship away.

"It is really sad," Noel says. "His son called me many times and asked me to help find his dad. He is still calling me."

The owner of the ship offered a reward.

Noel's sources were notified. It wasn't long before an informant called, saying he knew where the ship was, that the pirates had changed its name and repainted it and that it was being used in the "offshore trade"—running drugs.

The *Fu Tai*, now with a new identity, is reported to be sailing between Bangkok and Hong Kong; it loads heroin from small boats and takes it across the South China Sea to Hong Kong, calling in at the Philippines. It never goes into port and stops only to off-load its lethal cargo onto another waiting vessel and to pick up supplies and bunkers. With no authority on the high seas to stop it, it will forever continue its voyage until it sinks. "I asked the informant if he really thought we were going to try to recover the ship in those circumstances. If we got involved in something like that, there would be payback; they'd plant a bomb and it is all over—like in some Hollywood movie."

"And the boy's father—the engineer?"

Noel frowns, shakes his head. "I think he is still on the ship after all these years; he has probably never gotten off, like in a prison. The *Fu Tai* is a ghost ship and he just works day and night—never to go ashore. I don't think he will ever see his family again."

16

A Pirate by Any Other Name

How is it physically possible for anyone to steal an object that is larger than a city building, operated by a couple dozen men and women, and carries a cargo worth millions? And it just disappears. Nothing like this occurs on land.

It is easier than hijacking a truck. On the highway there is some law enforcement. At sea there is no enforcement, and a hijacked ship is used for years in criminal activities until she falls apart and sinks.

Ship hijacking is a crime usually far more violent than a random act of robbery at sea. And there is no known defense. Hijackers use modern military weapons to take down a vessel, while the crew is basically defenseless, armed with only a fire hose or two. In a hijacking there are often no witnesses.

A particularly brutal attack occurred in the South China Sea when the M/V *Cheung Son*, a Panama-registered bulk carrier from Shanghai to Malaysia, was hijacked on November 16, 1998. Seldom in the so-called Golden Age of Piracy of the seventeenth and eighteenth centuries was there ever a more bestial, cold-blooded act of murder on the high seas than that committed by those who took over this ship. The leader of the pirates wanted everyone on his team implicated, so he forced each in his gang to kill one crewman. The pirates lined up the twenty-three sailors on deck, hooded their heads with plastic garbage bags, and clubbed them, or shot them, or stabbed them to death. The bodies were tossed into the sea. Six of the bloated corpses, weighted down with metal engine parts, were later hauled aboard fishing boats, snagged in nets. Strangely, the purpose of the hijacking remains a mystery. The ship's declared cargo was furnace slag, of little significant value; the extreme violence of the attack, the fact that none of the original crew was permitted to live, has led to speculation that the ship may have been carrying illegal arms, since off-loaded, destined for a fundamental extremist group. The Public Security Bureau of the People's Republic of China eventually arrested the pirates after they found photographs of a party on board celebrating the successful hijacking.

The crew of the *Ten-yu* was also never heard from again. The Japanese-owned vessel was carrying three thousand tons of aluminum ingot when it was hijacked by professional Indonesian pirates armed with machine guns in the Malacca Straits on September 27, 1998. The sixteen hijackers were arrested by the Chinese when it entered their waters. To the amazement of many in the industry the Chinese authorities repatriated the criminals, provoking an international protest.[43] Among those released were the chief officer and the chief engineer, who according to the IMB had been arrested by the Chinese three years earlier aboard the *Anna Sierra*, a cargo vessel they also had hijacked.[44]

Some pirates, not wanting blood on their hands, often force the crew members off the ship knowing that chances of survival are slim; on the *Anna Sierra* the seamen were set adrift in rafts without food and water; on the *Inabukwa* they were marooned on a deserted island. There are some strange exceptions: After the cargo of diesel fuel was siphoned off from the hijacked *Petchem* in the South China Sea, the ship was abandoned with the crew, bound and gagged, still on board. And still alive.

The theft of a ship is frequently pulled off while it is riding at anchor. If you have a spare $300,000, you can go down to the docks in Manila, or more conveniently sit at the rooftop bar of the Pan Pacific Hotel, and pick out any one of a number of ships in the harbor and a syndicate will arrange for a gang to steal it. It is boggling: a ship lying peacefully at anchor, filled with cargo, waiting for a berth, its men going about their routine chores, pirated right under the noses of authorities. If you do not need the crew and have your own, then the crew is told to swim for it. The ship is sailed out to sea, and for the price the syndicate will change its identity and deliver it to some mutually agreed location within three days. This could never happen in the aviation industry. One wonders what the reaction would be if a crewed 747 carrying cargo—a DHL or FedEx plane—were to disappear. In the South China Sea a ship goes missing with a cargo just as valuable and a crew many times larger. And no one hears a word of it.

Can a ship just vanish? Turning it into a phantom ship, erasing its original identity, is relatively easy. A ship can be repainted anywhere, at sea, against a dock, or while hidden in some remote island anchorage. Yet it is not often the whole ship that is painted. Pirates slap a coat of paint over the company's distinctive multicolored funnel while the ship is under way, en route to a rendezvous with another pirate ship into which it will pump its stolen cargo. With scaffolding, pirates at sea lower themselves down the transom and paint over the original name and home port that is welded on the stern and slap on a new identity. Meanwhile others in the gang are painting over the ship's name that is stenciled on life rafts, life rings, and lifeboats, and on the name boards that hang off the bridge wings or are affixed to the sides of the wheelhouse.

The hijacked vessel gets a new registry; changing flags is an integral part of the process. Before the hijacking the syndicates will have procured a temporary ship's registration and a new home port from some banana republic in South America or any country in which corruption and lack of accountably are common. The flag of that nation is flown from the staff, and the original ship, once legitimately on the books, exists no longer. Registering with these flag-of-convenience nations not only serves organized crime but, it has been noted, terrorists as well.[45]

Chew Cheng Kiat, known in Singapore as David Wong, was the local kingpin for a crime syndicate based in Hong Kong, and Fujian Province, China. He arranged the hijacking of twenty-two vessels in the Malacca Straits and South China Sea. He ran his hijack operations just across the Straits at Batam Island aboard the M/T *Pulau Mas,* mother ship for smaller fast boats that tracked and attacked. Found on board the ship were fifteen handcuffs, fourteen ski masks, three knives, bogus immigration and ship stamps, and twelve cartons of paint. Placing his own local pirate as a sleeper on the ship he intended to seize, he would await a mobile phone call from the insider about the specifics of the cargo, the time of departure, the route the ship was taking, what antipiracy measures were in place, and when it was to leave territorial waters for the open seas.

One of the vessels hijacked by Wong and his gang was the M/T *Petro Ranger,* attacked by twelve men in 1998 north of the Horsburgh Light. The ship was transporting 9,600 tons of diesel fuel, and 1,600 tons of Jet A1 fuel from the Shell Bukom refinery complex to a terminal at Ho Chi Minh City. The cargo was worth $2.3 million.

The pirates followed standard operating procedure for an attack at sea: Using a high-speed motorboat, they crept up from behind in the cover of the radar blind spot, scaled bamboo ladders and ropes and grappling hooks, overpowered the watch on the bridge, disabled all communications equipment including satellite, telex, marine radios, and handheld walkie-talkies, then marched a hostage with a gun in the back down to the master's quarters.

The crew was bound and herded into the officers' mess, where they were confined for ten days. The pirates had prepared in advance false crew lists, manifests, registrations, and cargo ownership papers; they hoisted the Honduran flag, painted the blue funnel orange, and hastily slapped on the ship's new name—WILBY—over the vessel's original name welded on the transom. They also stenciled the vessel's new identity on anything that could be associated with the previous ship. The hijackers took the ship toward Haikou on Hainan Island on the southern coast of China, where it was joined by two tankers that siphoned off the cargo of diesel. The pirates were arrested after a Chinese patrol boat stopped the vessel to inspect the ship's papers.

The hijacking had been meticulously executed. The pirate leader, hired by Wong, was well dressed and well spoken; he later admitted he had been ordered into action by a syndicate with bosses in Singapore, Hong Kong, and China. After the cargo had been stolen, the

Petro Ranger was to have been turned into a phantom ship. The syndicate would have used the ship in cargo scams, or to possibly carry immigrants, drugs, or illegal arms.

Petroships, the ship's owners, had issued detailed antipiracy guidelines for its masters the year before. The *Shipboard Operating Procedures Manual* warned:

> The dangers of entering a piracy black spot can be significantly reduced if the ship's crew take relatively simple precautions. Above all, potential raiders will be discouraged by evidence of good ship security and vigilance.

The company told its captains that when passing through known piracy areas they must seal off all access to the ship, maintain an active patrol on deck, turn on deck lights, and keep fire hoses on standby. With these defenses in place how was it so easy to hijack this modern 12,000-ton tanker?

The master of the *Petro Ranger* insists he had followed company policy, that he had rigged the ship and prepared its crew for a passage through hostile waters.[46] Yet there is a contrary view.

Captain James Jeeris brought the *Petro Ranger* back from its captivity in China. "I read the captain's night orders, which the master told the A/B I was not to see. They did not include any antipiracy procedures; the chief engineer told me when I sailed the ship back to Singapore that there was never anything done on the *Petro Ranger* to defend itself against pirates on that passage."

Years later company officials are still dismayed that one of its masters would fail to take commonsense precautions and subsequently lose a ship.

It is also easier to hijack a ship if the syndicates have at hand detailed knowledge of the type and layout of vessel they want to steal, whether there exists an antipiracy plan, and to what extent it is being implemented.

The master of the *Petro Ranger* wrote that he was convinced someone within Petroships had informed the hijackers of the type of cargo he would be carrying, the time of his departure from the refinery, and his ETA at the pilot station at Vung Tau, Vietnam. Thus, if he shaped a course directly for the Mekong Delta, the syndicates would know exactly where he was at any given time. Much of the information, however, was obtainable from the outside; anyone could monitor the ship's request for a pilot on the VHF radio and know within a few minutes the vessel's departure time and thus its approximate ETA at its destination without an informant on the inside. And anyone with a good pair of binoculars in a tall city building could confirm the vessel's departure from the terminal or monitor the passage through the straits from the radio communication with the Vessel Traffic Information Service. Whether antipiracy procedures would be in force was known if you had information about the particular master of the ship. If the captain had not taken antipiracy measures before, why would he on this run? The captain of the *Petro Ranger* told reporters that the pirates appeared to know personal things about him. His way of doing things was also available information.

But if pirates place sleepers on the inside, the job of hijacking a $16 million ship with its million-dollar cargo becomes a walk in the park. David Wong admitted he had placed his own man aboard the *Petro Ranger* and other ships.[47]

It also makes the job easier if the pirates know the inside and outside of every ship, the layout of the accommodations, the location of the control rooms and the captain's quarters. One of the pirates, I discovered, had been a Petroships officer. Darman—often the Indonesian custom to use only one name—had been second engineer on at least four Petroships vessels. He knew how to run a ship.

Darman earned $1,800 Singapore a month, about $800 U.S., as an officer for Petroships. Not a bad salary for an Indonesian sailor. Still, word gets around in this business, and he had heard that the pirates who knocked off the *Cheung Son* were each paid $11,000 for their part in the massacre. He had gone to the gathering spot for seamen and the local pirate recruiting ground—the seedy Clifford Pier at the bottom end of Singapore City. Here longboats chug back and forth carrying sailors to their ships in the outer-port-limit anchorage, a forgotten sea of several hundred merchant vessels waiting for cargo, waiting for berths, or just rusting away as they swing on their anchors. It is beyond the jurisdiction of the Port of Singapore Authority, and the IMB estimates that in the OPL, at least twenty-five

percent of the ships at anchor have either been pirated, will be pirated, or have pirates living aboard.[48]

Darman could have sat on the low cement wall at the pier, smoking a Gudang Garam with the other Indonesian seamen, or he could
have wandered over to the gritty Beer Park that overlooks the channel and bought Lau Pa's tasty pig organ soup for about a buck. Here
the scuttlebutt is of ships looking for crew, of addresses for guaranteed clean hookers and their specialties, of a way to make a little extra
money on the side. And piracy today is easy extra money.

I decided to track down the engineer pirate. Working on leads
from those with whom he worked, I wrote in textbook Indonesian a
letter to his last known address in Medan, Sumatra, setting out times
(and financial incentive) for a meeting across the Straits in Singapore.
He might be back at sea in a straight job or possibly pirating another
ship, and the chances of meeting him were next to nil. I never expected that he would respond, still, I wrote that I would be at the bottom of Clifford Pier on certain dates and hours; I'd be wearing a
black baseball cap.

I sit on the waist-high cement wall day after day at the appointed
hour, scanning the faces of itinerant seamen, making eye contact. I
am getting to be a fixture—hookers, gay boys, itinerant seamen, and
beggars have stopped taking notice. One old man now greets me each
afternoon with "*Selamat datang, Kapitan.*" Welcome.

I have Darman's photo taken years before; it is either a mug shot
or a passport photo—small dark eyes, thin black mustache, receding
black hair. He does not look like a simpatico sort. Darman will have
to recognize me—I'll never be able to make him. Each afternoon I
leave empty handed and frustrated, certain the meet is never going to
happen.

Until the last day on the schedule. I sit on the cement wall
hunched over a newspaper, occasionally glancing down at the myna
birds that peck away on the cement under my feet. The glass and
steel of Singapore office buildings rise in front of me on the other
side of the bay.

A young Indonesian with orange-hennaed curly hair and a soft, pouty face passes in front of me, slows down, catches my eye, smiles, and continues on. Minutes later he is back. He hoists himself up on my wall a few feet away and stares out into the bay. The boy wears an orange T-shirt, black pants, and black running shoes with bright yellow laces. This is not Darman—too young, too frail. I look at my watch—hell, just about 6:00 P.M. and I'm nearly gone.

He jumps down and, suddenly reaching a decision, walks up to me and puts a soft hand on my arm.

"Mister John?" he says sweetly. "You come."

I follow the boy past Lau Pa's to a cutout under the cement stairs leading up to a skyway across the busy street. It is cavelike and dark but open for all the world if you were passing this way. But most people don't—in Singapore you don't stray, you don't walk on the grass. This concrete grotto is the sort of place that the homeless would choose, a hidey-hole out of public view, spacious enough for a cooking fire and a few scrounged mattresses. A stench of dead wet ashes and urine emit from within.

A balding man in his thirties sits cross-legged on one of the mattresses, drinking *kopi susu* from a straw that sticks out of a tied plastic sandwich bag. He has heavy lips under a thick mustache that wraps down around his mouth. He wears rumpled slacks and a short-sleeved checkered shirt. A mobile phone is clipped to his belt. He raises his eyebrows in greeting, continues drinking.

"*Anda Darman?*" I ask. Are you Darman?

He merely nods, mutters something in Indonesian.

"Mister Darman asks if you pay."

"I pay. He talk?"

"I talk," the man says in English. He looks up at me and offers a slow reluctant grin. His eyes are vacant, soulless.

I ask the boy if this man is really Darman. I look down at the tattered photo. There is a slight resemblance. The kid translates and the man barks something. He is not pleased.

"You speak English?"

"Little English."

"You were on the *Petro Ranger*—when it was attacked?" How do I ask if he was a pirate? There is no such thing as "piracy" to pirates. It is simply more piecework; there is not much difference between work that involves violence and punching a clock. It's a job.

"Yah, *Petro Ranger!*" The response is spontaneous and proud.

It is a difficult communication and the boy helps. From the stumble of conversation I am able to understand that he met friends here at the pier who knew people who were looking for a ship's engineer; he took a bus across the causeway to Jahore Baru in Malaysia, where he applied for a job. Then, he says, he was sent across the Straits to Pulau Batam, where he became a pirate. Darman does not seem to regret helping to hijack the ship; it is a simple fact. Morality, from what I can tell, does not figure.

"Who were you working for?"

"Petroships."

"—When you went aboard the *Petro Ranger*."

"Chinese men."

I tell the boy to ask why he attacked the *Petro Ranger*.

The boy looks at me, a little frightened. Then he translates.

"Money. *Banyak, banyak*—much money," Darman blurts in English. Then he speaks too fast in Indonesian to understand. The boy adds quietly: Four thousand dollars.

I say that I heard he made good money for Petroships and the boy translates. Darman laughs bitterly, says, "Petroships no good."

"Why no good?"

He rattles off something quickly and the youth translates. "Mister Darman say they let him go because he not speak good English. Mister Darman leave now."[49]

I pull out a wad of bills from my pocket and bend over and hand them to him. He takes the money and slips it into his shirt pocket. I almost get the impression that he is waiting for the next in line behind me. The boy stands in my way. He also wants money. I push past and get out into the hot evening air and breathe freshly.

Out on the street I step back out of the way of a bus coming from the right; it is the British system here and sometimes I still forget. Billboarded on the side of the bus in red and black letters with a Jolly Roger: "PIRATES—SINGAPORE'S FIRST 3-D COMEDY. LIVE IT! FEEL IT!" I wonder if the world doesn't need a little of that romance.

The Chinese in Hainan Island—after confiscating the remaining cargo on board the *Petro Ranger* as "evidence"—released Darman and his mates without prosecuting. Malaysian authorities had already begun extradition proceedings against the twelve pirates and were dumbfounded when they learned that the Chinese had sent the pirates back home to Indonesia. Repatriating the suspects was in contravention of the 1988 Rome Convention to which China was a party; the convention obliges states to submit piracy cases for prosecution without exception.

The master of the *Petro Ranger* said later that a number of those same pirates were seen pirating ships again in the Malacca Straits. Eric Ellen, director of the IMB at the time, charged that release of the suspects was part of "a deep plot to cover up China's participation in criminal activity. This is not the first time that Chinese ports have been used to shelter hijacked vessels."

I throw my gear into my seabag and take a launch across the harbor to the sister ship of the *Petro Ranger*—the *Petro Concord*. The passage ahead will take me from Singapore across the South China Sea to Ho Chi Minh City, the same route of the *Petro Ranger*, and past the spot where she was hijacked.

17

Into the Dead Zone

Petro Concord, South China Sea

If a voyage down the Malacca Straits on the *Montrose* was an exercise in caution and awareness, then a passage across the murderous waters of the South China Sea on a smaller tanker is a passage in abject fear. Ships out here are far more alone, more vulnerable, than in the congested and tightly regulated channels. Located just on the other side of the Straits, the South China Sea is a violent, unregulated no-man's-land, the private game reserve of organized crime; it is in these international waters that the hulking beasts of the sea like the *Petro Ranger* are hunted down.

After departing Singapore there are no precise traffic lanes beyond Horsburgh Light. Ships depart the refineries and the container terminals laden with their precious cargoes and shape a course through a body of water that is larger than the Gulf of Mexico. Boxed in by Malaysia, Indonesia, Thailand, Cambodia, Vietnam, the Philippines, China, and Taiwan, the South China Sea region has become what the U.S. regards in the facile terms of headline writers as a powder keg. Hainan Island lies in the north, the site of the 2001 midair collision between a Chinese jet fighter and a U.S. spy plane; it is where many hijacked ships have been brought, where the hijackers took the *Petro Ranger*. The oil-rich Spratly Islands, claimed by China, Taiwan, Vietnam, Malaysia, the Philippines, and Brunei, the scene of frequent violent conflict, lie on the direct shipping route to Hong Kong, Korea, and Japan. Abu Sayaf rebels attack ships passing the Philippine coast with mortars and rocket-propelled grenades and kidnap tourists off resort islands. No law, order, or any moral code is enforced in the South China Sea; this is an unpatrolled black hole where unarmed vessels and their civilian crews simply fall off the edge of the planet.

A passage through these hostile seas is a lesson in combat readiness that other vessels might do well to follow.

The M/T *Petro Concord* will be transporting cargo similar to that of her sister ship—3,000 tons of kerosene and 8,000 tons of jet fuel—valued at $2.5 million. The Jet A1 is enough to fill 141 late-model 747s, or enough to send a single 747 to the moon. And back. The kerosene, when peddled on the black market, is enough to make someone very rich.

On this passage I was to understand the fear of many seafarers plying this dangerous sea; perhaps it was the careful preparations for battle, perhaps it was when the captain admitted that he was afraid, that I, too, felt the tension. There was little doubt from the very start of the three-day voyage that the captain and his crew were going to do everything they could to prevent pirates from stealing their ship and cargo.

The *Petro Concord* is a handsome vessel. Built in 1995, she is four hundred feet long, somewhat longer than a football field. She is raked slightly aft and her cargo deck leads to a jaunty raised prow; she could be a little sister to the *Montrose*. The *Petro Concord* is not large as tankers go these days. Weighing in at 12,000 tons, she is puny compared to the *Montrose*, but then most ships are. A VLCC carries twenty-five times more cargo and was designed to deliver crude, that's it. Very important. Tankers like the *Petro Concord*, however, transport the refined products—jet fuel, diesel, fuel oil, and gasoline—to nearly every port in the world; these are the ones that deliver the goods.

The *Montrose*, more automated, is normally manned by a crew of seventeen to twenty-one. The *Petro Concord* has a crew of twenty-three. Petroships says it could man their tanker with less, but because of the ship's hectic schedule and fast turnaround and because of the extra men needed for the nighttime and sometimes daytime piracy watch, the *Petro Concord* has more.

She is a colorful vessel: her hull is black, her bottom red, and her boxy superstructure behind her long deck a fresh-painted white; the large blue detached funnel with a six-foot-high white *P* is behind all of this. Her deck, rust free and clean, has been recently painted a forest-green; a silver-and-white metal catwalk runs the length in the middle of the deck over thick gray pipes intercepted by bright red valve wheels. A long, thin yellow pipe that carries fire-fighting foam and a thicker red pipe that carries seawater run parallel to each other under the catwalk; the foam and the water are mixed at the two reddish-orange swivel-fire cannon mounted on the walkway. A small gray five-ton crane to lift the filler pipes to the manifolds reaches awkwardly out of the catwalk in the center of the deck.

The master of the *Petro Concord* is Than Maung Myint from Burma. He has been at sea for the past twenty-five years, more than half his life, and he has held the rank of captain for the past twelve. He has never been pirated at sea. He doesn't intend to be. Mindful that our sister ship was hijacked, his own antipiracy defenses are taken a step or two farther than company policy.

The *Petro Concord* is as defended as it can be. Unlike many ships, this captain has written his own specific antipiracy plan—very thorough, created from the lessons of the previous hijacking. It defines antipiracy duties while at sea, at anchorage, in port. There are some similarities to those precautions taken on the *Montrose*.

List of Action to be taken on Sighting Pirates

1—Raise the Alarm on the ship's whistle/bell and also shout.

2—All deck and accommodation lights to be switched on.

3—Alert all ships in vicinity and call nearest coastal station.

4—Use water jets to deter pirates.

5—Create wave at stern by altering course port and starboard.

6—Fire warning rockets.

7—Alter course to nearest port.

If pirates board:

1—Men on pirate watch run to accommodation and shut door behind them.

2—All crew to assemble at the bridge.

3—Stay calm and do not attempt heroic. [sic]

On this ship, particularly, these measures are well founded. The *Petro Concord* has been unlucky; it has been attacked four times in the past three years, twice in 2000.

The most recent incident was the most serious. The *Petro Concord* was steaming away from a Singapore refinery and had just dropped off its harbor pilot when it was surrounded by a pack of speedboats that had trailed the ship into international waters. As she crossed the territorial boundary, pirates scaled the hull like spiders and climbed aboard. The master radioed marine police for help. They responded that they were watching the attack through their binoculars, but, sorry, they were unable to do anything because the ship had left their jurisdiction. They suggested the captain try to return to Singapore. As the ship began its turn, the pirates dropped their apparent plans to hijack the vessel and escaped instead with mooring lines and paint.

Another attempt was made while the ship was anchored at the mouth of the Mekong Delta as it waited for a river pilot. Armed bandits held two of the crew hostage and stole mooring ropes, a fireman's suit, and a bicycle off the deck. In yet another incident she was boarded while tied to the pier at the oil terminal at Nha Be, where we are going; they stole paint from the bosun's locker and some of the crew's clothes.

⌒

I have been "signed on." I have filled out the indemnity forms stating next of kin and I have agreed not to hold Petroships responsible in case of my death. I've tossed my kit in the little cabin located just in front of the ship's funnel—usually reserved for an extra officer or the overnight stay of a harbor pilot—and I join Captain Than, his chief officer, and some refinery officials who are monitoring the loading of the jet fuel in the cargo control room.

There are electrical storms in the area. Brilliant flashes and sonorous booms fly over the harbor with tropical intensity. A squall line of low, dark cloud churns just above the surface and rolls toward us. The thunder reaches inside the CCR, over the normal sounds of the ship, the rumbling of the engine on standby, the quiet hum of the air conditioning and circulating fans. Chief Officer Noah Ageyi Owusu from Ghana stops punching the loading figures into his calculator and looks up at the blackened sky and the rain that pelts the windows and sweeps horizontally across the deck. A jagged bolt of lightning rips across the harbor. Noah, with a few years on him, has a gravelly voice and eyes that seem perpetually concerned, and he is not taking any chances: it's his call. One spark could do it. He radios the terminal to stop pumping the fuel until the squall passes.

Neither Noah nor Captain Than seems particularly concerned about the delay; lifting such a cargo with only one pipe in such conditions takes time. This ship is chartered at $10,000 a day from the moment loading begins, so it is not coming out of Petroships' pockets.

The ship's antipiracy briefings are held just prior to sailing and every night the ship is at sea. The slow loading process here in Singapore offers Captain Than an opportunity to call the war council at 2400—midnight—in the cargo control room. It is attended by Noah, the chief officer, his second-in-command, as well as the chief engineer, the second officer, the third engineer, and the two A/Bs. We make an odd bunch—a Burmese, two Bangladeshis, two Indonesians, two Africans, and me, the Yank.

Captain Than announces that he will station four of his crew with walkie-talkies on the decks with instructions to communicate with the bridge every fifteen minutes. They are to alert the officers on watch of any vessel that might be suspect—fast boat, slow boat, fishing boat, *prahau*. All hatches before we sail will be secured except the one over the steering room, a precaution in case of an unlikely steering failure on the bridge. With four men on piracy watch there is no need for dummies strapped to the railings. I question Captain Than about the efficacy of the dolls and he has a good laugh.

The *Petro Ranger* was hijacked halfway between Horsburgh Light and the Anambas Islands. A penciled X on the chart taken from the pirates marked the spot—02.20N–104.55E—where the attack was to take place. The pirates were accurate within a couple nautical miles, not that their accuracy represented any great navigational feat. The pirates zipped out of a Malaysian cove on their speedboat, following directions on their inexpensive handheld GPS.

Mindful that crime syndicates know of our route and our cargo, may even have a better idea when we will get under way than we do and thus can plot our expected position at any time, the captain announces, "I will change my course; I will not follow the shortest route—to avoid the pirates I will alter my course." He looks significantly at each of his crew members. "My ship will not be hijacked. If they know where we are going, they will have to look hard for us. I keep three or four hours in my pocket to change course." Until private mobile communications improve, this is still a pretty good move; out there we are beyond mobile telephone range, and even if a sleeper were equipped with a handheld GPS, he probably could not get in touch with his gang once we were beyond the line-of-sight range of his cell phone.

The captain confides later on the bridge that while the most direct route is within ten miles of the Anambas Islands, he will go west after passing Horsburgh and stay about twenty miles off. Twenty additional miles on a speedboat with radar is not a hell of a big difference. Off the Somali coast pirates armed with rocket-propelled grenades and antitank weapons usually take their speedboats up to fifty miles offshore to attack passing ships.

Chief Noah, the West African, fills in some of the details for the crew: "If you see pirates coming on boats to the ship, sound the general alarm, alert all ships in the vicinity. Use the helm to create waves, port to starboard, port to starboard. If they are already on board make friends!" He even suggests inviting the pirates for a cup of tea. The laughter seems too ready, too short. Then he turns to me: "Anyone who is free can walk around the decks to beef up the watch."

Noah is a quiet older man with a scratchy voice and dark earnest eyes, receding hair, a mustache and goatee that are beginning to turn white. Born the son of a farmer in a wattle hut in the bush, he worked and studied his way up to the top. He is qualified as a ship captain—he is licensed by the British government to command nearly any merchant vessel. "I was lucky," he says, "I had the bush way of training—respect for authority, hard work, no stealing, and no complaining." The company knows he is adept at handling this crew of many languages and cultures and says that chief officers like him are harder to find than qualified masters, and so they have asked him to be patient—Petroships needs him more than he needs them.

After 2000 hours every night we are to bunker down in the citadel. All doors to the decks except one are dogged shut, then barred by a steel pipe, impossible to open from the outside. There are no windows on any of the doors except to the bridgewings. It appears that the *Petro Concord* is more difficult to penetrate than the *Montrose*. Captain Than keeps one door open in the event that pirates board and the men on patrol need to escape to the protection of the inside.

The captain says that he knows the pirates expect the leeward door to be left open, so instead he might decide to leave the windward door unlocked. He won't even tell his own officers during this antipiracy meeting which door it is—not until the last minute. He seems to be pushing caution to its limits, but again there is concern that one of our crew would tip the syndicates of the location of that open door before we left the Singapore transmission range. Once the pirates know the quickest way to get inside, it is only a matter of minutes before they take over the ship.

Chief Officer Noah, second in command of the *Petro Concord*, is responsible for implementing antipiracy procedures. "Who knows what's going on—inside, outside, who knows?" he says. "Somebody on the hand phone could call and tell them anything they need to know. It all boils down to inside work."

Noah admits careful screening of the crews is always a problem; Petroships, with a reputation in the industry of better-than-average salaries and conditions, tries to keep their personnel loyal to the company as long as possible. Yet sometimes even a better-than-average wage for a seafarer, as I discovered with Darman, doesn't nearly match that offered by the syndicates.

There is no discussion about resisting the pirates; there are no fire extinguishers and no knives. It is assumed that no one needs to be told not to fight back.

I ask the captain how concerned is he really about piracy—after all, only a small percentage of ships are attacked. "Very concerned," he says with some emphasis.

Afraid?

"Very. I would feel better with a gun, but on a tanker, I don't know."

It is getting close to departure and I am getting increasingly nervous. Perhaps it is because it could happen, that it has happened, and that it will happen again and nobody is doing very much to stop it. In the year 2000 there were eight hijackings in this area. In the first nine months of 2001 there were fifteen. One of the ships that disappeared was the *Hualien No. 1* with twenty-one crewmen aboard. Noel Choong believes pirates changed the name of the vessel and threw the original crew overboard. The vessel, it is almost certain, is today falsely registered and working the seas as a phantom ship.

We are prepared, yet few of those aboard believe that our meager defenses could hold off determined, heavily armed pirates from boarding us, robbing us, and, if it is their pleasure, like the butchers of the *Cheung Son*, clubbing us and dumping our bodies into the sea. I cannot really think it will happen. Yet the captain is apprehensive. The crew is visibly nervous. I am a little scared. I wish we would get under way.

Noah has briefed me about the lifeboats, the life jacket in my

242 JOHN S. BURNETT

cabin, and the signals. Seven short blasts of the ship's whistle followed by one long, and I take to the lifeboats. A continuous ringing of the bells and I'm to get to the emergency stations. For pirates? "Either— both," Noah says. "You'll know." Noah tries one on me; I'm sure it has worked before and I chuckle. Every ship he is on, he says, is his ark. Sure. But he turns serious when discussing pirates. "I am afraid," he says. "It's my life, my safety; this is no game." Then he grins. "But if they get aboard, I can always come up from behind. It's dark and I'm black, so they'd never see me."

On the way up to the bridge by the outside ladders, I pause to watch the tugboats pull us away from the pier. Our cargo stinks. The overpowering sweet acrid stench of kerosene is everywhere. I wouldn't dare light a match; it still seems a miracle to me that the *Valiant Carrier* didn't explode.

The interior of the ship's spacious bridge is a glassed-in eyrie with a wide view of the sea through large reinforced tinted windows that slant outward. There is no steering wheel on this ship like on the *Montrose*—it is merely a three-inch vertical joystick; the ship is steered as one might move a raised mouse button on a laptop. The traditional telegraph with the big handle that sends orders down to the engine room has been replaced by a long row of backlighted push buttons:

Ahead   **Astern**
Full/Half/Slow/Dead Slow/Stop/Dead Slow/Slow/Half/Full

The pilot enters the bridge, it is the same flamboyant Singapore Indian with pressed white slacks, white safari shirt, and white gloves who brought the *Montrose* into Bukom. Today he appears less like a horseman riding through the Kashmir than a Mississippi riverboat gambler—tuft of white hair under his lip, bushy eyebrows, pointed white goatee, and handlebar mustache. He greets the captain with a dulcet good morning and takes command. He is even more colorful in daylight.

"Port ten!" he orders. His left hand rises to his shoulder in a smooth single motion and falls outward, palm out. He is a traffic cop with panache.

"Port ten degrees, sir," repeats the young Malaysian cadet. He taps the joystick and the ship, more responsive than the *Montrose*, begins an immediate turn to the left.

"All ahead full!" he orders. He raises his arm and motions forward as if he were leading a cavalry charge.

"All ahead full, sir." The cadet punches a button and a buzzer sounds briefly, confirming the change.

"You have some traffic out there," the pilot says, turning to Captain Than.

"Amidships."

"Amidships."

The pilot performs these theatrics to my amusement, perhaps for my amusement. Captain Than appears unimpressed. Getting us to the shipping lanes is not a difficult job—a landlubber could have gotten us this far.

"Well, I think you have it now, Cap," he says.

"Thank you, Captain," Than replies. "See you next time."

The pilot picks up his computer bag and disappears down the stairwell to the waiting launch that motors alongside.

Captain Than removes the phone from its cradle on the console: "VTIS, VTIS, this is the *Petro Concord*."

"*Petro Concord*, VTIS."

"VTIS, *Petro Concord*. We are approaching channel from Bukom to cross to eastbound lane."

"*Petro Concord*, you have a VLCC westbound, two miles, a car carrier four miles westbound, and eastbound you have two vessels, a sand barge, five miles, another vessel six miles. Exercise caution, *Petro Concord*."

I think I'd rather try darting across the LA freeway.

"*Ocean Neptune, Ocean Neptune*, this is VTIS," the radio warns the VLCC to our right. "Be advised you have a vessel entering your westbound lane—a tanker."

We cut between the VLCC and the car carrier and take a position between the sand barge and the container ship going our way. The Vessel Traffic Information Service continues to squawk instructions and warnings to other ships passing, crossing, exiting, entering the many channels and fairways of the Straits. When a ship strays out of its lanes and wanders into oncoming traffic it is advised by the stern radio voice, in a tone usually directed at unruly schoolchildren, to return to its track.

We are in the eastbound lane finally—in line with ships astern, ships ahead, motoring at about the same speed. Barring some unexpected trouble, we are safely on our way out to sea. A small sailboat, in line with the traffic approaching, bobs in the wake of passing ships. As it passes below I see a man and a small boy in the cockpit; the boy sits on his hands, staring in wonderment at the line of big merchant ships. There have been so many times I wished I were back on the *Unicorn*.

"Full away," the captain orders the helmsman. It is the order to the engine room to switch from diesel fuel to fuel oil. There will be no more maneuvering, no more dashing across crossing traffic, and it is assumed no chance of a sudden stop. The *Valiant Carrier*, three times our size, was steaming under this unforgiving fuel oil when it was attacked. Captain Monteiro probably could not have brought his ship to a crash stop before it hit the reef; turning sharply while under way probably saved the area from serious environmental damage.

I notice on the bulkhead, on each side of the wheelhouse, information about a crash stop and what it would mean to the *Petro Concord*. For this smaller vessel:

CRASH STOP
STOP DISTANCE: .9 MILES
TIME TAKEN: 6 MIN 7 SECS
COURSE CHANGE BY: 110 STARBOARD

It would take six minutes to come to a complete stop. That seems like a very long time were a collision imminent.

"Engine room, this is the bridge. Full away at 1027 hours."

Two *prahau*, small two-man fishing canoes, work the middle of the crowded shipping lane.

"Very dangerous," the captain says, looking down as they rock violently in our wake.

"Do you try to avoid them?"

"Difficult in the channel. But I try to. Maybe baby pirates."

Horsburgh Light is a small mark in the distance. It is a convergence point for most ships going into and out of the South China Sea. Beyond Horsburgh a ship is in international waters, and there is no one to call for help in the event of a hijacking—no coast guard, no navy, no marines, no police. Beyond, a ship enters a dead zone from which it might never return.

An old dot matrix printer starts spitting out a message on the telex behind the chart table. Than walks to the machine, tears off the spooled paper, reads it, signs it off on the bottom, and then hands it to me. It is the daily IMB piracy situation report. Included in the litany of violent events is one that is of some particular interest to us:

AT 1955 LT IN POSITION 00:37.0S–05:25.04E OFF RIAU ISLAND, INDONESIA. WHILE UNDERWAY, ARMED PIRATES BOARDED A GENERAL CARGO SHIP AND HIJACKED HER. THE SHIP ALONG WITH HER 22 CREW AND HER CARGO WORTH US $2.1 MILLION ARE MISSING.

I read the report in silence and put it back on the chart table and look up at the captain. "Not far away," he says. With a pair of dividers I measure the distance on the chart—the ship was hijacked about ninety miles south of our present position.

18

Murder Not Uncommon

Petro Concord

This charge into no-man's-land seems a bit skewed, out of sync. Petroships Chairman Alan Chan says his crews face guerrilla warfare when they enter the South China Sea. There are some similarities. At night those predatory warriors, armed with automatic weapons, sneak out of their lairs, creep up from behind, and, under cover of darkness, attack. In these waters at night, if statistics and history are accountable, we enter a virtual war zone.

Why should this crew, the crew on any ship, have to worry about getting killed? These guys are simply doing a job. If they wanted to go to war, they could have joined the military.

But we are safe for a while. It is daytime, and so far as is known, there have not yet been any daylight hijackings.

⌒‿⌒

Captain Than has a wonderful, man-in-the-moon face, with big brown eyes and a big smile. It is an intelligent face, but it reveals nothing of the man himself. He seems to be a shy man, and it is certain he is not sure how to deal with his new crew member with the laptop.

I have told him about the passage on the VLCC and he is curious about the master's accommodations. He chuckles when I describe Captain Postma's quarters; Than offers to show me his. The bedroom and dayroom are compact little chambers, closetlike compared to Postma's. The ship's safe is in a cabinet in his room. This captain doesn't use it either. It looks brand new and never closed. A double-locking system is identical to the one on the *Montrose* and the *Valiant Carrier:* combination and key. Captain Than acknowledges there is cash on board—$1,900 U.S. and about $1,000 Singapore, and he says he has hidden it well.

He has a Geronimo button in his dayroom, a small wall-mounted Inmarsat C automatic distress alarm that, when the protective hood is lifted, and the red button is pressed for five seconds, transmits a mayday signal to search-and-rescue coordination centers in the region, with the ship's ID code and precise location. There are other Geronimo buttons that only he and his officers know about, something like the silent alarms next to bank tellers.

The satellite locating device recommended by the IMB is also aboard this ship. After hijackers took control of the *Petro Ranger,* one of their first moves was to disable all communications equipment. What these brigands had neglected was the fax machine; after Petroships in Singapore stopped receiving the twice-daily position reports from the captain, they faxed the ship. When they saw that their fax had been received but went unanswered, they knew then that their ship was still afloat. The pirates discovered the query and destroyed the machine. Petroships again faxed and, receiving no confirmation of a successful transmission, deduced that their ship had been hijacked. Following the hijacking Chan equipped every ship in his fleet with ShipLoc, the satellite tracking device. He considers it cheap insurance. Chan says in most cases the master and crew aren't told it is aboard their ship for fear that the pirates will force them to reveal its location and, once known, will disable it.

Captain Than knows the transmitting unit is aboard his ship. He claims he doesn't know where it is. Its location is fairly easy to figure out: It may look like an electric junction box but it has an antenna sticking out of it, so it is probably up on Monkey Island—on the roof of the bridge—with the radar, radio, and satellite antennae.

"Better I don't know, really," the captain says.

"But you do know. . . ."

An enigmatic look, a slight grin.

I suggest that the company is afraid that pirates would torture him to find it.

"Yes, I think so."

And if it comes to that?

He throws his hands up in the air—"I give up my ship."

Than is no old swashbuckling skipper of a tramp tanker calling into remote and seedy ports. He is an educated man, with a university degree in a science that takes him as far away from the sea as possible on earth—geology. He went to sea in 1975 to escape the repressive regime of General U Ne Win, who turned Burma into a police state; being a seaman was pretty good money then and it was one of the few professions for which passports were issued. So he started again from scratch and became a cadet on a government merchant ship. When he is not commanding a ship, he is a visiting lecturer at the Institute of Marine Technology in Yangon, formerly Rangoon.

He appears to be a loner; whether it is his personality, or because of rank, or because only one other on the ship comes from Burma and speaks his native language, is not clear. His solitude is nowhere more apparent than during mealtime, a rather miscellaneous event. There is no officers-only mess as on the *Montrose* or on the tiny *Papa Zulu Four*. A ship is not an egalitarian society—there is a well-defined command structure as found in any quasi-military operation. But this is an Asian-built ship run by an Asian company manned by Asians. There is no decorous protocol observed here, no flummery accorded the office: even though he is Buddhist, the captain eats the same halal food as all his Islamic crew, from engine-room greaser to chief officer. The Indonesians and the Malaysians sit at one table, deftly finger-eating their food as is their tradition, prattling away in their language; the non-Muslims, the Hindu, the Buddhists, the Christians, and others generally eat at the next table using knife, fork, and spoon. It is a natural separation for this most important daily event in a sailor's life. After a meal the captain washes his own dishes as we all do—unlike on the *Montrose*, which, despite a smaller crew, assigns a steward to wash dishes, serve the food, and daily clean the officers' quarters. In port a television on a wall-stand at the end of one table rattles away twenty-four hours a day; it provides a welcome distraction from forced chatter between crew and officers, officers and captain. Captain Than doesn't seem to be unpopular—there is simply little small talk; a member of this crew, even an officer, doesn't ask the captain how many children he has or whether he likes the ship or how long he's been at sea.

He says he has decided it is time to leave the sea, to return home to his wife and two daughters. The current military regime in Myanmar is nearly as bad as that which he fled—where an unlicensed fax machine can land you in jail—but he thinks international sanctions are forcing it to loosen its totalitarian grip; one day, the captain says, there will be democracy and a climate for private enterprise. He will start his own business in a field that he knows so well—a shipping agency for the companies that send their vessels to Rangoon once the country opens up to the rest of the world.

Later, on the bridge, he admits, "I do love the sea—when the weather is good. But I sometimes get seasick." A tanker captain who gets seasick; he is an honest man.

It is a stunning afternoon, bright, tropical; the sea shimmers in the sunlight as it rolls softly across our course. Towering cumulonimbus build over Borneo on the right; the tops of these massive clouds appear to explode upward with a force before my eyes—roil, twist, expand higher, until they can go no farther.

Three of our crew sit on their heels on the poop deck, propped against the railing, and watch another cut the hair of one of their colleagues. The barber, the A/B, wears blue coveralls and a blue New York Yankees baseball cap and works with red-handled children's paper scissors and an old comb with a few teeth missing. He works with precision. The guys ramble on about something, sometimes laughing—a joke in Indonesian; they offer big smiles and one waves tentatively. It is a warm, companionable affair.

The *Petro Concord* has the feel of a ship at sea; she rides a swell and gives way to the sea, unlike a VLCC that defies it. You feel the vibrations of engine, the turning of shaft, the bite of propeller, the occasional shudder as a crossing sea smacks against an oversized rudder; you hear the steady quiet roar of air conditioning, the throaty rumble of the big diesel. She smells like a ship, of lube oil and grease, of fuel oil, kerosene, and the sea and preparations of the midday meal.

To most seafarers a ship is an object of some beauty, one of those inanimate constructs of steel, alloy, and wood upon which men proffer qualities human and beyond, a thing of certain spiritual essence. Perhaps it is because a sailor is afraid of the sea, knows he will always be less than the sea, insignificant, less important here than anywhere else on the planet, and fears that he may die at sea. Whether on a crab boat in the Bering Sea icing up and close to capsizing, or on a clapped-out old tramp off the French coast battling a midwinter Atlantic storm, on a modern VLCC in the Persian Gulf twisting and wrenching in a Bay of Bengal typhoon, or on a sailboat in the middle of South Pacific pissing yourself because you probably won't be able to get out of the path of the dangerous semicircle of a cyclone, your ship is all that stands between you and the creatures in the sea who will nibble and pick apart your rotting flesh. Out here a man, a woman, is truly alone. On land we have become inured to the reality of death; we see it all the time—earthquakes, floods, and famine wipe out thousands and we have come to ignore death or to minimize it; yet at sea, no matter what the ship, we feel we are closer to our maker. To those who cross the seas, the ship is more than a mere universe, it becomes part of the essential core of our being, and we imbue our vessel with our own unique spiritual traits that we pray are strong enough to carry us through the worst conditions. It is why men have always called a ship "she."

When the *Petro Concord* is under way, there is little noise outside except for the rush of the passing sea. Quiet save for the occasional rattle from the tall rows of vent pipes sticking out of the cargo deck. These pipes stand like single old-fashioned streetlamps with outstretched cruciform arms grasping little red teats capped with the bronze bullet tips. When the jet fuel and kerosene expand in the heat inside the tanks, the inflammable vapors vent through these bronze caps of the pressure vacuum valves in a sudden noisy fidgety clatter of metal against metal. It was the gaseous fumes emitting from these vents that so concerned Captain Monteiro and it is why no "naked lights," not even a disposable lighter buried in a pocket, are permitted on deck at any time.

Up at the bow, I crane over to watch the ship slice through the seas; the bow wave rises nearly to the anchors. A couple of dolphin chase the wave, play tag with this rumbling piece of machinery called a ship. I remember on my first ship when I was a teenager—I wasn't very useful then; I worked as a "wiper" in the engine room of a Panamanian-registered rust bucket, an ancient World War II T-2 tanker; it was mere grunt work, cleaning oil and grease off the walkways and the machinery, squirting a grease gun, turning valve wheels, performing minor maintenance tasks that any teenager, any aspiring seaman, could learn. I spent much of my off-watch hours out on deck, staring out at the horizon, daydreaming. In high school I was called a dreamer; often I dreamed about the sea. From prep school the only way you were to go to sea was through the Naval Academy—but never, God forbid, by working your way "up through the fo'c'scle." Today, thousands of sea miles later, I still stare out across the sea and daydream. I have never understood why so many seafarers spend most of the time off watch cloistered within their cabins, in the rec room or mess, when they could be outside searching, looking, staring, daydreaming. Considering how much time a seaman spends at sea, the sea itself really takes very little of their attention.

The indigo-blue water rushes smoothly past; the surface is not far below the deck—only about ten feet; in a heavy crossing swell we would be awash. At sea speed our ship's wake is much less than I expected; the wave from the bow is hardly noticeable, there is no midships wave and our propwash is not even whitewater—much different from years past when a ship "plowed" through the sea, creating a rolling bow wave that, on a flat sea, could be seen and felt for miles. A large bow wave means greater resistance. And resistance means money to the shipowner. To reduce resistance naval architects came up with the idea of extending the bow below the waterline, adding a bulblike protrusion. This relatively new design keeps the stern of a ship from squatting and allows flatter trim amidships. The bulbous bow, now found on most vessels, probably has saved shipping companies more money in the long term than any other recent development in naval architecture. But it has also been a boon to predators planning to hijack a ship. Without a midships wave and stern wake it has become considerably easier for a speedboat to tie up alongside or onto the stern while a vessel is under way. The poop deck of this ship is only about fourteen feet above the surface, about the same distance as the *Montrose;* pirates could raise a household stepladder from another boat and climb aboard in a lick.

A lone figure in white coveralls leans against the railing of the ship's catwalk, looking out over the sea. It is our chief engineer, Vincent Chibueze Udoye, the tall Nigerian who commands the crew in the engine room. He must be daydreaming, for there is nothing out there but the horizon. I am reluctant to break into whatever abstracted musings he may be having, but he catches my eye and waves me up.

"Fresh air?"

"I come out and look at the sea to sort myself out," he says.

"Rare for a sailor."

"I suppose. But in the engine room I might as well be working in a factory. I need to get out."

Vincent is an imposing man, built like a prizefighter, with quick eyes and a shiny bald pate that he absently rubs. In my scant dealings with him I have noticed a driving enthusiasm for matters over the horizon—that there is just too much out there to learn to sit still. He is a person who is excited about what he knows and that which he has learned, he is eager to pass on; he is a natural teacher. Given the opportunity, he'll expound on the various flash points and kinematic viscosity ratings of the cargo that we carry and expect that his enthusiasm is yours.

He is a chartered engineer. This means his skills are recognized worldwide. Petroships knows they are lucky to have him, and they frequently raise his salary as incentive to stay on. But it is in his eyes:

he'll not be spending the rest of his life at sea; he has served his time. He admits he was thinking just now about his family, his two-year-old daughter and his wife who live in the UK. They progress, they go forward, and they develop, he says, while he stays on a bloody ship watching them pass him by.

As we talk, a large tanker a couple of miles astern begins to overtake us. We have been aware of the ship for some time; it has grown from an indistinct smudge on the horizon to this point where it is clear she intends to pass. Our speed is about thirteen knots, so it must be going nearly twenty. As it closes on us, it is identifiable as a VLCC loaded to capacity, bound either for the Philippines or Japan. So this is how the *Montrose* looks under way; low and flat in the water like a floating runway. It is not the length that strikes me but the width of the thing. It seems as wide as the *Petro Concord* is long. Laden, she looks like an iceberg; most of her bulk lies beneath the surface. I now begin to feel how crews on other ships must regard the *Montrose*— awed and intimidated. On board I'd had no idea.

The entire ship, hull and superstructure, is painted a pea-green, and the bridgewings, extending from a small wheelhouse on top, do look like the narrow wings of an aircraft, not stubby protrusions like ours on the *Petro Concord* but suspended walkways supported by thin corbeled struts that reach out over the boat deck.

The vessel appears to be running parallel but it is deceiving, for we can see she is beginning to crowd us. Vincent stops in midsentence and stares. Our deck crew, clad in their blue coveralls and hard hats, have stopped working on the large red valve wheels and stand over their buckets of grease to watch with some admiration and curiosity the passage of this magnificent vessel. The VLCC dwarfs us and we are made to feel very insignificant indeed. As important as our cargo is and as many 747s that we can fuel, we are made virtually unworthy by this contemptuous leviathan. Against this ship we are reminded that we are only 12,000 tons and this ship next to us is 300,000 tons. Indeed, it could swallow us for lunch; the bunkers she carries for her engine alone are nearly as much as our entire cargo.

It is now abeam of us and closing; there is no one on its decks, no silhouette visible through the windows on the bridge—like a ghost ship it just seems to steam unguided.

"Good Lord! It is going to cross our bow," Vincent is incredulous. "This is going to be close."

It is the burdened vessel—we are the stand-on vessel and we have the "right of way"—on two counts: it is overtaking us and we are on its starboard. So absurd is the situation that I cannot feel threatened. This cannot be happening. How could it? Two ships, both loaded to the gunwales with flammable cargo, out in the middle of the South China Sea in daylight, in perfect visibility, with an absolutely flat surface, no encroaching traffic, no restrictive lanes—about to collide. The supertanker keeps on coming, makes no effort to avoid us. Out here might makes right.

The *Berge Sigval* from Stavanger, Norway—for its name is now quite clear—is going for it; it will attempt to cut across our bow at about a thirty-five-degree angle. At our present closing speeds it is unlikely that it will succeed without hitting us. Most of our ship's crew, called out by their mates, are topsides, leaning out over the railing, staring with startled eyes at the tanker. I notice that both Vincent and I are grasping the railing with our knuckles nearly white. I fervently hope our watch standers on the bridge, the Malaysian cadet and the youthful Bangladeshi third officer, have alerted the captain and that he has taken over the helm; I look up at the bridge but can see nothing through the tinted glass.

The *Petro Concord* suddenly begins to vibrate, the whole ship shudders. In answer to my unspoken prayer we are reducing speed.

Incredibly, the *Berge Sigval* just keeps coming. Because we are slowing, it doesn't look like it will hit us directly, but now it doesn't look like we can avoid ramming it amidships. A fleeting thought: I wonder what happens when two tankers collide? Do they blow up? Just catch fire? Just spill millions of gallons of their different highly volatile payloads? Without altering course the VLCC starts to slide just in front of our bow. It is going to be very close. Our ship suddenly turns sharply to port, directly toward the tanker's flat stern, then slowly farther over until we just miss the ship's transom. To someone watching the drama on another radar the two ships would have merged as one on the screen.

"My God, I've never come so close," Vincent mutters. In his fifteen years at sea this is as near to a collision with a VLCC as he ever wants to get; he adds wistfully that not so long ago, he aspired to be chief engineer of such a ship. Later I hear that while some of the crew thought that we were going to be eaten alive by this jolly green monster, they were also in awe of it, remarking to each other that wouldn't it be something to work on a fine ship like that?

The imperturbable Captain Than doesn't want to make much of the incident. "Close," is all he'll say. He cites Rule 18 of the International Collision Regulations, which states a vessel shall keep clear of another "restricted in her ability to maneuver." This would work in the Malacca Straits, but it is a little weak out here; the ship had us in its sights fifteen miles away, and with miles of unlimited sea room and a slight course change to starboard—of only a single degree—it could have kept well clear of us. And for this rule there are others more applicable—overtaking and starboard position—that for these circumstances give us unassailable priority. Captain Than finally took evasive action, reducing speed, turning in, and avoiding it by what the photographs later show was a very narrow margin indeed. "She was bigger—we were smaller," Than says simply of his prudent action. During the *Berge Sigval*'s incautious challenge and during the *Petro Concord*'s evasive maneuver, neither captain so much as radioed the other, no one on either bridge went out to the wing to signal, shout, or otherwise act if anything was out of the ordinary.

Bergesen d.y. Group, of Oslo, which owns the *Berge Sigval*, prides itself as the world's "largest independent shipping company in U/VLCC tonnage."[50] It claims its vessels are "manned by highly trained and experienced crews." If so the officers on watch, on this day, appeared to have been sleeping off their Singapore shore leave.

According to casualty reports a ship bumps into another somewhere in the world at last once a day—often, inexplicably, during the same absurdly perfect conditions as we have today. In fact in conditions such as these the fully laden VLCC *Maersk Navigator*, carrying crude to Japan, collided with the bulk carrier *Sanko Honour* at the northern entrance of the Malacca Straits. It spilled nearly eight million gallons of oil, about the same amount released by the *Exxon*

Valdez—the two ships were well out to sea and pollution to the land was avoided. There was no explanation for the accident.

⌒

Vincent takes me on a cook's tour of his domain, down into the steamy bowels of the engine room.

This is not a double-hulled ship—too small—so no water ballast tanks, no manly challenge to descend into hell's hole. Merely a tour of an engine room. Delightful.

He proudly explains every gauge, every dial on the panel in the control room that answers the commands from the bridge; he reveals the best operating temperatures for diesel and fuel oil, the size of the pistons in the big Mitsubishi diesel; he shows me the fire-fighting foam storage room, takes me to the steering room, where the electro-hydraulic ram turns the ship's large rudder, and finally down to the sphinctered end, to the vessel's huge spinning stainless steel shaft that turns the propeller—the end result of all this heat and madness. The innards of a ship this size have changed little since I was down here so briefly in my youth (after one trip in the engine room I knew I had to get out and work the deck). While I still find it as fascinating as any kid, I am more interested in finding out whether, with all our anti-piracy precautions, we can be penetrated.

For a ship that prides itself on doing all that is possible to prevent pirate ingress, the *Petro Concord*, like the *Montrose*, I discover, is far from secure. While some pirates might find it difficult to board with fire hoses blasting and the decks lit up like a Vegas casino, it would not be difficult for them to find a way inside once on board.

The hatches, skylights, and vents are secured from below with chain and cinched tight by turnbuckles.

But not in the CO_2 room—the sterile chamber that houses thirty-four red man-sized cylinders of carbon dioxide, huge extinguishers to smother a blaze in the engine room. The overhead steel escape hatch opens up on the poop deck. A thick rope loops through the handles of the hatch and is tied to the bottom rung of the steel escape ladder. It looks solid and the rope is tight. But I wonder aloud whether lashing the hatch with rope could keep out determined pirates. I once tied down the fo'c'scle hatch of the *Unicorn* in East Africa only to have it cut by a thief; it was a fool's way of doing things. Rope stretches. Later, topsides, Vincent and I heft the roped-down heavy steel cover. With little effort we are able to lift the hatch just high enough for a pirate to slip the blade of a long knife through the opening and cut the rope.

And the engine-room skylight is not just unlocked, it is held open by a half-ton chain block attached to the steel ladder welded to the funnel. "We never close it," Vincent says. And for good reason. The engine room here in the tropics often seems hotter than hell itself. After a three-day passage normal working temperatures down in the hole for the men wearing coveralls, work boots, and hard hats reaches 43°C (116°F). "When it's closed, it gets up to 48 degrees (126°F). We have to let the gases out of the engine room," the chief engineer explains. The only time it is closed is during a tropic downpour when the ship is in port.

If I were a pirate and determined to get into the ship, it would be no big thing to abseil down the inner wall of the skylight, kick away, and grab on to the railing of the catwalk a few feet distant. A mistake could result in your death, but it doesn't look all that hard. Hollywood could make it happen.

The engine crew could get their fresh air and the pirates could be kept out if a welded rebar grill were hinged to the inside and padlocked to the frame. The bosun could build that within his four-hour watch.

And taking over the ship without violence is not all that hard either. From the engine room it is a short distance to the air conditioning room. Large enclosed fans blow chilled clean air throughout the accommodation bloc. Fresh air is never pumped in from the outside because of the possibility of sucking up toxic fumes, so it is circulated and recirculated—a closed loop. Vincent opens a small steel door to the big fans and sprays lemon scented air freshener into the blowers. Instantly the stink of chemical lemon permeates the entire accommodation bloc, the galley, the mess, the crew's cabins, the bridge, and the cargo control room. A pirate in the early morning hours could scale down the engine room skylight, creep along the steel grating to the air conditioning room, strap on a mask, and spray some knock-out gas into the air circulation unit and pull off a hijacking without resistance.

It all sounds a bit over the top, but if the pirates and terrorists have been so clever as to hijack ships and airplanes, plunder cargo, and commandeer ferry boats with near military precision, what is to stop them from taking over any ship afloat?

Later, over coffee in the mess room, Vincent says he had always known what he was going to do with his life. In Lagos as a child, he recalls that he walked barefoot to the docks and watched the ships arrive from strange faraway ports—Hamburg, Rotterdam, London, Baltimore, New Orleans, places he had heard about in school. "I really wanted to go to sea—but then I didn't know what it meant to become a seaman. Still, I love the sea." Now, professionally and personally, he has had enough. The fear of piracy, he says, has a lot to do with his decision.

Whether on a tiny sailboat bobbing in the middle of the ocean, a *Montrose*-sized crude carrier rumbling down the Malacca Straits, or a product carrier in a sea where murder is not uncommon, those who work the ships, wherever they are in the world, on whatever sea, don't need to be reminded how dangerous it is. Out here their fear is real. Hell, I feel it. And I sense Vincent's fear. There is no one to call for help if attacked. A ship goes missing, its crew is never heard from again. What of it? The nagging disquiet of normal at-sea loneliness is brought home a thousandfold when you also are afraid. This seems all so unnecessary—we are civilians, we shouldn't have to be on a war footing just to deliver some goods that the world can't live without. For many the attraction to the life at sea is no match for the demons of their isolation and the fear for their lives. They are alone out here. But then the sea is the world's greatest wilderness.

There is a sudden scream from the adjoining room. I jump up and find some of the crew watching a video in the rec room.

This is the most popular gathering place for the crew aboard ship; it is one of the few areas where smoking is permitted. There is a tired festive atmosphere about the place—red paper Chinese lanterns swing with the ship's motion, relics of a Buddhist New Year celebration long forgotten, and the walls are decked with gold, red, and silver paper decorations proclaiming *Selamat Hari Raya*, remnants of the feast at the end of Ramadan that occurred even before the Buddhists celebrated theirs. The cheap wood plastic paneling is plastered with industrial safety warnings. And the poster with fierce-looking pirates climbing aboard that accompanies the Videotel training film. On this ship who needs to be warned?

There are a couple of couches, a card table, and chairs. A broken rowing machine is jammed into a far corner, a contraption that the crew ignore like old wreckage. Ali and Suli, two of the Indonesian crew, are staring wide eyed at the video, reciting and mimicking the words in *The Perfect Storm*, which, along with *Titanic*, they've seen until seawater pours out of their dreams. Firefighters, I suppose, watch movies about burning buildings, and pilots about airplanes. But absolutely, many seafarers watch movies about the sea, even if they do show hundred-foot waves curling over a small fishing boat and saccharine tears spilling as the great liner sinks below the sea. Darman probably sat with his mates in an identical room, watching the same films. I wonder if they have aboard any movies about pirates? *Hook?* Disney's *Blackbeard?* Do pirates watch movies about hijackings?

We have just had another antipiracy meeting; the captain was on the bridge and Noah and Vincent held the chair. The atmosphere was quiet, somber; we are near the spot where the *Petro Ranger* was hijacked, where other ships have disappeared.

Noah announces that wire cable has replaced the rope securing the hatch over the CO_2 room—impossible to open from the outside. Then he reminds this small group of defenders to use full hose, not the spray.

Every ship has its resident comedian, and one is needed tonight. Ours is Ali, known as Ali Baba, the square-faced Indonesian A/B with the frizzy hair. "It's better I use a gun, Chief," he says, throwing out his chest like a tough guy.

"You find one, you use it." Noah has little patience. "The way we stop them is to see them first. So vigilance. Keep your eyes open!"

Another Indonesian character walks in, his eyes a little puffy, his black hair and mustache plastered wet against his face. He is a little embarrassed. He was off watch and he overslept.

"Suli! Where have you been?"

"He's scared of pirates," Ali Baba offers, making big shocking eyes. The crew laughs nervously.

"Pirates afraid too," Suli says. And the others agree.

19

In the Dark of the Night

Petro Concord

The fear of an attack is so strong tonight that I wonder if its very intensity doesn't make the event a certainty. We are prepared. But such preparations, such a battle plan, haven't stopped them before.

The rumbling vibration of the ship's powerful engine, a sensory combination of sound and feeling—unfailing and steady—soothes, mitigates the nervousness, the fears. And the smell of dinner: *gule kambing*, goat meat stewed in coconut milk, *soto ayam*, chicken soup, *ikan bilis*, knuckle-sized whole whitebait with peanuts, and deep-fried prawns and rice—wafts through the corridors and sneaks into my cabin like an invited guest. Comforting. But outside the hoses shoot a withering stream of high-pressure water into the night, bright lights seek out every shadow, and the Aldis lamp directed from the bridge scans the waters beyond; crewmen on patrol check in with the bridge by walkie-talkie every fifteen minutes. It is a strange sensation, waiting to be attacked.

While every ship is vulnerable, some are more so than others. The very size of the *Montrose* gave us an unwitting, dangerous sense of security. We were nine stories above the sea, and even though our transom was low to the surface, we could be forgiven for feeling invincible. After all, there are hundreds of ships out there and most of them are easier targets than a VLCC. On the smaller *Petro Concord*, however, we steam through these waters with no delusions, no false sense of security. We know that we are a soft target. Piracy is taken very seriously by this captain and crew. The fear this night is not imagined, not by me, not by the boys who have to patrol the poop deck looking for pirates and praying they won't find any.

Ali, the grinning Indonesian with the jokes, says a friend of his was killed by pirates, or at least he thinks he was. The ship his mate was working had been hijacked and neither the ship nor the crew were ever seen again.

We are at 02.30N–105.06E, approaching Pulau Pulau Anambas, a small group of volcanic islands that litter the area like spilled crumbs. They lie in the path of most ships steaming through the Orient. Attacks on vessels passing these islands occur frequently, often with tragic results. The tanker *Theresa*, about the same size as our ship, had been steaming past a fleet of fishing boats when the chief officer noticed two echoes on the radar screen break away from the pack and approach his ship. Despite the antipiracy measures, thirty pirates armed with U.S.-issue M-16s on two small boats forced their way on board and overwhelmed the deck patrol. They shot out the bridge windows, shot the third officer, looted the ship of all cash and crews' valuables, and returned to their boats five hours later.

We should be abeam the Anambas group at about 2230 hours. We are on full alert. The present conditions favor the pirates—there is little wind and the sea is dead calm, with a slight swell from the northeast; lightning backlights thunderheads over Borneo to our right.

Our poop deck is fully illuminated, as are the waters astern. Fire hoses, wired to the railings at the corner of each side of the poop deck below and at the forward part of the superstructure, shoot a steady high-powered stream about twenty feet outboard until their force is spent by the wind.

With our battle plans in place it still seems inconceivable that any pirates would consider attacking us. Our defense is a strong one. Yet we know they are out there and we know that it might happen—

probably not in the next few hours but, according to the captain, just before dawn, when most of us need to get some sleep and those patrolling the decks are at their least alert. We hope that if they see us looking for them, they might go elsewhere. That is what we hope.

Suli is patrolling, not stalking, but just walking around. He stops, gazes up at the crystal night sky, then resumes his stroll. His presence is enough. He is a slight fellow but from a distance adequately fearsome in his blue boilersuit, a white T-shirt he has wrapped as a headpiece, and a walkie-talkie sticking out of a breast pocket. Tonight is his anniversary—he has been on the *Petro Concord* for a solid year. His wife has had a baby that he has never seen. A year on this ship without a break—seems like a prison sentence to me.

Suli can escape, of course; he can sign off anytime he likes—he is not a prisoner. But on land without work, or sweeping a Singapore or Jakarta street, he would face a more serious desperation.

I enter the blacked-out wheelhouse from behind a heavy curtain that separates it from the lighted chart and radio section. I announce myself quietly—I've not been asked to, but I feel it is the right thing to do; I wouldn't want someone unannounced to walk into my dream. There is a vestal, vaguely deific atmosphere about the bridge of a ship at sea at night—strangely sacrosanct and inviolable, a place of invisible movement, of confessional tones and preferred silence. Talk is limited and an infrequent command softly spoken.

It takes a while for my eyes to adjust. The silhouettes of the captain, his second officer, and a cadet glide through the darkness. The clear outline of the ship's wide nose slices through the black water ahead and splits the calm seas in a long, frothy phosphorescent wave that splays out from each side. Low clouds torn from a faraway squall slide in front of a gibbous moon. A slash of lightning briefly lights our faces. There are ships nearby: a vessel a few hundreds yards away on the starboard side is about to pass; she is lit by a horizontal string of lamps along her deck, beneath the stacks of boxcar-sized containers. A liquid natural gas carrier that passed us a few minutes ago had its guard up—its poop deck was brightly lighted and its hoses fired outboard. We are not alone out here. But we are. In spite of the traffic we know with certainty that no ship will come to our rescue during an attack. Nor would we go to theirs. Out here we are on our own.

One of the two watch standers walks out to the bridgewing and scans the faint horizon; the other bends to the radar. There are some showers ahead, and they turn up as a messy blob on the screen. The solid return is the container ship off the starboard side. But there are two other small echoes that don't seem to be moving. Those are probably fishing boats. I look up from the screen into the darkness ahead. Moments ago they were running before us with regulation navigation lights. Odd, but the boats seem to have vanished. I no longer see their red and green running lights. No reason that I can think of to turn out the lights, especially when a big tanker is bearing down on them. But then maybe I was seeing things.

The young cadet, who had been stationed at the radar screen, walks out to the bridgewing and with the ship's binoculars scans the seas around us; he had seen the targets.

"Fishing boats wouldn't turn their lights off, would they?" I ask the captain.

"They would and they would get close, very close, to look us over. If they see that we are not prepared, maybe then they become pirates. If they see that we know they are there, well, they go back to fishing."

How the two spook boats can be there one minute and gone the next is a mystery. There is no sea to speak of, only a low swell from the northeast. Nothing that could hide the navigation lights or a couple of echoes. They were only intermittently detected by the radar, the type of return you would get from large rubber dinghies or low-slung wooden boats. They could have been small fishing boats or speedboats. Whatever they were, they were on a course to cross our bow when they vanished; perhaps they have passed in front us and are motoring away toward the islands. Captain Than and I search the darkness ahead. The captain is very much in control, very smooth, yet as he stands beside me on the bridgewing, I sense something different in his presence, a stiffness. We should have night vision glasses to see anything in this light. The talk is hushed but tense. They must be out here someplace. They can't just disappear.

"Captain!" The second mate's loud voice, his tone, raises the hair on the back of my neck.

Captain Than joins the officer at the radar screen. I look over their shoulders. Two tiny green targets seem to be moving, and as the radial arm of the radar makes its 360 degree sweep, it is apparent they are coming this way. Another sweep: The targets are moving quickly toward us—angled and closing on our stern. There is an apparent blind spot off our starboard quarter. One target, then the other, disappears within it. They are gone. But they are out there.

The captain rushes out onto the bridgewing. "Suli! You look! Tell others—quickly, aft!"

He returns to the radar inside the bridge. My heart is in my throat. I hear running of feet, a frightening sound on a ship. Below, Suli and Ali are wrestling with the fire hoses; they direct torrents of water off the poop deck down toward the sea where they expect pirates will try to board.

We know the boats are just beyond the protective barrier of light that we have created around the back end of our ship. We are now all outside. We wait, expecting them to burst through the wall of light any second. I wonder if we shouldn't be locked down, inside—they can't get us if we lock ourselves in. No one says a word. We wait and search. The evening is warm, but the sea air is chilling. They are out there somewhere. Stalking. Sussing us out.

I follow the captain inside and to the radar screen. Our eyes follow the radial sweep for the targets; we can't find the bloody things. How close are they? Maintaining their positions within the blind sector, they hold off our stern somewhere out there. The wait is terrible, something I imagine like the minutes before a battle. What the hell are they doing? A large ship passes us about a mile off our starboard. Will its brightly illuminated poop deck help us find the two boats hanging off our stern? I try to pierce the barrier of shimmering artificial light that we have created behind us but I can't get through, no matter how hard I will it. I think of that SWAT team in Nigeria and the pirates bursting through the stern lights and attacking. And I wait and expect to see them charging at us any second. The sea breeze is that much colder.

The captain stands by my side, scanning. Now I feel his tension.

"Captain!" a voice comes from inside the bridge. "Captain, look!"

I follow Captain Than into the bridge and to the radar.

The captain grunts something unintelligible, taps the screen with his forefinger.

Two small targets hover at the edge of the blind spot and onto the screen. They seem to be falling back.

The cadet on the wing calls the captain outside. I see the navigation lights of one boat, then the lights of the other, suddenly come on. In the haze and through the glare of our own spotlights, we can see the faint shadows of the small boats; they are too far away for us to make out what type of boats they are. Ten minutes they had followed us, sniffed at us—checked us out. Now they hang back, still following, with the unabashed impudence of stalking muggers who are changing their minds at the sight of a cop. What are they? They turn and head off toward the other echoes on the screen that make up the fishing fleet, at a speed faster than most fishing boats. Evidently they were not out here fishing.

We pass the Anambas without further incident, but the stalking remains uncomfortably with us. If those boats had intended to hijack us, if they had been assigned to take our ship, they probably could have done so with or without our antipiracy defenses. If they were fishermen, opportunists, looking for a score, then they passed us by for easier game, for another ship without such obvious piracy precautions in place.

We are sailing out of pirate territory now, but I'm told the gauntlet does not end here. We have been weaving in and out of Vietnamese fishing fleets for the past few hours. The captain writes in his night orders to avoid them at all costs. He says the fishermen are reported to be shooting at passing ships that come too close to their nets.

We have completed our mission. We are tied to the oil terminal pier at Nha Be, a few miles downriver from Ho Chi Minh City, and we have begun discharging. We will never know whether any fishermen took potshots at us, although we passed through groups of substantial-looking fishing boats. There were no bullet holes anywhere near the bridge that we could find.

It is late at night; a heavy mist envelops the ship and I feel the need to stand in it. Out on the bridgewing I stare at Vietnam; a goose-stepping armed guard with rifle on his shoulder marches the length of the glistening terminal pier below; the lights of Ho Chi Minh City brighten most of the sky to the north and to the east, over the little tributaries and channels that wind through the mangrove swamp of the Mekong Delta, it is dark and mysterious and junglelike. Distant lightning teases the imagination.

Last night we were either "pirated" or we picked up a stowaway. A stowaway is worse. If the stowaway is Vietnamese and we find him, then we can hand him over to the local police: best-case scenario. But if he is a Filipino who boarded when the ship called in at the Philippines some weeks ago, then Petroships would have to find a country that would accept him. Few countries would. Captain Than tells me that some stowaways have been known to remain on a vessel for as long as a year, locked in the cabin when in port, free to roam the ship when at sea.

One Shell tanker had picked up a stowaway in Dar es Salaam, Tanzania. They tried to get rid of him in a half-dozen ports in the Mediterranean and Europe but no one would take him. The ship had to keep him on board until it returned to the East African port many months later.

"Greek ships—they find stowaway," Captain Than says, "they throw overboard. That is easier. They don't want the problems."

I ask him what he would do if he found a stowaway.

He smiles. I don't get an answer.

The crew, both deck and engine, are turning the ship inside-out looking for the guy, but on a ship there are nooks and crannies, many places to tuck into.

Evidence of boarding was first discovered by Vincent, who interrupted breakfast. "We've got strange footprints by the funnel, Captain. Also down in the engine room."

The captain, Vincent, Noah, and I rush up the steps two at a time to the boat deck outside my cabin. Barefoot tracks are stenciled in black soot and caking white salt on the deck, as distinct as if they had been painted on a city sidewalk. The prints disappear through the steel door of the funnel. They are round trip tracks, and it is unclear whether the tracks are from someone coming out—a stowaway—or someone going in, a thief. Perhaps a stowaway got hungry and was looking for food or needed air, was getting claustrophobic or wanted to see what port this was. He could only have climbed out of the engine room if the engine had cooled down. Otherwise he would have fried as he squeezed himself through the eight-inch space between the funnel housing and the main engine exhaust.

Where could a stowaway board? Not in Singapore. Who in their right mind would want to forsake Singapore for Vietnam? A stowaway, however, could have climbed off of one of the three bumboats that tied alongside us yesterday, whose occupants tried to peddle Rambo T-shirts, beer, soft drinks, and silk. It would not have been difficult for one of them to sneak aboard and disappear inside.

During our search of the engine room Vincent suggests to the captain that perhaps it is someone planted on board who will be involved in a hijack. Now, that does seems improbable, but you can't fault the man for his creativity.

On the drying deck it appears now that the footprints lead from the poop deck below, enter the funnel door, and return back down to the deck, evidently to an awaiting boat. So we were boarded by shoreside thieves in the night from boats alongside—pirates in the loosely defined sense. It is odd that nothing significant appears stolen, although one of the crew says his running shoes placed outside his door are missing. Perhaps he will be able to buy them back in the local market. The thieves may have fled when one of the engineers on watch turned a corner. But it shows how easy it is to board and enter this ship without getting busted: We are tied to the pier of a high-security national petroleum depot that is surrounded with gulaglike watchtowers and guards who patrol the dock with their assault rifles; our stern lines are strung to a mooring block that is just in front of the shore police, and we have two young Vietnamese guards on board with AK-47s. The evidence is that the pirates climbed aboard from the river side of our ship. Our armed guards wouldn't have nabbed them; from what I've seen, our guards spend their time drinking tea, watching television, eating, and sleeping. They don't go outside.

It would be a natural assumption that these thieves were armed at least with a blade or two. As often occurs and is seldom reported, a member of the crew goes out on deck in the middle of the night and bumps into them. The crewman is knifed, injured, or killed and the pirates escape. I shudder to think what would have happened had any of us stumbled onto one of the bastards. It didn't happen, after all, thankfully. Yet bumping into shore-based thieves after they've boarded a ship is a near daily occurrence in ports throughout the world—in Miami, in Newark, in Barcelona, in Antwerp, in Nha Be—and it is just one of the additional hundreds of assaults that go unrecorded. It is a cinch that the boarding here, this petty theft, will never be reported. After all, the cargo was delivered and the conveyor that had begun in the Middle East ended here without anyone getting killed.

20

Attack in Real Time

Kuala Lumpur

Those who work and live at sea well know that their ships, the cargo they carry, and more importantly, their lives, are at risk. I know firsthand their concerns. But I also wanted an industry perspective on piracy, so I became a fly on the wall at the Fourth International Meeting on Piracy and Phantom Ships held in Kuala Lumpur, Malaysia, in late June 2001, where shipowners and insurance executives, investors and lawyers, diplomats, military and law officers sought some solutions to the crime that was a threat not only to their industry but to the global economy.

Organized by the International Maritime Bureau, its director, Captain P. K. Mukundan, hoped at best that the conference might alert the public that there is a very serious problem out on the world's seaways with an enormous potential for disaster. At the end of the conference, alas, there was no more public awareness that piracy existed than before the meeting. Yet it wasn't a waste of time. During the conference Mukundan and his crew saved a ship and probably a number of lives.

Muku, as he is called, welcomed the delegates with bad news. Piracy was out of control, the numbers of attempted boardings, actual boardings, and hijackings were skyrocketing. He told them more seafarers were getting killed or injured each year. The owners whose ships had been hijacked or robbed and the preachers and the unions who represented the men and women who work the sea didn't have to be told.

Muku, a genial, even-tempered ship's master, has spent years out there; the safety of his crew and his ship are paramount, as it is to nearly every captain; he probably would be the last man off the ship. As an ex-seafarer he tried to set the tone and put the crime into human terms. On the wall-sized screen he showed his first slide.

It was of a naked seaman from a ship hijacked in the South China Sea whose body had been washed ashore. The seafarer had been bludgeoned, knifed, and shot before being kicked overboard. The corpse, picked apart by fish and surface crabs, was bloated like a Thanksgiving Day Parade balloon—it appeared that if you stuck a pin in it, it would gush gallons of saltwater and seaweed. It was barely recognizable as a human being, as a man whose family still prayed for his return.

The next slide was of an officer who had tried to defend his ship. There was not much left of him either—a parang had neatly cleaved his head in two. The body's one open eye conveyed all the terror this man felt before feeling no more. This was the expression of a man rousted from his bunk with a knife to his throat and told that if didn't cooperate, he would be killed.

The photographs were an encouraging start. I had been hoping that this was going to be a conference not of frequent fliers on company-paid junkets but of compassionate members of the industry who also were concerned with lives. But I could not help but wonder if these slides would have the opposite effect, stressing less the sanctity of life than the anonymity of death, of how little we count on earth. Apparently it did, for with nary a raised eyebrow we moved right along with speeches that suited the delegates' own agendas:

"It has been estimated that losses in piracy amount to about sixteen billion dollars U.S. The total sum of sixteen billion means roughly two and half dollars for every human being. That is for one year and that is the cost to the world," intoned one shipowner.

Nothing more than a resolution or two was expected from the conference—had not pirates themselves provided a little assistance.

⁓

Muku informs me during a coffee break that two ships have just been attacked in the Straits, one of them hijacked.

The timing is propitious. Perhaps these attacks, occurring at a time when this international piracy conference is being conducted within miles of the events, will help put the word out that piracy at sea is no longer romantic fantasy built from three hundred years of legend but exists today, cold brittle fact.

As head of the IMB, Muku often wonders if he is not just pissing into the wind. More ships are hijacked, more seafarers are getting killed, and there is another feel-good conference about what to do about piracy. Time, Muku knows, is not in his favor. He knows that piracy must be stopped before a ship like the *Montrose* is taken over, careens into another, breaks up, and plays hell with the world economy and wreaks havoc on the environment. He knows that human nature is basically assessment oriented and reactionary and few will take notice until that catastrophe, or one like it, occurs—or until Hollywood makes it a Big Deal through computer graphics.

In the first instance, the M/T *Tirta Niaga IV,* southbound to Singapore, developed engine trouble and anchored for repairs on the Indonesian side of the Straits just off the deepwater channel. She had all the chances of an injured whitetail deer among a pack of wild dogs; it wasn't long before she was surrounded by dozens of small boats from nearby communities. Dirt-poor villagers armed with long knives and clubs swarmed aboard and captured the ship. It was apparently a spontaneous attack on a luckless vessel that had anchored off their *kampung;* it was too good to pass up, the riches had come to them. Their booty was not the cargo—nearly 3,000 tons of refined palm oil that would have been a bonanza for a crime syndicate—but the captain himself, and so they kidnapped him.

The crew was released and, without the master, sailed the vessel across the Straits into Malaysian waters. The kidnappers were demanding a ransom of a billion Indonesian rupiah for the captain, about $95,000 U.S.

This one isolated event, the first hostage-taking in the Straits in recent memory, is ominous. The implications are far reaching; the event, in fact, could increase the number of attacks against ships in the Straits and start a trend in hostage-taking, an unmanageable escalation. The *Tirta Niaga IV*'s owners are negotiating for the captain's release, but their dilemma goes well beyond how much to pay the kidnappers.

If the ship's owners were to meet the demands and pay the ransom, precedence will have been set and the pirate syndicates now forming would realize that such hostage-taking is easy money. While internationally it is generally the policy of governments not to accede to demands of kidnappers or terrorists, the shipowners have no such constraints—they are dealing for the life of their employee, a captain of one of their ships. But the significance to shipping on the Malacca Straits is not lost on them. If they do not pay the ransom, their captain is, in all likelihood, a dead man.[51] If they do pay, then copycat kidnapping against the crews of passing ships probably soon will follow. Ship companies whose vessels use the waterway are following the developments closely. The *Tirta Niaga IV* is owned by a small company. A VLCC or a gas carrier leased by an oil major would be a tempting target—the master of such a vessel would fetch far more.

The second attack is a hijacking. A hijacking means that the crew of a ship has been neutralized. *Neutralized* could mean ending up as a slide show exhibit before a conference of industrialists. "The crew," Muku says, "they may be all right, they may be dead." But I see by the almost mischievous glint in Muku's eyes, something is different. "The ship, the *Selayang*—we are tracking it on the computer."

Back in the autumn of 2000, pirates hijacked the tanker *Petchem*, injuring some of the crew, changing the ship's name, repainting the funnel, and pumping out its cargo of diesel to an awaiting syndicate ship. The vessel was found adrift in eastern Singapore waters the next day. Noel Choong had said at the time that had the ship been equipped with a satellite tracking device, the marine police could have arrested it before it had sailed out of Malaysian waters.

Because the *Petchem* was transporting cargo for the oil majors, its owner knew he could not afford another hijacking. Whether it was a result of pressure from the charterer of the vessel, Shell Malaysia Trading Sdn. Bhd., or whether it was because of Noel's advice, the shipowner installed the transmitting unit aboard the *Petchem*'s sister ship, the M/T *Selayang*. But it did not stop pirates. When the *Selayang* departed the terminal at Port Dickson on its regular run down the Straits to Labuan, on Malaysia's section of Borneo Island, she was transporting 3,500 tons of diesel fuel. Just abeam of Pulau Karimun, pirates in a lightning strike boarded the vessel, attacked the crew, took control of the tanker, and sailed it away.

For some reason the shipowner didn't discover his ship missing until days later. "How can you not keep track of your ship?" wonders Noel. It was evident that the owner of the *Selayang* did not require twice daily position reports such as those filed by the *Petro Concord*. The owner finally called Muku and Choong, furious that despite the "gimmick" tracking device he had installed, another of his ships had been hijacked. One of his fleet hijacked carrying cargo for an oil major was unfortunate, but two—the shipowner knew he would have a lot of explaining to do. Noel told him that the transponder could not prevent a hijacking but that it could help recover the ship before the cargo was siphoned off. This was the first time a ship equipped with such a device had been pirated. It would be a good test of the unit's effectiveness.

For the past two days Muku and the Piracy Reporting Center have followed the hijacking on a computer. And today I have been brought aboard. We have an eye in the sky. A thin line inches across a computer screen. It is the *Selayang*, commandeered by pirates. This is a hijacking in Real Time. Wherever the pirates take the ship, wherever they attempt to hide, whatever course they take, we follow them on the screen. We are the cat crouched in the shadows watching a mouse at play. The hijackers have no idea. They cannot escape.

We can only wonder about the intention of the pirates. Will they merely steal the cargo and then release crew and ship like they did the *Petchem?* Have they already begun to erase the ship's identity, repainting the funnel, scratching out its name on the stern and bridge sign-boards and replacing them with a new name and home port of their own? If they are remaking the vessel into a phantom ship, then the crew is in deep trouble and may not have much time left. Where are the pirates taking her? If the hijackers do not discover and destroy the satellite transmitter, we should soon find out.

Muku and Noel are thinking the same thing: A trap could be set, the fourteen crew members rescued.

The computer line reveals the vessel's course since it was hijacked. After Karimun she turned south along the Sumatra coast, weaving through a myriad of islands, then out into the South China Sea on a determined line toward Borneo. The next day it doubled back north-west toward Singapore. Its new direction, Muku thinks, indicates that it has received orders to rendezvous with another vessel to transfer the stolen cargo.

From the Piracy Reporting Center only a few blocks away, Noel sends an alert to the region's navies, to all ships at sea, every maritime law-enforcement agency, and to the Office of Naval Intelligence in Washington, D.C., describing the ship and where it was last officially reported.

Muku holds a hurried conversation with Malaysian marine police chief Muda, one of the delegates, who phones Superintendent Aziz of the Southern Command and orders him to prepare a strike force to storm the vessel if it enters Malaysian waters. Aziz asks Muda how he knows the ship's location, even wonders if the Americans are supply-ing satellite intelligence. Muda, laughing, admits there is a tracking device aboard and that for the first time they have real-time intel. "We'll go in as soon as it enters our territory. All we can do is to wait," Muda assures the IMB director.

Port Dickson is only a few miles up the coast from where I spent the night on Jamal's patrol. The ship was hijacked right under his nose. Apparently the wily tentacles of his intelligence network don't extend as far as the Jakarta, Singapore, or Hong Kong syndicates—or to the military in Jakarta. Jamal is more of a behind-the-lines man; he gets his information from the field, not from the situation rooms of the military or the boardrooms of the crime bosses.

The ship wasn't in Malaysian waters very long. The pirates probably had instructions to slip over to the safer waters of the Indonesian
side of the Straits shortly after they hijacked the vessel. I can imagine
how frustrated, how angry, Jamal must be. And probably a little hum-
bled. No doubt he is hoping the ship will return to his turf so he can
make the kill—and perhaps it will; the pirates have no idea we are
watching them.

Who are these pirates? Are they part of Bhudi Sunil's newly
strengthened gang from Pulau Karimun, hired by the syndicates as a
test of his ability to hijack a ship? Is this hijacking part of the new order on the Malacca Straits? Is this the first in a new series of hijackings, the first act of piracy by a newly formed syndicate? Was a lost
command involved? Did they use military-issue weapons? Is this an
escalation of the war?

Or is this a continuation of the old one—a carefully planned heist
of a ship organized by the Jakarta/Singapore/Bangkok syndicate
without involving Bhudi's boys? It all depends on their MO: type of
guns used, where the gang is from, and how good their seamanship.
If the ship is arrested in Malaysian territory, then Jamal and his crew
have methods of extracting the information they need without too
much difficulty.

The thin line on the computer screen reveals a drama we can only
imagine. That impersonal dark thread takes on near animastic quality;
stare at it hard enough and the line peels off the screen and slips into
our imaginations and becomes that hijacked ship at sea. Thus can we
envision the terror of the crew at this moment, tied up, blindfolded,
cowering against the bulkhead, beaten; perhaps some are already dead.
This is not a drama we will hear about secondhand, a life-and-death
event that occurred some time ago; this is going on now in front of
our eyes. We can imagine that a crewman is being tossed overboard.
We are unable to help. In the conference room few are aware of the
drama that is unfolding.

The detailed printout[52] of what we see on the computer is compelling; the jerky, uneven line represents every course change, every
tentative turn of the wheel, every action taken by the pirate crew. It
represents every discussion, every decision, made on the captured
ship's bridge; perhaps there is an argument among the pirates them-

selves: Head this way! Go that way! No, this way! The printout shows an erratic course that runs north, turns suddenly south, doubles back again. The line wobbles a bit where Muku says it looks like it is lying ahull, simply drifting. Either the syndicate's plans are not yet firmed up or are being rewritten. He thinks they are waiting for instructions.

The thin black line begins to move again, takes a sharp turn north, and angles toward the same area where pirates had stolen the cargo from the *Petchem* so many months earlier.

The U.S. naval attaché at the embassy in Kuala Lumpur calls Noel and asks for additional information on the hijacked vessel. Some of the ships of the Seventh Fleet are in Singapore and they can assist. "They offered to look for it," Noel says later. "But I told them we knew where it was. I am pleased they offered." This may be one of the first times the U.S. has taken an active interest in a hijacking where American interests were not at stake.

Because we know where it is, this is one ship that will not be permitted to hide in some deepwater cove, to find a safe harbor in a syndicate-friendly port. This is one that will not be permitted to change its identify and flag and disappear as a phantom ship.

Muku's patience is running out. It is a personal thing and he can wait no longer. There is a crew on board who are afraid for their lives and thus far we have been impotent, just watching. Muku calls the Naval Command Center in Jakarta and asks if they have received the IMB alert. If so, have they seen the ship? It should be near their naval base at Batam Island—only a few miles away. He provides the latitude and longitude within decimal seconds of a degree.

Are you sure it's there? they ask.

Absolutely positive.

How do you know?

We have sources.

Okay, we'll send some ships.

Hours after contacting the Indonesians, as the thin little line on the computer appears about to touch Malaysian waters, the ship makes a U-turn and begins tracking back to the south. The hijackers have been tipped off. A snitch within the Batam or the Jakarta command centers has informed the crime bosses that the IMB knows the ship's

position. Someone has called the pirates on his hand phone and ordered them to get the hell away from the Malaysian Coast at best
speed, forget the rendezvous with the syndicate tanker, go south deep
into the safety of Indonesian waters in the Java Sea. We can hardly
believe it.

The news on board the pirated ship that it has been spotted must
be causing more than a little consternation among the hijackers. It is
easy to envisage. Someone is following us! They know where we are!
How do they know? What are we going to do? Where can we go?
One of the pirates may be on the bridgewing—his rifle on his shoulder, still wearing a ski mask—scanning the sky with the ship's binoculars for an airplane that he thinks is tailing them. The pirates inside
pore over the radar; perhaps they see a target in the distance and
think they are being dogged by a ship from some navy.

The mere line on the computer screen has become for us a large
rumbling oil tanker full of panic-stricken thugs who order an emergency turn at full speed; chairs, dishes on tables, glasses, any objects
not tied down are flying through the ship; the crew, blindfolded and
bound, are hurled across the floor in the sudden maneuver. The fact
that they now know they are being tracked worries us: panicky pirates
mean violence and death on board. A chilling lesson from the short
history of modern piracy.

There is still no word from Jakarta. Where are the Indonesians?
Muku calls the Jakarta and Batam centers every ninety minutes, pleads
with them to seize the pirated ship and rescue the crew. He hits a
stone wall.

"We know where it is—within a half mile!" he says over the
phone. "We want you stop that ship!"

And the Indonesian Naval Command responds that:

—*We are looking but we can't find it.*

—*The weather is bad, the visibility is poor.* (A phone call shows the
weather to be good with some showers in the area.)

—*The seas are too high.*

—*We don't think it is where you say it is. Are you sure it's there?*

—*Beyond any doubt*, Muku says, as he watches the slow-moving
line inch closer to the Indonesian coast of Borneo.

His eyes widen, incredulous.

"Please! You must arrest that ship. It is in your waters. We don't know what is happening out there—this kind of delay is dangerous to the crew." The concern on his face deepens as he listens on the phone; it is evident he fears what the crew is going through—assuming they are still alive.

He taps a button on the phone, slips it into his pocket, and turns to me. "Now they say that the ship is going ten knots and they don't have any ships in the area that can go faster than eight knots. They can't catch a fully laden tanker?" He is not a profane man, but his face has *Bullshit!* written all over it. We wonder aloud what kind of navy this is?

Muku receives an angry phone call from the owner of the *Selayang*, who demands to know what the hell is going on.

"He was hysterical—very rude," Muku says. The IMB director offers to hire a small plane to locate the ship. "But it comes down to cost at the end of the day—we can find the ship even if the Indonesians can't. I told him that in my view the Indonesians are doing nothing."

Muku, his patience at its limit, stops giving the Indonesians the ship's position. Without real-time information it will be revealing to see what the ship does, what the Indonesian military will do. "All the Indonesians are doing is giving our intelligence to someone who is feeding that back to the ship."

A couple hours later, when the Indonesians get no more position reports from the IMB, they telephone him. Noel fields the call:

—*Where is the ship?* they ask.

—*We don't know. We lost it,* Noel says.

—*How are we going to stop it if we don't know where it is?*

—*We'll keep looking.*

—*Where are you getting your information—from the United States?*

Noel hesitates, stammers: *Yes, that's it. From American intelligence sources.*

The Indonesians seem satisfied.

The tracking line on the screen inexplicably stops, goes nowhere further. What are the pirates doing? What are they waiting for? Do they think that they are no longer being followed? Have they begun to off-load? We would know if this were an airplane that was being hijacked. CNN would have chartered its own plane to follow the drama. Viewers would be on the edge of their seats watching this blow-by-blow high-seas chase. But this is no airplane and there are no cameras to show whether it is discharging the stolen oil into another ship, or whether the crew is being executed on deck. Were cameras recording the hijacking, the Indonesian navy probably would be out there seizing the vessel, capturing the pirates, and heroically rescuing the crew. The syndicates are aware that the rest of the world doesn't know this sort of thing occurs at sea today, and they assume they will forever be safe from the prying eyes of the media and the concern of the world.

Muku's frustration with the Indonesians is turning to anger. He is on a slow boil. He is a highly intelligent, patient man but I am seeing his limits. We discuss his dilemma—I am the hothead and I suggest he has an unbeatable hand. As chairman of this high-profile international antipiracy conference attended by 170 delegates from thirty-six different nations, he wields a bit of clout. There will be a media briefing later in the day and it will be attended by the wire services, television, and the press.

⁓

The conference adjourns to the commercial harbor of Port Klang on the Straits some miles away, where the Malaysian military has thrown the delegates a little dog-and-pony show—a demonstration of how their commandos will rescue passengers on a cruise ship hijacked by pirates and terrorists. It is a break for the conference delegates, but it is no break in the efforts to get the Indonesians off their backsides and into action.

Lieutenant Commander M. Zaenal, the recently appointed chief of the Indonesian navy's Command and Control Center on Batam Island, is one of the delegates. He has not yet taken over the command but he is as close to military authority as we are going to find on this day. Zaenal is a charming and well-spoken young officer with a proud military bearing. I wonder if this man will help put an end to piracy or be a part of it.

Zaenal sits just in front of us on the bus back to town. Muku leans over his shoulder. "I don't think your navy intends to do anything about this ship. You have a ten-minute presentation to the conference when we get back. I expect you will tell the conference that you have captured the ship. If you do not announce you have arrested the ship I will go public and ask why not."

Zaenal turns to face Muku. The two stare hard at each other. The Indonesian shakes his head and grimaces.

"May I use your phone?" he asks Muku.

Muku hands him his mobile and Zaenal covers the mouthpiece with a cupped hand and speaks in hushed tones. Later he turns to Muku. "We have dispatched planes and ships. That is all I can say."

Muku blows through his teeth in frustration and mutters. "God, who knows who he talked to?"

Prior to Zaenal's speech the French representative of the locating transponder ShipLoc describes the gadget to the conference. He startles the delegates with an illustration of its effectiveness. On the wall screen he shows the rest of the gathering what we've been dealing with—the strange course of the runaway ship from the moment it was hijacked days ago to the present. The thin black line takes it down the Straits, north, suddenly south and around the bottom end of Borneo, then north again. "As you can see," he points out, "the ship is at this moment off Samarinda, Borneo. It is still going north. We have known where it was since it was reported missing." The delegates, who had been so concerned about their own agendas, sit in absolute amazement. There are few in the room who do not now fully imagine what must be unfolding aboard that ship at that very moment.

The Indonesian military now knows how we have been tracking the *Selayang*. It had to come out. But it will be a two-edged sword. In the future pirates will be forewarned that many ships, like those of the Petroships fleet, will be so equipped. It is unlikely that hijackers will believe that a master of a ship, like Captain Than on the *Petro Concord*, does not know where the unit is located. They will torture or kill to find the little gray box; once found it will be disabled, the ship successfully hijacked, and piracy may have won another round.

After the break Zaenal gives his speech, and this is the one that everyone listens to. They hang on nearly every word. He tells them that Indonesia's military has thirteen thousand miles of coastline and seventeen thousand islands to patrol, that while it will never accept international patrols in its territorial waters, it needs international financial assistance to beef up its forces to control its seas (he might have told the delegates that its present naval force of only 114 warships, most of them World War II vintage, is less than half the number needed).[53] He finishes and receives a polite applause. He never mentions the hijacking.

"Questions from the audience?" Muku asks. Silence. Most want to know when the Indonesian navy is going to arrest the ship and save the crew, but no one wants to take the officer to task.

"No questions? Really? Then I do have a question." If ever there could be a collective hush, then there is one now. "What is the Indonesian navy doing about the hijacked ship—the *Selayang*—that is now in the hands of pirates in Indonesian waters? We know where the ship is—your navy knows where the ship is. Why haven't they arrested it?" Muku's tone is none too gentle.

None of the delegates who normally shuffle and cough and move papers or mutter into their mobile phones makes a sound.

"We have dispatched planes and ships—I just ask that you please be patient." That is the extent of Commander Zaenal's response. Quickly he takes his seat before anyone can ask another question. Muku shakes his head in dismay and the conference breaks for coffee.

"I think that is bloody terrible," Muku says during the break. "The ship has passed between two lighthouses on the southeast coast. We should tell them in Jakarta to have the keepers look out their windows; they can watch the ship go by."

During the waning hours of the conference Muku writes a biting statement for the press conference, charging the Indonesians with complicity, that it appears pirates have found a safe haven in Indonesia. It is a strong statement, one that posits by implication that the Indonesian navy is in league with the pirates. Muku sits at the head table on the stage, nervously tapping his fingers, waiting for the last speaker to finish. He answers his silently vibrating mobile phone. It is the commandant of the Indonesian navy in Jakarta, who tells him that they have just seized the *Selayang*. Most of the crew is unharmed and ten armed pirates have surrendered. The ship is being towed into Balik Papan by the navy. Some of the oil, however, is missing.

The ship's name, the Indonesians say, has been painted over and it has become the *Wang Yung*, an indication that the pirates were going to turn it into a phantom. Muku, beaming, makes the announcement and he receives a standing ovation.

Captain Mukundan won this round because of the threat of public pressure, because of the high-profile piracy conference, and because he had tracked the ship smack into Indonesian waters with the satellite device. It is assumed that the Indonesian navy did in fact use Muku's information to follow the hijacked ship; some cynics think their warships even accompanied it or, worse, had intended to escort it to a safe rendezvous where it would help discharge the cargo into a waiting ship. Muku would never charge the Indonesians with that. But he does expect that Indonesia will exact a high price for capturing the ship and the pirates; he expects that most of Shell's valuable million-dollar cargo will have disappeared when the ship is returned to its anxious owner.[54]

Muku junks his caustic remarks to the press and instead hastily scribbles some words of praise for the cooperative Indonesians.

Muku, Noel Choong, and their staffs are pleased. They have saved the lives of the crew of one ship, seafarers who may never know that this time somebody out there was watching.

AFTERWORD

The Enemy Within

Hijackings, hostage taking, violent acts of robbery, cold-blooded murder on the high seas—these are the terrifying ingredients of piracy.

There has been traditionally an ill-defined distinction between piracy and terrorism. Following the attacks on the World Trade Center and the Pentagon, governments worldwide finally began to take notice that there had been a war at sea long before September 11. The inevitable conclusion was reached—there is very little difference between the two crimes.

The International Maritime Bureau and others in the maritime industry have called the bombing of the USS *Cole* in Aden harbor an act of piracy. That attack hammered home that we can no longer afford to ignore piracy, or deny its close relationship with terrorism. The stakes are too high.

Ships have often been targets of "terrorists"—pirates who have attacked not just for greed but for political and religious purposes. Piracy and terrorism have long had historical connections.

Between the sixteenth and eighteenth centuries feuding Moslem and Christian rulers funded "corsairs" to raid shipping in the Mediterranean; the Moslem raiders operated out of the Barbary States of Tunis, Tripoli, and Algiers in North Africa, and the Christians out of Rhodes and then Malta. The navies of both groups were essentially marauding pirates who were able to operate with impunity because their activity was justified in religious rather than political terms. It was a form of holy war.[55] In the eighteenth century, in the years following the American Revolution, the United States was forced to pay $18,000 a year "tribute"—protection money—for safe passage past the North African pirate states. Finally, in 1804, in battles immortalized in the Marine Corps Hymn (*"From the halls of Montezuma to the shores of Tripoli . . ."*) this piratical extortion was put paid by British, French, and U.S. navies.

A notorious act of political piracy occurred on October 7, 1985, when four members of the Palestine Liberation Front seized the Italian cruise liner *Achille Lauro* and demanded Israel release fifty Palestinian prisoners. Five days later they killed Leon Klinghoffer, an elderly American passenger confined to a wheelchair, and threw the body overboard. Egyptian and PLO officials negotiated safe passage from Egypt for the terrorists in return for the release of the hostages and the ship. U.S. Navy fighter planes intercepted the Egyptian aircraft carrying the hijackers and forced it to land at a NATO airbase in Italy. The hijackers were arrested and tried by Italian authorities. The U.S. government requested the terrorists' extradition. The arrest warrant charged the terrorists with hostage-taking, "piracy, and conspiracy to commit piracy."

It was this incident that in part triggered creation of the law dealing with political piracy—the Convention for the Suppression of Unlawful Acts Against the Safety of Maritime Navigation. The convention, which seeks to ensure the prosecution and extradition of those who commit crimes against ships, is the basic law dealing with maritime terrorism. Today there is building sentiment within the industry, especially among those owners whose ships have been attacked by mere pirates, to deal with piracy, political piracy, and terrorism under one law.

Terrorist attacks on ships before 9-11 include a plot in June 2001 by Basque separatists posing as tourists to blow up the ferry *Val de*

Loire on a passage from Spain to the UK with two thousand passengers aboard and another by the same group to plant a car bomb on a ferry nearly as large from Valencia to the Mediterranean island of Majorca, which failed because the car in which the bomb was packed broke down at the last minute. The Toronto-based Cuba Cruise Corporation in 1999 canceled its winter sailing schedule because of terrorist threats against their cruise ships[56]; separatist Tamil guerillas have attacked international shipping off Sri Lanka during their fight for an independent homeland; the Abu Sayaf in the southern Philippines, linked to Al-Qaeda, has for years attacked passing ships, including large passenger ferries and cargo vessels with heavy weapons. Piracy for political purposes has also included the bombing by French saboteurs of the Greenpeace vessel *Rainbow Warrior* in Auckland, New Zealand, in 1985 prior to its protest voyage to the nuclear test site in the South Pacific. And eight activists from Greenpeace in the summer of 2001 forced their way on board the Norwegian tanker *Anna Knutsen*, carrying U.S.-owned oil outside Le Havre, France; they were protesting American policy on climate change negotiations. Even the United States was accused of committing an "act of piracy" in January 2002 by Syria when the Sixth Fleet, looking for terrorist suspects and weapons of mass destruction, stopped, searched, and later released two Syrian cargo vessels in the Mediterranean after they had displayed "suspicious behavior."

Yet the threat that concerns many is of a terrorist attack on a ship in one of the world's strategic waterways—the Panama and Suez Canals[57], the Strait of Gibraltar, and the Malacca Straits. While the War on Terrorism focuses on protecting American harbors and ports, the Malacca Straits are the sea lanes most vulnerable to terrorist attack. This, the world's most congested channel, cuts through the heart of political and religious unrest.

Growing religious polarization in the secular but predominantly Islamic nations of Indonesia and Malaysia, through which the Malacca Straits funnel, is a serious concern. A mujahideen network, trained in Afghanistan and well established in Southeast Asia, feeds upon the discontent of the huge, impoverished Muslim populations of not only Indonesia and Malaysia, but the Philippines, Thailand, Cambodia, and even Burma. Religious turbulence coupled with economic instability stirs an explosive cocktail in these nations. For the first time U.S. military officials are openly expressing fears that as a result of political and religious conflict, attacks on passing ships could evolve from mere crimes of robbery to calculated political crimes that would pose an even greater risk to global security.[58] Indeed, it was not long after this concern was revealed that their fears were realized.

Whether coincident to the terrorist attacks on the U.S. or as part of an overall strategy, the Free Aceh Movement (*Gerakin Aceh Merdeka*—GAM), the Islamic fundamentalist group in Indonesia's province on Sumatra, warned vessels transiting the Malacca Straits they would have to seek permission to pass. It was this extremist organization often linked to Al-Qaeda that forced Exxon-Mobil Corporation to shut down its Sumatra operations in 2000 following months of persistent attacks on the company's onshore facilities. To underscore their demands GAM indirectly claimed responsibility for the attack on the M/V *Ocean Silver* and held half of the crew for ransom.[59] The assault on the ship was the first recorded act of piracy for political as well as for financial gain in the Straits and it marked a disturbing development for the region. The ransom money, according to intelligence sources, was to be used to finance GAM's landside fight for independence, which it has waged since 1976. The attack on this ship and others since highlights the ease with which politically motivated organizations can attack vessels in these international shipping lanes.

While this piracy was for money to fund the movement, it did underscore fears that terrorist-sponsored pirates could do a lot more than take hostages to further their cause. They could use a ship itself in an attack—as a weapon. Terrorists turned passenger planes into aerial bombs. They can, with far less effort, turn ships laden with crude oil, jet fuel, liquid natural, or petroleum gas into very effective and destructive floating bombs that could destroy strategic waterways, industrial complexes, or inner harbors in large cities. Terrorists/pirates attacked and nearly sank a state-of-the-art warship; could they not have equal success with any other ship afloat? As pirates have shown for the past decade, taking over a ship is easy.

Terrorists will employ tried and proven pirate methods to gain control of the vessel. The attack will either be a stealthy boarding

288   John S. Burnett

from another ship or fast boat or an inside job—techniques that pirates have mastered over the years. The targets: a cruise ship or a VLCC or one of the many gas carriers that steam routinely unnoticed through narrow shipping lanes or that call into city harbors.

Shipowners today are on high alert for such a possibility. Before 9-11 their security procedures had been based on risk assessment—it hasn't happened to us and the odds are that it won't. That attitude is out the window. They realize now that they must prepare their defenses for the unforeseen, the unimaginable. No longer can they think in tightly ordered ways, casting an eye on past history and probability statistics. Today they are trying to imagine what they previously could not conceive, looking for ways to defend against an attack conjured up in creative and diabolical minds. They find themselves trying to think out of the box, to outcreate those who want to kill and destroy. This is a difficult task for those who traditionally have based their security policies on crimes with some historical precedence. How do you plan for a crime that has not yet occurred, the inconceivable? No one expected terrorists to drive a fuel-laden commercial jet into a skyscraper. Had anyone thought to defend against a terrorist walking onto an airplane with a few ounces of plastic explosives in his shoes?

There are scant security precautions in place aboard a huge crude oil tanker or a volatile gas carrier. Nobody goes through an airport-type screening before boarding a VLCC, and at this writing no passenger takes his shoes off for inspection when joining a cruise ship and nobody is searched for a belt-bomb when boarding a packed city ferry.

The stunning successes of pirates during the past ten years demonstrate that all ships can be attacked successfully either by sea or from within. And it is expected that terrorists will use the same methods. A modern warship like the USS *Cole* in Aden Harbor (bombed—explosives packed in a small boat alongside); the VLCC *Chaumont* (taken over—pirates from small boats scampered up bamboo poles in the middle of the night); the *Selayang* and others (hijacked—carried out in part by sleepers among the crew). No matter how well protected, every ship afloat—and this includes those that carry enough reactor fuel to build a few nuclear devices—is physically highly vulnerable. Terrorists, like pirates, give no warnings, no demands, and there will be no time for negotiations. The acts are committed methodically, coldly.

So aware are the *Montrose*'s managers that they now continuously evaluate the approaches that their ships take every time they enter a port. "We want to keep the bazookas out of the hedges," said Bill McKnight, the head of the company's emergency response team.

That is a conceivable threat. The least defensible, however, is the one at the hands of an insider, a member of the crew who could bring aboard a bomb, in a suitcase or in his shoes. Or a sleeper as a member of the crew who could single-handedly take control of a ship and turn it into a bomb. The use of insiders has been a technique perfected by ship hijackers for many years. Instead of crime syndicates planting sleepers to hijack a vessel, terrorist cells plant insiders aboard who go about their business doing their jobs without suspicion for months or longer until receiving the signal to strike. There is reason to believe that there may be those currently aboard ships at sea prepared to carry out such an attack, one that would close the world's most strategic waterways or lay waste to a populated area. The shipping industry knows it has become a target, that its vessels are potential weapons, and it is nervous.

Without up-to-the-minute reliable counterterrorism intelligence, the identity of a sleeper is nearly impossible to detect. Counterterrorist agencies are seldom one step ahead of those they are trying to catch. Frequently, a suspect is not a terrorist until he is caught in the act or until after he has committed the crime, as has been historically demonstrated. Those who try to anticipate, to foil a terrorist attack, know that they have to be lucky all the time; a terrorist has to be lucky just once.

It is a common belief that most ships are crewed by men and women who work directly for the shipowner. They are not. Most ships at sea today are crewed by seafarers selected by body shops that are often based in countries with radical groups: Pakistan, Indonesia, Malaysia, India, the Philippines, among others. Many of the applicants for jobs at sea with few or no qualifications pay agencies to get them on the rolls. Screening of these seafarers is bypassed. Officers buy their certificates to get on a ship at quite incredible sums for jobs that are quite exploitive in nature.[60]

Graham Shaw, whose company assesses risk on maritime jobs for the insurance industry and whose commandos ride shotgun on cruise ships, believes that passenger vessels will be the next terrorist target, abetted by sleepers working as crewmen.

"Cruise ships have up front the visual trappings of security. But an attack is much more likely from within. The crews of those ships are not hired by the cruise companies but by manning agencies. You have a thousand crew members on a cruise ship—laundry crew, dining room crew, galley crews, officers, seamen—from all over the world."[61]

One such ship that has raised concern, despite its security force of a couple of Gurkhas, is the recently launched M/V *The World*. Billed as the first oceangoing luxury resort, it is a ship only for the very rich and famous, with apartments costing from $2 to $6 million each. The ship, with a crew of mixed nationalities, is to spend 250 days at anchor or in ports worldwide; some fear the vessel may become a soft target.

Owners and operators of vessels have little involvement in the selection of those who crew their ships. The change in manning policies stems in part from the legacy of the *Exxon Valdez* disaster. Since the tanker ran up on Bligh Reef in 1989, oil companies have been shedding their shipping companies. Exxon-Mobil, the world's largest oil company, has begun to farm the job of transporting its oil to outside non-American operators, and it must rely on those shipowners, whose officers come from far corners of the globe, to guarantee the safe delivery of their cargo.

Terrorists in September 2001 targeted symbols that represented the economic and military might of the United States—the World Trade Center and the Pentagon. There are those in the maritime industry who fear an easy target for terrorists today is the lifeblood of the western world, its supply of crude oil. While on passage aboard the *Montrose* I saw that it would be quite simple to block the Malacca Straits or any other of the world's vital waterways. Just a slight turn of the wheel by a mere degree or two could do it. The course change would have gone unnoticed until the ship was on the rocks or had collided into another vessel. During that night, weeks before 9-11, I was thinking only of some suicidal nutter behind the wheel, not some indoctrinated terrorist.

McKnight acknowledged that his company, which also operates the largest fleet of LNG tankers in the world, was paying greater attention to the origins of its ships' officers. Crew vetting, he said, was handled by the manning agencies and was "informal."

"We don't ask ourselves what kind of clothes an engineer changes into when he's off duty," Bill said. "We don't shine torches into people's eyes asking, 'Are you with us or against us?'" But he also said that a sleeper aboard their ships was a possibility and a concern.

None of the officers on the *Montrose* worked directly for or were responsible directly to the oil company.[62] Five of the officers were Pakistani, two were Filipino, two Croatian, two British, and there was a Dutchman. The junior officers, from Pakistan and the Philippines, seemed to be eager, well-qualified, educated, and dedicated men. Some of those deck officers to whom I spoke dreamed of a command of their own. The sixteen Filipino ratings on the ship were supplied by United Philippines Lines of Manila. The Pakistanis, all officers, were selected by Terra-Marine Agencies in Karachi, a reputable body shop. Terra-Marine provides about 4,000 officers and 1,500 ratings to some of the industry's largest oil tankers and maintains that its seafarers go through "a unique and thorough screening process, after which they are dedicated for the company's employment only."

While it is unlikely that a ship operated by the company would be the victim of an inside terrorist act, there are dozens of other vessels registered under flags of convenience that carry crude oil, gas, or chemicals and that ply these channels daily; many are older ships crewed by seafarers of questionable background and qualifications.

Concerned that terrorist sleepers live and work among ships' crews, the U.S. Coast Guard has proposed to a UN regulatory body, the International Maritime Organization, a Seafarers Verification Scheme that would, under international law, provide maritime authorities with the identity and background of all crew members aboard vessels entering American ports. The seafarers identity papers would include biometrics on the document such as a fingerprint or a retina scan.[63]

The Coast Guard also is trying to translate the airborne attacks on the World Trade Center and the Pentagon into similar attacks from the sea. "If they can do that in aviation, what's the parallel in the maritime domain?" USCG commandant James Loy said.

The agency was paying special attention to "tankers carrying nasty stuff"—petroleum, chemicals, and liquid natural and petroleum gas. "It's all about rogue ships," Loy said. "How do you deal with the potential of a rogue ship?"[64]

Captain Mukundan of the International Maritime Bureau echoed Loy's concern. Well-placed insiders, he said, like those used by pirate syndicates, could take over a tanker or a gas carrier for suicide missions and turn the ships into missiles. Liquid natural gas tankers, for example, have the potential of being powerful weapons. Shortly after September 11 the LNG tanker *Matthew*, bound for the Distrigas terminal in Everett, Massachusetts, carrying 33 million gallons of highly explosive supercooled gas—enough gas to heat thirty thousand homes for a month—was turned away from Boston Harbor by the Coast Guard because it was such a tempting target for terrorists.

Mukundan painted a dark picture. "A gas carrier waiting in the port for the pilot; a small boat comes alongside, and terrorists, like pirates, board, take over the ship, put the ship on autopilot, and run it full speed toward the terminal; the terrorists jump overboard. It is not difficult as long as you have a straight line to the target, a straight line of approach."

Bill McKnight, who tries to drill into his captains and crew the necessity of antipiracy/antiterrorism defenses, admits that the September 11 terrorist attacks have changed the attitude at the oil major. Today antipiracy precautions are in effect "wherever we are—globally."

"Our attitude has always been risk based," McKnight says. No longer. "Today we are working on the infinite scenario. We are trying to plan for the bigger than credible. Now somehow we are trying to plan beyond the spectacular. It is an extremely difficult time for us."

This ship company had once scoffed at the idea that anyone could hijack a VLCC. However, the situation today is different, and McKnight and his crew are evaluating two types of satellite locating devices. The inconceivable notion of hijacking a VLCC now falls within the "bigger than credible."

Yet despite the new security measures—and some are considerable—ships, from local city ferryboats to the largest vessels at sea, remain as vulnerable as city skyscrapers.

There have been some voices raised that this investigation will provide a blueprint to pirates and terrorists. Pirates and terrorists don't need a do-it-yourself manual. There is nothing within that is not already well known to those determined to take down a ship, to turn a ship into a weapon; those who fight piracy and terrorism are learning from them. On the other hand it is hoped that an investigation such as this might encourage the world to take its head out of the sand, to sit up and take notice that piracy and maritime terrorism are not something found only in the history books but occur at sea every day with terrifying potential.

Many of those who helped make this book possible are still at sea. Some have gotten over their experiences and continue with their lives. Yet for others there is a permanent scar that is sometimes difficult to ignore. I know. One captain told me shortly after a pirate rammed a gun down his throat that returning home made it even worse:

"I tried to work it out. Nothing like that had ever happened to me. My wife was there and she listened. But down at the bar, when I began to talk about it—when I spoke of it to my friends in the neighborhood, they couldn't understand. They laughed, thought it was a joke. 'Piracy? You mean like bootlegging CDs?' someone asked me. If you return from a war, then everyone knows there is a war, no matter how unpopular. There is a war out there but no one knows it exists."

A master of a hijacked vessel who was beaten, drugged, and kidnapped said upon his release, "Now I know what it is like to be raped."

Captain Donny Monteiro and his family appear to have gotten on with their lives. Donny has swallowed the anchor and now owns a ship-survey and marine-insurance business in his native city of Mangalore, a port on India's Malabar Coast. Ironically, Mangalore was a staging area for pirates who plundered European shipping in the seventeenth and eighteenth centuries. Today it is a port with very little activity, and Donny wears that faraway look of a man whose heart is back at sea. When this story appears, he will probably be on the bridge of another ship.

The family returned to their comfortable and secure home in Mangalore as soon as little Vanisha was discharged from the hospital in Singapore. It is a bright and airy apartment overlooking a tropical public garden.

Vanisha has been sitting primly in a big chair as her mother, Vimala, relives the attack. Vanisha has a quick smile, but she is a little shy; her close-cropped black hair is as silky as her mother's and her pert, childishly flirtatious eyes are beguiling. "It was a miracle," Vim says. She looks over at the little girl and holds out her hands: "Come." She hugs her daughter tightly and closes her eyes. Her voice is just above a whisper and her eyes are a little damp.

"Until recently," Vim continues, "she always told her classmates that she got the scar when she fell out of bed as a baby." Vanisha learned the truth when she was about six and she is now affectionately called the Pirate Child by the neighbors. She is not embarrassed to show the scar, a short, obviously deep wound over her left eye.

Vim says her own life after the attack became "a blank." She found strength from the support she had to provide to Deepak and to Vanisha, but it was not enough. She was for years a soul lost among the living. More than once, when Vanisha slept in the next room, she panicked and searched the house for her.

She has been on a ship only once since that terrifying night. "I was with Donny in bed. The ship was tied to a pier, but it rolled a little in the water. I awoke suddenly and grabbed him: 'Donny, the pirates are here!' "

Young Deepak is a quiet teenager, a straight-A student and a bit of a computer nerd who still wears oversized glasses that give him a brainy, studious look. He is working on a mustache, a new brush with a few dark bristles. Deepak remembers the events well: "Mama gave me all of her jewelry and stuff and she said, 'Stick to me.' I heard the bottles breaking in the other room, furniture being thrown, and I thought, *They are hurting my dad!*" He pauses and focuses on some distant point on the floor. Perhaps he is reliving the terror. It is a long time between words. "I could see blood on the floor—I saw Vanisha hurt and I cried. I thought she was dead. I wanted to go after them, kick them, hit them, but I didn't have any weapon. I have always wanted to kill them."

The lad once gave a fifteen-minute talk to his class about the attack. His classmates listened, rapt, incredulous. When he finished, the class remained silent. Then from the back of the room, one of the students blurted, "There aren't any pirates! We don't believe you!" To this day his classmates still aren't convinced that pirates exist and they think he made up the story.

Unicorn

Following this investigation Jackie and I returned to the *Unicorn*, which we had kept on the East African Coast near Dar es Salaam. After a rather blustery passage across the channel from the mainland, we are now anchored in a little cove on Zanzibar Island. Being back on the *Unicorn* is a joy, yet somehow it is not the same as it was. The boundless freedom that we once knew as blue water sailors is no longer there. Physically there is little to stop this adventuring. Caution, however, certainly slows it down. It has been ten years since I was attacked in the South China Sea. Piracy has gotten worse, more violent, more frequent. And it occurs everywhere—it is as if there is some sort of coconut grapevine by which thugs on one continent have communicated to those on another that piracy is easy to do, easy to get away with. A rogue's sport.

That is not to say that all boats and ships are in peril. It is still relatively safe here, for example. We still buy crayfish from passing fishermen for a pittance, we still row ashore and wander through the wattle hut villages, play with local children, buy locally grown tomatoes, yams, onions, and sometimes a chicken.

Jackie and I are sitting together out on deck under a full moon, leaning back against the cabin, staring at the jungle that clings to the hills on the other side of the lagoon. The still air is humid and thick, redolent of the smells of this East African tourist island, a strange mélange of dank rain forest and the unseen flowers within, salt air from the exposed reef, and the heady smells of the new crop of cloves coming into blossom. It seems very peaceful. But we feel the disquiet.

We have been discussing how to bring the *Unicorn* back to the States. We want to go through the Suez Canal and the Mediterranean, but that now is out of the question. We heard over the HF radio that a convoy of sailboats sailing up the Red Sea (few make that passage alone anymore) were forced to turn back because one of them was strafed by machine guns from pirates who tried to board them. Closer to "home" up the coast, a tanker was attacked by armed pirates even though it was anchored well offshore in the Mombassa Roads. Here on Zanzibar, while anchored off Stone Town, the island's main port just south of us, Roger, a French friend, and his wife were attacked in their sailboat by machete-wielding thugs. In the predawn hours pirates sailed up in an Arab dhow, and alongside, then silently climbed aboard his boat. Roger is one who did not get the message—never resist—and jumping out of the sack he grabbed his own machete, and in what must have been a terrifying duel evoking battles with Blackbeard, fought back. He drove them off his boat but not without getting badly injured. Pretty stupid thing to do— whether on the *Montrose* in the Malacca Straits or on a sailboat off the Mexican coast or anchored in some African creek, there is hardly anyone foolish enough to fight back.

So we are a little more nervous about heading out than we were a couple of years ago. We don't have the benefit of the daily IMB piracy reports. But who needs to be warned? I suppose we are more like those on the *Petro Concord*—we are always on our guard. I don't think anyone sleeps lighter than I do.

The reflection of the moon cuts a shimmering swath across the water that leads directly to the *Unicorn*. A splash, a fish jumps and lands heavily, and I wonder—is it the hunter or the hunted?

A couple of large dugout canoes with villagers returning from the port slice across the golden reflection, the paddlers' rhythmic pace smooth and strong. One of the boats stops and drifts and the other catches up. Their deep, quiet chatter crosses the silent night. A voice is raised and another, an animated discussion. They are moving on, together side by side, a little stronger, a little more determined. Strange, they are no longer going to the landing of their village but are beginning to carve a wide circle. They are coming this way.

June 2002
Stone Town
Zanzibar

NOTES

Introduction

1. In many parts of the Arab world, where the consumption of alcohol is prohibited, the drug of choice is khat. The bitter leaf, chewed, is a stimulant, its effect not much different than that of the coca leaf. Many nations in the Middle East subsidize the growing of the narcotic and encourage its consumption to keep restive populations at peace.

2. "She was boarded, she was looted, she was scuttled till she sank. And the pale survivors left us by the medium of the plank."—John Masefield, "A Ballad of John Silver." Saltwater Palas & Ballads (1936)

Walk the plank is used here figuratively to mean "forced to jump overboard." There never was an instance recorded (except in the rather fanciful rhyme above) in which anyone was actually made to walk out on a plank of wood extended from the side of a ship. In fact, it is said that many of the cruel events of piracy today are far more violent than those recorded during seventeenth and eighteenth centuries.

Chapter 1

3. "The *Montrose*" is leased from a company in the Caribbean.

SHIP'S PARTICULARS:
Port of registry:

Keel laid: Launched: Delivered:
Call sign: Length overall: 332m (1089 ft 02 in)
Breadth Molded: 58m Depth Molded: 31
Main Engine: Sulzer   MCR: 36000 KWH@ 73.4 rpm
Propeller: four-bladed right-hand cunial bronze 10.2m diameter
Service speed: Laden 15 knots   Ballast: 16.5 knots
Charter consumption: Laden 95 mt/d   Ballast: 95 mt/d
Anchors: 17380kg   Cable: 14 shackles on each
Height of mast above keel: 62.10m
Bow to bridge: 279.50m (917 ft)
Stern to bridge: 52.50m (172 ft)

4.   Full instructions when passing through piracy areas as well as what to do during an actual attack follow:

ANTI-PIRACY PRECAUTIONS

Anti-piracy precautions will be in force whenever the vessel is sailing at night in the area from Pulau Rondo off Sumatra, in the South China Sea Area as far east as Taiwan (including all Indonesian and Philippine waters) and in any other areas such as off the island of Socotra, the coasts of Brazil, certain coasts off West Africa and anywhere pirates have been known to operate.

During these periods, the aft deck floodlights will be on and a high standard of vigilance maintained, with regular observation of the after decks by the bridge watches. At least two hoses should be rigged on the Sunken Deck to help deter boarders. All doors into the accommodation and engine room spaces will be secured either with locking bars or locked from the Outside with padlocks where suitable fittings are available. In the event of an emergency, these locked doors can be opened by unscrewing the wingnut on the inside of the door and pushing the securing bolt outwards.

It is recommended that cabin doors are locked at night.

Bridge watch keepers are to be particularly vigilant and closely monitor the approach of small craft as well as listening for pirate alerts on the VHF. This will probably mean not getting involved with other activities during night watches. A pirate attack message should be prepared and set up for quick transmission via Sat-C. The position information in the message should be regularly updated. Please remember that a pirate attack does not qualify as a Distress unless life is threatened.

If an attack seems imminent sound the general alarm and send the message following this up with an all ships call on the VHF if there is time.

A PA announcement should be made at thus time to remind personnel to remain INSIDE and muster in the accommodation.

Muster Point in the no. 1 deck alleyway
In the event of a Fire Alarm being activated during these periods, the usual alarms will be sounded (and) all personnel should proceed to the usual Fire Muster Points on the sunken deck.

Remember that the best defense against a pirate attack is vigilance. If you are threatened by armed men, it is not advisable to resist them.

If pirates succeed in entering the accommodation do not place yourself or others in further danger by resisting or antagonizing the attackers.

On the flip side of the **Precautions** are:

ACTIONS TO BE TAKEN
IN THE EVENT OF A PIRATE ATTACK

—Raise the alarm by sounding the General Alarm;
—Make a PA announcement to advise personnel of attack and to muster inside the accommodation;
—Bring lockouts inside the bridge and lock bridgewing doors;
—Start fire pump;
—Send pre-formatted pirate attack message via Sat-C to National Piracy Center;
—Use VHF Channel 16 to attract attention from other vessels and request assistance if required;
—Check security of all external doors (internally);
—Set up a citadel for the security of personnel;
—If pirates on board, consider stopping main engine for safety of navigation if likelihood that personnel may be locked up.

Chapter 2
5. During the dark days following the terrorist attacks on the U.S., there was heightened concern about the continuous flow of oil from the Middle East. Data from the Analysis of Petroleum Exports, a tanker tracking product from Lloyd's Information Services, revealed that as much as sixteen percent of the world's crude oil supply originates in so-called "sensitive" Middle East countries such as Iran, Iraq, Yemen, Syria, Sudan, and Libya.

6. The *Exxon Valdez* disaster, in which the master's judgment was considered by some to have been impaired by the few drinks he had consumed ashore before departing Valdez, has made shipowners much more aware of the effects of alcohol at sea. The corporate policy is clearly outlined: "*A high stan-*

dard of self-discipline is required from officers and crew who are always on call should unexpected circumstances occur, irrespective of the type of ship or trade involved. In addition the company's reputation and business interests can be seriously undermined by an incident in which the abuse of alcohol is implicated or inferred, or in which the adverse effect of alcohol on ship's personnel is witnessed by shore-based authorities, customers, and the general public." The Group sets a limit of 40mg percent per 100 milliliters of blood *"AT ANY ONE TIME (emphasis theirs) . . . This is in line with the maximum limit imposed by the United States Coast Guard."*

The master of the *Exxon Valdez* was determined to have alcohol in his blood several hours after the accident but he was found not guilty of operating a vessel under the influence of alcohol by a jury in Alaska.

7. The PRC compiles a weekly piracy report and can be accessed at www.iccwbo.org/ccs/imb_piracy.

Chapter 3

8. *Poop deck* is a common nautical term with an uncertain origin. The *Oxford English Dictionary* defines it as the aftermost deck of a ship, the stern. But I think there might be a more alimentary explanation. Great wooden motorless Arab dhows with lateen sails once were the main vehicles of commerce between Arabia and East Africa; today they still sail between Zanzibar and the Tanzanian mainland, transporting cloves and other spices. In Indonesia *penisi,* dhowlike boats with huge plastic sloop-rig sails, ply the Java Sea between Borneo and Java, carting rain-forest timber. Both types of ships have a poop deck in common. In Indonesia the poop deck is an extension on the after part of the hull where sailors perform their daily ablutions. On African dhows sailors squat on a small extended deck attached to the stern below the main deck. I passed a dhow in the Red Sea off the coast of Sudan whose poop deck was an eyesore of a half dozen bare bums. Apparently the crew had eaten something that hadn't agreed.

Chapter 4

9. "Many pirate attacks go unrecorded. Although estimates are difficult to calculate, it is believed financial losses from maritime crime will be as high as $16 billion this year."—John Brandon, assistant director of the Asia Foundation, Washington, D.C.

Chapter 5

10. Captain Karun Mathur of the Maltese-flagged *Erika* was detained after his ship broke up and sank off the Brittany Coast in December 1999. The *Erika* spill spread oil over 400km of French coastline and caused an estimated £600 million damage.

11. Master and officers are, however, not without culpability. As of February 2002, a French court was due to sentence First Officer Vladimir Chernyshov on charges of endangering lives, causing accidental pollution, and failing to observe safety rules after his container ship Melbridge Bilbao ran aground off the Brittany coast when he fell asleep on the bridge. NUMAST Telegraph, February 2002.

12. The complete report can be found at the State of Alaska's website: http://www.oilspill.state.ak

13. Following 9-11, the International Maritime Organization recommended that ship operators appoint a ship security officer who would assess the potential threat in ports, terminals, and sea areas on ship's voyages. While the SSO could be the master himself, NUMAST and others warned that the security tasks placed on an existing officer would be a burden and recommended the creation of an additional position trained in antiterror, antipiracy defenses.

Chapter 5
14. The yacht was identified later as the *Daisy Duck*, British.

Chapter 6
15. The IMB specifically recommends ShipLoc, built by Collecte Localisation Satellites, a French satellite service company, but there are other similar devices on the market. For further information: http://www.cls.fr or shiploc@cls.fr.

16. *Piracy & Armed Robbers—A Master's Guide*, video producer Robin Jackson, writer/director Barney Broom, can be ordered from Videotel Marine International, 84 Newman Street, London W1T 3EU, Tel: +44 171 299 1818, e-mail: Mail@videomail.com. The book of the same name can be ordered from the International Chamber of Shipping, 12 Carthusian Sr., London ECM 6EZ, e-mail: post@marisec.org.

Chapter 7
17. Dr. Frank Barnaby, nuclear physicist, who worked from 1951 to 1957 in UK's Aldermaston Nuclear Weapons Establishment, said that fresh plutonium MOX fuel can be handled with little difficulty and plutonium can be extracted in any reasonably well-equipped laboratory using standard chemical processes. The U.S. Department of Energy Office of Arms Control and Nonproliferation said in a 1997 report: "It is important to understand that fresh MOX fuel remains a material in the most sensitive category because plutonium suitable for use in weapons could be separated from it relatively easily."

18. The environmental group Friends of the Earth warned after the terrorist attacks on the U.S. that the ships of the Pacific Nuclear Transport were "sitting ducks" and that their onboard weaponry was "no match for a determined terrorist."

19. Nor are these ships invulnerable to accident. On March 25, 2002, the *Atlantic Osprey*, one of the BNFL vessels designed to carry MOX, caught fire while in the Manchester Ship Channel in the UK. The ship met Type B international atomic-energy safety guidelines that require these vessels to withstand fires of up to 800°C. However, a fire aboard ship is often considerably hotter. When the *Nagasaki Spirit* and the *Ocean Blessing* collided in the Malacca Straits as a result of pirate attack, the fires aboard those vessels, according to the salvors, were well in excess of 1,100°C.

Shaun Burnie of Greenpeace said the UK was lucky that the ship was not carrying MOX. "The next time it could be on a ship loaded with plutonium off Bremehaven, Germany, or in the Panama Canal with a nuclear cargo."

20. Blackbeard, who terrorized the Atlantic Coast in 1718, was perhaps the most colorful of all pirates. Virginia Governor Alexander Spotswood offered a £100 reward for the capture of Blackbeard, dead or alive. Eighteenth century novelist and journalist Daniel Defoe wrote in *A General History of the Robberies and Murders of the Most Notorious Pyrates*, a best-seller in London in 1724, that the beard of this famous brigand was like "a frightful meteor, covered his whole face and frightened America more than any comet that has appeared there for a long time." His beard, never trimmed and very long and jet black, reached down from his eyes to his chest. Blackbeard parted it and plaited it into little tails with colorful ribbons. *The Pirates*, Time-Life Books, 1978.

Chapter 8
21. Captain Brian Hoare, Stolt Nielsen.

22. From an interview with the British officers' union NUMAST, February 1998, and Videotel antipiracy training video.

Chapter 9
23. Postmortem on Captain MacKereth, conducted September 25, 1992 by the Institute of Science and Forensic Medicine, Singapore.

24. Few realize that launching a life raft at sea is sometimes as dangerous as staying on a vessel in peril. According to the UK's Marine Accident Investigation Board, twelve seafarers have been killed and eighty-seven injured as a result of lifeboat launching accidents on British ships during the past ten years.

25. Belgian/Dutch Documentary *Piraten!* (Panorama Series), CTC Production. Coproducers: AVRO, Aegis Productions, WDR/ARD, CoBoFonds, Setu Films (India). Camera: Ruud Denslagen, Eindreacteur AVRO: Marijke Rawie, copyright AVRO/CTC 2000.

26. Ships collide nearly every day somewhere in the world and they don't blow up. What was the ignition source for this inferno?

Steel against steel and the volatile gaseous state of those empty tanks in the *Nagasaki Spirit* could have done it. But one official who witnessed the final days of the *Ocean Blessing* said it was more likely a result of the large shipment of illegal arms and ammunition the container ship was carrying to the Middle East.

A "box ship" is a mystery ship; anything could be inside those containers. The contents within the containers must be stated and declared, for insurance, for customs, for the shippers, for the shipping company, none of whom may be aware of the actual contents of the boxes. And not every one of the millions of containers that make up most of the world's commercial shipments is ever inspected by anybody. Often a declared shipment of cloth or tomatoes or machine parts or personal effects could be drugs, illegal immigrants, guns, or even a nuclear device.

While one of the 1,500 containers on the *Ocean Blessing* was known to be carrying disposable gas lighters, there were, according to authorities I spoke with, a number of containers with much more dangerous cargo. The manifest listed five containers of Chinese burlap; there was also a container or two of "diplomatic" cargo, goods beyond the reach of customs authorities.

Following the collision and after the fires were put out, the *Ocean Blessing* was sold for scrap, then towed by a Chinese tugboat to India, where it was beached in front of a breaker's yard. Indian customs law requires that the scrapyard obtain a light displacement certificate indicating that the ship is, as she lies, worth no more than the value of its steel.

The Department of Customs Revenue, the government watchdog that keeps an eye on its own officials, discovered there was not mere undamaged cargo destined to "fall off a truck" but evidence of a large illegal weapons shipment.

"There were Chinese arms in those containers," said one official who said he still fears for his life. "Five containers were declared as burlap but there were arms and ammunition and I suppose explosives that was either going to Iraq, or, I was told, to some extremist group to overthrow the Saudi government."

The *Ocean Blessing*, with its mysterious cargo, never quite made it into the breaker's yard. When Indian government investigators began sniffing around, the owner of the scrapyard, apparently in close contact with Chinese arms merchants who were thinking of other more local uses for the arms that they felt could still be salvaged, fled without a trace. Today the ship lies derelict in thirty feet of water in front of where the scrapyard used to be, battered by the angry surf from passing typhoons; each year pieces of the *Ocean Blessing* still wash up on the beach. Locals know that there is a lot to salvage, but Hindus fear the evil spirit that lurks within the wreck; it has become a "fish reef," but even local fisherman won't go near the ghost ship. The only way to get to those Chinese crates, still stacked tight within the holds of the ship, is to take it apart on shore. Some officials in the Indian government know exactly what lies beneath the waves. And they are just as happy that the ship sank finally and that there will be no way to find out.

In 2000, 11.6 million shipping containers, 11.5 million trucks, 2.2 million railcars, and 211,000 vessels passed through U.S. ports; the containers carried on trains, ships, and trucks account for more than ninety percent of the overseas cargo coming into the country. Officials fear that a container containing a weapon of mass destruction could be unloaded from a ship and transported on a tractor-trailer across country through populated areas without inspection on its arrival into the U.S. According to the Coast Guard, less than two percent of the containers are checked. In testimony before Congress, Senator Joseph Lieberman, D-Conn., said; "The ease with which a terrorist could smuggle chemical, biological, or even nuclear weapons in a container, without detection, is, in a word, hair raising."

27. Naphtha is a highly volatile liquid obtained during the refining of petroleum and is often blended to make gasoline. Called white oil, it also is used to make plastics, solvents, and various chemicals. It is highly explosive when exposed to open flame. Captain Betts says oil companies spike crude oil with naphtha when coming from the Persian Gulf "to avoid paying taxes" on the import. "You can carry LPG in for free," he says. Some crude oil, like Saudi Khafji Crude, has some naphtha naturally blended within.

28. When the *Exxon Valdez* piled onto Bligh Reef in Prince William Sound, there was no explosion, no fire to burn off the spill, and 10.8 million gallons of North Slope Crude Oil spread rapidly, driven by wind and current. Most of that amount, according to the National Oceanic and Atmospheric Administration, evaporated, dispersed into the water column, or degraded naturally. Only sixteen percent, about 1.7 million gallons, reached shore, yet 1,300 miles of shoreline were despoiled and the local environment had been affected for years. The area damaged in that ecological disaster covered 10,000 square miles.

29. (Ibid *Piraten!*, note 25)

30. The original report of the attack stated that the ship had run down the channel out of command; reports that were revised indicate that the bridge remained secure and under control of the watch stander.

31. There are two alternative routes, were the Malacca Straits closed. The Sunda Straits around the southern end of Sumatra into the Java Sea past the smoldering Anak Krakatao volcano are rent by strong currents and riptides and overfalls. Vessels like the *Montrose* with a draft in excess of eighteen meters can't cross over the irregular and shifting channels. Drill rigs and fishing fleets, unregulated channels with heavy ferry traffic between Java and Sumatra, and rogue cargo vessels make the passage a hazardous one even for smaller big ships. Many navigation charts available for the passage are of questionable accuracy.

The second passage, the Lombok-Makassar Straits, is much farther east. The route winds down Sumatra, east along the south Java coast, north through the Indonesian Archipelago along the east side of Borneo toward the Philippines. The Straits are navigable for giant ships, but the many additional days required to make the passage to Japan and the rest of industrialized Asia would severely increase the cost of transportation of the product and thus its cost to the consumer.

Chapter 10
32. A Smithsonian Environmental Research Center study found that a typical liter of ballast water from an oceangoing ship contained some 830 million bacteria and more than 7 billion viruses. *Vibro cholerae*, the bacterium responsible for cholera, was found in the ballast water of all ships tested after entering the Chesapeake Bay from foreign ports.

Chapter 11
33. There are 2 million illegal immigrants in Malaysia of a population of 23 million. Most of these have been spirited across the Malacca Straits from Indonesia during the past ten years. There is no other practical way to get into Malaysia except through Thailand and that is rarely done; Thais are a different people with different religion, language, and appearance.

In January 2002 two police boats, pursuing an Indonesian longboat carrying fifty-four illegal immigrants including several women, were bombarded with firebombs. When police attempted to board, they were attacked by the desperate immigrants armed with parangs and axes.

34. These boats exchange cut timber, copra, and palm oil from Indonesia for cartons of soft drinks, live chickens, and kerosene in Malaysia, an age-old tradition of commerce between the two nations.

35. **Article 105** of the United Nations Convention on the Law of the Sea (UNCLOS) allows the seizure of a pirate ship or aircraft:

> On the high seas, or in any other place outside the jurisdiction of any State, every State may seize a pirate ship or aircraft taken by piracy and under the control of pirates and arrest the persons and seize the property on board.

Article 111 permits hot pursuit within limits:

> The hot pursuit of a foreign ship may be undertaken when the competent authorities of the coastal State have good reason to believe that the ship has violated the law and regulations of that State. Such pursuit must be commenced when the foreign ship or one of its boats is within the international waters, the achipelagic waters, the territorial sea, or the contiguous zone if the pursuit has not been interrupted.

It is quite specific where that pursuit must end:

> The right of hot pursuit ceases as soon as the ship pursued enters the territorial sea of its own State or of a third State.

36. The Royal Malaysian Marine Police have been effective on their side of the Malacca Straits. In 2000 there were seventy-five reported attacks in the area. In 2001 the figure dropped to seventeen. There was no noticeable decline on the Indonesian side, where Jamal and his team are forbidden to enter.

Chapter 12

37. The Singapore marine police have good reason to be cautious. The Singapore government revealed on Jan 13, 2002, that it had uncovered a plot by the clandestine Jemaah Islamiah, part of Al-Qaeda network, to bomb U.S. naval vessels in a special "kill zone" along the city-state's northeast coastline as well as American, British, Australian, and Israeli embassies.

38. The Americans did show up. Briefly. In October and November 2001, U.S. Navy frigates escorted merchant ships through the Malacca Straits that carried "cargoes of high importance or value" to the war effort in Afghanistan. Admiral Dennis Cutler Blair, commander of the U.S. forces in the Pacific, said he was concerned that these supply ships in the Straits were vulnerable to attack from armed extremists linked to Al-Qaeda who use Southeast Asia as a base. The number of attacks during these months in Indonesian waters of the Malacca Straits did not decrease.

39. Captain P. Mukundan, Director, International Maritime Bureau, agrees: "The Japanese would go right in. They'd just do it" without regard for international restrictions. "I think they [the littoral states] would let them get away with it."

40. In the first three months of 2002 the use of guns in the Malacca Straits in fact did increase. In one such incident the crew aboard a livestock carrier took cover as pirates, attempting to board, sprayed the bridge with automatic gunfire. The incident occurred on Jamal's patch.

Chapter 15

41. The link between Asian crime syndicates and Al-Qaeda is the heroin trade. Organized crime buys, moves, deals the heroin, much of it originating in Afghanistan. Monies are said to find their way back to terrorist cells, the Abu Sayaf being one of them; the Jemaah Islamiah in Malaysia and Indonesia, accused of attempting to blow up American interests in Singapore, another. Al-Qaeda is reported to control up to eighty front companies in fifty countries, including its ownership or control of twenty-three merchant vessels. The fleet, according to intelligence sources, has been used to smuggle high-quality Afghan heroin and hashish to the West and throughout Asia. One of these ships owned indirectly by the Al-Qaeda network was used to provide logistic support for the terrorist bombing of the U.S. embassies in East Africa; the fleet gives terrorists the ability to transport personnel and equipment, including biological or nuclear weapons, into any littoral state in the world.

42. For a more detailed look at organized crime and maritime fraud see *Shipping at Risk*, Eric Ellen, International Chamber of Commerce, 1997. This is probably the most comprehensive and up-to-date overview of maritime crime on the market today.

Chapter 16

43. Three South Koreans were arrested by South Korean Maritime Police and charged with acquiring stolen cargo from the *Ten-yu*. The police said those arrested admitted buying the ship and aluminum from two Chinese Indonesians and selling them to a Chinese company in Myanmar via another company in Singapore—a clear indication of the involvement of organized crime. (See *Golden Venture*, page 220.)

44. Those who figured in the hijacking of the *Ten-yu* also were involved in the hijacking of the *Alondra Rainbow*, a current cause célèbre among those trying to control the activities of the syndicates. On October 22, 1999, pirates armed with swords and guns attacked the *Alondra Rainbow* only hours after it departed Kuala Tanjung, Sumatra, on the Malacca Straits. The crew was set

adrift in a life raft and found ten days later by a passing fishing boat. The captain on a tanker who had received the alert from the IMB Piracy Reporting Center in Kuala Lumpur spotted the ship heading into the Arabian Sea. Indian authorities were called and a coast guard vessel was sent to intercept the ship. Despite warning shots fired across her bow, the *Alondra Rainbow*, renamed the *Mega Rama*, continued to flee. An Indian navy ship joined the high seas chase and, after pumping a few shells into her, was able to stop and board the stolen ship. The fifteen Indonesians pirates attempted unsuccessfully to destroy the evidence by setting fire to the ship and scuttling her. Between the time of hijacking and its arrest, $4.25 million worth of aluminum ingots, of high value on the black market, had been illegally off-loaded. At least one of the Indonesian pirates and possibly another had been involved in the hijacking of the *Ten-yu* in September 1998. The pirates were charged with high seas piracy by a court in Mumbai.

45. David Cockroft, general secretary of the International Transport Federation, December 9, 2001: "When a ship is registered with one of these flags, a curtain of secrecy descends. It's as valuable if you're a terrorist as if you're a money launderer, someone who wants to sink a ship for insurance purposes or work its crew to death before abandoning them unpaid. As long as governments and the United Nations turn a blind eye to the way FoCs (flags of convenience) allow criminals to operate anonymously, ships will be used to transport everything from drugs and illegal immigrants to the supplies used by the Al-Qaeda men who blew up the U.S. embassies in Kenya and Tanzania."

For hijacking purposes registration papers for a ship targeted can be bought from a flag-of-convenience nation's embassy or consulate; only cash and a description of the vessel is required.

The *Karine-A*, arrested in January 2002 by Israeli intelligence agents in the Red Sea, was flying a flag of convenience. Registered in Tonga, a tiny kingdom in the South Pacific, the vessel was carrying fifty tons of weapons and explosives to Palestinians from Iran.

A ship that landed in Italy in March 2002 carrying 928 asylum seekers from Iraq had been registered with six different FoCs over the last fifteen years.

46. The master of the vessel wrote in his book (*Petro Pirates*, Captain Ken Blyth with Peter Corris, Sydney: Allen & Unwin, 2000): "*. . . I was mindful of the danger and when I wrote out my night orders, which each officer was required to read and sign on taking over his watch, I stressed that an alert pirate watch was to be maintained. I also made the point verbally to the officer of the watch and requested him to do the same when he was relieved.*"

47. Wong was sentenced in August 1999 by a district court on Batam Island, Indonesia, to six years in jail for masterminding and financing piracy

operations. First Admiral TNI Sumardi, director of Guskamar Armabar, Indonesian Intelligence.

48. Captain Jayant Abhyankar, deputy director of the ICC International Maritime Bureau in an interview November 14, 2000.

49. Petroships confirms Darman was let go because of his poor knowledge of English, the international language of seafarers and shipping. The international Safety Management Code, which became effective in July 1998, requires seafarers have a working knowledge of English. The code covers mainly tankers and bulk carriers and was designed to improve safety performance aboard vessels.

Chapter 18

50. In September 1999 the *Berge Sigval* was awarded the coveted "Green Award," which offers the ship financial incentives such as reduction of port dues, import duties, etc., for ships that practice "clean and safe shipping and environmental awareness in the tanker shipping industry." From the Green Award Foundation Annual Report, 2000. The vessel nearly lost its award on this day.

A number of ship masters shown the photos have reacted with amazement at the seamanship, or worse, arrogance. Unless the watch stander had fallen asleep or become ill without anyone being informed, a near miss like this in such perfect conditions is rare. To a man, no one knows how a ship like the *Berge Sigval* could take such a chance.

In September 2001 ten merchant ships sank on seas throughout the world as a result of fires, collisions, or heavy weather. This is about average for a month.

Chapter 20

51. Captain Simon Perera, fifty-eight, of the *Tirta Niaga IV* was released some months later after the Singapore-based charterers paid $30,000 in ransom.

The kidnapping in fact did kick off a spate of copycat hijack and hostage incidents. It was only a couple months later that rebels armed with grenade launchers, members of the Islamic separatist group Free Aceh Movement (GAM), held the crew of the *Ocean Silver* for ransom. In another incident pirates seized a crew of six from a tug off Bandar Aceh and some months later hijacked a tug and barge and kidnapped a crew member off a tug at Karimun. The IMB believes that there are considerably more cases that go unreported because owners and crews were "being threatened and warned not to report to the authorities."

52. The charts of the *Selayang*'s course:

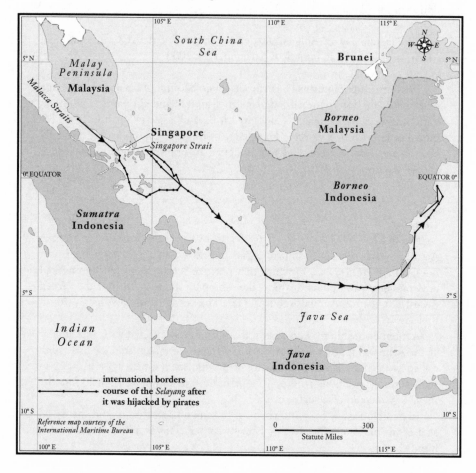

53. *Maritime Asia, Lloyd's List,* June 2001, by Siswanto Rusdi: Sarwono Kusumaatmadja, chairman of the Indonesian Maritime Council, defended Indonesia's efforts against piracy: "The first problem is that Indonesia lacks sufficient patrol boats, while the water territory that should be covered is so huge. This means there are areas without any control at all. These areas are suitable as pirates' base camps."

Hindering effective law enforcement efforts at sea are the interagency squabbles between the Ministry of Transportation and Telecommunication, the national police, customs, and the Indonesian navy. None is specifically empowered to fight piracy or to bring captured pirates to court.

54. The *Selayang* was held by the Indonesian navy, who charged the owner $100,000 to release the vessel. The navy said the payment would assure that

the ship, the crew, *and* the pirates would be released without a police investigation, a process that would otherwise tie up the ship and crew and the cargo indefinitely. A total of 200 tons of diesel fuel had been off-loaded onto fishing boats during one of the tanker's mysterious stops.

The crew was unharmed; Noel Choong, PRC director, said later that like the attack on the *Petchem*, the hijacking had been an inside job. Many of the crew had mobile phones and probably phoned their confederates the departure time of the ship from the terminal and its ETA at the spot where the attack was to take place, off Karimun.

Afterword

55. M. J. Peterson, *An Historical Perspective on the Incidence of Piracy*, a paper presented before the Marine Police Center Conference on Modern Piracy, 1985, Woods Hole Oceanographic Institution.

56. *Ships Monthly*, February 2001, published by IPC Marine Division, London.

57. The Suez Canal is particularly vulnerable although rigidly patrolled. Egyptian police on November 17, 2001 arrested armed pirates as they tried to hijack a ship while transiting the canal. Every vessel passing through the canal, including sailboats, must have aboard a pilot from the Suez Canal Authority. Many ships' masters consider some of these pilots of questionable character and reliability—usually weary, slack-jawed functionaries who for a few cartons of Marlboros, some whiskey, and an envelope of anything from five dollars U.S. to several hundred dollars in *baksheesh*, will perform their jobs adequately. It is not called the Marlboro Canal for nothing.

58. Admiral Dennis Cutler Blair, U.S. Pacific Fleet Commander, November 27, 2001.

59. In an interview with the Associated Press, GAM spokesman Tengku Ishak said, "Even though we are not fully independent yet, we have the power to block ships. . . . If shippers do not want to seek permission from us, then they should not blame the GAM if cases such as experienced by the TB *Ocean Silver* are repeated. . . . The Indonesian government could not protect ships passing through the Straits of Malacca but the GAM could." GAM has been fighting since 1976 to end Indonesian rule on the northernmost province of Sumatra, a region of extensive oil and gas reserves.

Indonesia is considered a recruiting and training ground for Al-Qaeda, and some intelligence officials believe that GAM has links to the group. Indonesia is believed to have been the center of operations for attacks planned on American targets in Singapore in early 2002.

60. Andrew Linington, NUMAST.

It is not only the developing world where seafarers buy their documentation. The U.S. Coast Guard arrested two men in early 2002 in connection with the theft of a machine used to make merchant mariner documents. Some 650 blank licenses were also missing from USCG offices in San Juan, Puerto Rico.

61. Captain Mukundan of the IMB is also concerned about the vulnerability of cruise ships. He recalled that two months before the attacks on New York and Washington, Al-Qaeda had planned an aerial attack on the cruise ship that housed world leaders assembled in Genoa for the G8 summit. The leaders of Russia, France, Germany, Japan, Britain, and Canada stayed on the luxury cruise liner *European Vision*, chartered by the Italian government; President George W. Bush stayed in a hotel on land. Other cruise ships in the harbor housed the 1,500 delegates. Mukundan expressed astonishment when told that the Greek government had announced it intended to hire thirteen cruise ships to house many of the participants of the 2004 Olympics.

62. The European officers of "the *Montrose*," including the master, no longer work directly for "The Group" but for an independent manning agency based on the Isle of Man.

"You won't find many British on British ships anymore—unlike the Americans who hire only Americans. But there is nothing left of the American merchant marine, is there? There is no romance going to sea; people don't want to get their hands dirty."

63. The USCG recommendations submitted January 15, 2002 to the Maritime Safety Committee, 75th Session of the UN. The agency also has suggested vessels install stern radar systems "to warn of approaching vessels used by hijackers." This recommendation, as well as equipping ships with a satellite tracking device, are tools long advocated in the fight against piracy. It took a terrorist event to trigger realization that ships are exceptionally vulnerable and must be protected.

Additionally, the Maritime Transportation Anti-Terrorism Act of 2002 imposes strict security on foreign ports, shipping lines, and seafarers. Among other things, the law requires foreign-flag vessels entering U.S. ports to give ninety-six hours prior notice to the Coast Guard. Operators of commercial vessels arriving in U.S. waters from foreign ports will have to provide detailed specific information about passengers and crew. Vessels built after December 31, 2002, must be equipped with a position indicating transponder; such a device will become mandatory for older vessels after December 31, 2004.

64. *Washington Post*, November 27, 2001, by Edward Walsh.

GLOSSARY

A/B—Able Bodied seaman

Abeam—opposite the middle of a ship

Amidships—the middle section of the ship

Beam—the width of a ship

Bilge—the very bottom of the inside of a ship

Bow—the very forepart of a vessel

Bridge—the control room from which the ship is navigated

Bulkhead—a ship's partition or wall

Draft—the depth of a ship from the waterline to the bottom of its keel

Gangway—Accommodation ladder/diagonal steps from deck to pier or launch

GPS—Global Positioning Satellite

Knot—a nautical mile per hour, equal to 1.15 mph and 1.85 kph

Lee—the sheltered side

Limberhole—large cutout holes in the ship's frame that allow bilge water to flow freely

M/T—Motor Tanker—the vessel carries flammable cargo

M/V—Motor Vessel

Port—left side of ship

Port (starbd) quarter—the quadrant at the afterend of the ship's beam

SBM—Single Buoy Mooring: an offshore mooring to which tankers tie up and attach their filler pipes to load and discharge their cargo

Shrouds—lateral support for the mast

Starboard—right side

Steerageway—the minimum speed at which the vessel responds to the rudder

Stern—the aftermost part of a ship

S/Y—sailing yacht

Transom stern—the flat horizontal back end of a ship, from deck to sea

VHF radio—the short range ship-to-ship/shore radio commonly used in the maritime industry. Range is about 20 miles depending on height of antenna

Watch, officer's—the period he or she serves on duty, usually four hours on, four off

Watch stander—the officer on watch

Wheelhouse—the room containing a ship's steering wheel, today interchangeable with Bridge

Windward—facing the wind

BIBLIOGRAPHY

Blyth, Captain Ken, with Peter Corris. *Petro Pirates: The Hijacking of the Petro Ranger.* Sydney, Australia: Allen & Unwin, 2000.

Botting, Douglas. *The Pirates.* Alexandria, Virginia: Time-Life Books, 1978.

Ellen, Eric, ed. *Piracy at Sea.* Paris, France: ICC Publishing, 1989.

———, ed. *Shipping at Risk.* Paris, France: ICC Publishing, 1997.

Ellen, Eric, and Donald Campbell. *International Maritime Fraud.* London, UK: Street & Maxwell, 1981.

Eyres, D. J. *Ship Construction.* London, UK: Heinemann, 1978.

Howarth, Stephen. *Sea Shell: The Story of Shell's British Tanker Fleets, 1892–1992.* London, UK: Thomas Reed Publications, 1992.

International Petroleum Encyclopedia. Tulsa, Oklahoma: PennWell Publishing Co., 2000.

International Safety Guide for Oil Tankers and Terminals. London, UK: International Chamber of Shipping, 1996.

Lawrence, Bruce. *Shattering the Myth: Islam Beyond Violence.* Princeton, New Jersey: Princeton University Press, 2000.

Lewis, David. *We, the Navigators.* Honolulu, Hawaii: University of Hawaii Press, 1975.

Slocum, Joshua. *Sailing Alone Around the World.* New York: Penguin Classics, 1999.

Sobel, Dava. *Longitude.* London, UK: Fourth Estate Limited, 1998.

INDEX

ACKNOWLEDGMENTS

I wish to thank those nameless and faceless souls in the oil company's headquarters who temporarily opened the doors to their corporate shop; the time spent inside was revealing. And to those good men and women aboard the VLCC with whom I sailed.

I want to thank Alan Chan of Petroships for his cooperation; a courageous man. Perhaps telling this story will help to keep his ships and the men and women aboard them out of harm's way.

And a warm thanks to Donny and Vimala Monteiro, for their candor and hospitality—never forgotten.

A special appreciation to those who provided so much yet asked that their identities not be revealed.

I particularly would like to thank Mitch Hoffman, senior editor at Dutton, whose conviction and editorial direction held this project together, through calm and storm—all writers should be so lucky. In addition my thanks to Carole Baron and Brian Tart of Dutton, who supported that conviction; to Todd Keithley, whose encouragement and good efforts got this project off the ground; and to Andrew Pope, wayward artist, who first persuaded me to tell this story. To Jane Dystel and Ellis Levine.

The assistance of many others was important to the project. Among them are: Marcel Zandstra, whose support from the very first days and during 9-11 won't be forgotten, and Andrew Torchia, ex–Associated Press warhorse who had the moxie to act as stand-in to meet some pirates while his wife, Marion, stood in the shadows armed with a police whistle.

And particularly to Captain Potengal Mukundan of the International Maritime Bureau; Eric Ellen and S. Lin Kuo, who put me on a straight course; Michael Grey of *Lloyd's List*; Chris Austen and Brian Phelan of Wellington Offshore; Paul Teverini; Steffen Tunge of Stolt Nielsen; Chris Richards of the Singapore Oil Spill Response Center; Andy Torchia for his Singapore digs and brother Chris Torchia and Rohan Sullivan, journalists all and all helpful; Muhamad Bin Muda and Aziz B. Yusof of the Royal Malaysian Marine Police; Captain James Jeeris, Captain Kevin Miranda, and Captain Cheang Boon Hai; Captain Anil Deshpande; Captain John Swain and Captain Kaare Traeland; Michael Haughey of Control Risks Group; Steven Bond of VideoTel; Captain Ken Bales of Semco, Singapore; Andrew Lininginton of NUMAST; Jon Whitlow of the International Transport Federation; Chris Horrocks and Simon Bennett of the International Shipping Federation/International Chamber of Shipping; Professor Sam Menefee of the Center of National Security Law, University of Virginia; Chef Manmeet Singh Bali and crew at the Taj Manjarun, Mangalore; Alistair Johnston of the Informa Group; Mark Bruyneel; Cristof for use of his NYC center of operations; Linda Childress and Herb McCormick at *Cruising World Magazine*; Paul Gelder of *Yachting Monthly* (UK); in Tanga, Tanzania, Lut and Al-noor; and Lyn and Gebhard Waltenberg, who kept a keen eye on the neglected *Unicorn* during my absence. Thanks to Ruth Reichl and Jocelyn Zuckerman of *Gourmet Magazine*, who encouraged me to write again.

And to Jacqueline, who showed so much patience during those long days that extended into longer nights, allowing me to meet the improbable deadline. Without your support it would have been a grueling year.

JSB

ABOUT THE AUTHOR

John S. Burnett is a former reporter for United Press International who has written for many popular publications, including *National Geographic* and *The Guardian* (UK). He has served with the United Nations in Somalia as a relief worker and has lived for years in East Africa. He now lives with his wife Jacqueline in the Netherlands.